Truth, Politics, Morality

'What is the place of truth in politics? Cheryl Misak argues that if we would defend liberal freedoms we must not shy away from the truth. Misak develops and defends a lucid, well-informed and attractive version of Peirce's pragmatist theory of truth and convincingly shows that if this theory is correct, non-cognitivism in morality may be resisted and Schmitt's challenge may be rejected as epistemologically faulty. *Truth, Politics, Morality* will be valuable reading for anyone with serious interests in liberalism, democracy, or truth.'

Henry Richardson, Georgetown University

'*Truth, Politics, Morality* is a delight to read. It seems no easy task to write a book on a pragmatist's account of moral epistemology and its bearing on moral problems that is accessible both to those specializing in moral philosophy, and to those specializing in epistemology, but Cheryl Misak has succeeded admirably. The account Misak gives of knowledge and truth is sophisticated, but readily understood; her discussion of its application to moral inquiry is plausible, and often persuasive. The book is very clearly written, with a lively style.'

Robert L. Frazier, Christ Church, Oxford

Cheryl Misak is Professor of Philosophy at the University of Toronto. She is the author of *Truth and the End of Inquiry* (OUP) and *Verificationism* (Routledge).

Truth, Politics, Morality

Pragmatism and deliberation

Cheryl Misak

London and New York

First published 2000
by Routledge
11 New Fetter Lane, London EC4P 4EE

Simultaneously published in the USA and Canada
by Routledge
29 West 35th Street, New York, NY 10001

Routledge is an imprint of the Taylor & Francis Group

© 2000 Cheryl Misak

Typeset in Times by Taylor and Francis Books Ltd
Printed and bound in Great Britain by Biddles Ltd,
Guildford and King's Lynn

British Library Cataloguing in Publication Data
A catalogue record for this book is available from the British Library

Library of Congress Cataloging-in-Publication Data
Misak, C. J. (Cheryl J.)
  Truth, politics, morality : pragmatism and deliberation / Cheryl
Misak.
    p cm.
    Includes bibliographical references and index.
  1. Truth. 2. Political science–Philosophy. 3. Ethics.
  4. Pragmatism. 5. Inquiry (Theory of knowledge)
I. Title.
BD171.M515 1999   99-16328
121–dc21   CIP

ISBN 0–415–14035–8 (hb)
ISBN 0–415–14036–6 (pb)

For Sophie and Alexander,
who make the big things simple

Contents

viii   *Contents*

Acknowledgements

This book is in a way the final chapter of my D.Phil. thesis on pragmatism and truth, which was submitted at Oxford University over a decade ago. I had intended then to say something about moral judgement, but David Wiggins, who supervised that thesis, showed me just how far I had to go before I got anything close to right enough.

Since then, I have had the pleasure of trying out my thoughts in the Law and Philosophy Reading Group, which meets weekly at the University of Toronto over very civilised and friendly lunches. Its participants number heavily in the list of friends whose comments made for an improved final version: Judith Baker, David Bakhurst, Peter Benson, Alan Brudner, Bruce Chapman, Roger Crisp, Joe Heath, Brad Hooker, Chris Hookway, Bernard Katz, Mark Kingwell, Andrew Kernohan, Jenny Nedelsky, Hamish Stewart, Ernie Weinrib, and Melissa Williams. Donald Ainslie and Arthur Ripstein were especially conscientious in taking me to task. My graduate students at the University of Toronto and audiences at the American Political Science Association, Bryn Mawr College, the C.S. Peirce Society, the 1997 SUNY Buffalo Farber Conference, and the universities of Cambridge, Cape Town, Frankfurt, Oxford, Queens (Kingston), Reading, Sheffield, St. Andrews, Waterloo, Western Ontario, Witwatersrand, and York have also helped me say something closer to what I have to say.

Sustained writing time in Heidelberg, Cape Town, and Cambridge was made possible by the Alexander von Humboldt Foundation, the Social Sciences and Humanities Research Council of Canada, the University of Toronto Connaught Committee, and St. John's College, Cambridge, as by my college discipline representative, Jackie Brunning, and my head of department, Mark Thornton. Glenn Tiller was an excellent research assistant and Adrian Driscoll and Anna Gerber at Routledge were excellent editors.

I owe a rather extreme debt to Dr David Mazer and his colleagues in the Intensive Care Unit at St. Michael's Hospital, Toronto, who spent the better part of April 1998 hauling me out of septic shock. Were it not for them, nothing for me, least of all this book, would have been possible. Thanks also to Dr Louise Perlin and to the ICU nurses, especially Maureen Baye. It is heartening to find that superb and humane treatment can be had from a single tier public healthcare system, even one starved of funds by a succession of governments.

In an only slightly less literal sense, this book would also not have been possible without David Dyzenhaus. It has had the constant benefit of his critical gaze, careful editing, and felicitious examples. But even more importantly, he makes every day part of the good life.

Some of the material here builds on other work of mine and I thank the publishers for permission to draw upon it: *Verificationism: Its History and Prospects* (Routledge 1995), *Truth and the End of Inquiry* (Oxford University Press 1991), 'The Transcendental Turn in Truth and Ethics', *Transactions of the C.S. Peirce Society* 1994, 'Deflating Truth: Pragmatism vs. Disquotationalism', *The Monist* 1998, and 'Pragmatism, Empiricism, and Morality', in S. Lovibond and S. Williams (eds) *Nature, Truth and Value: Essays for David Wiggins* (Basil Blackwell 1996).

Note: Reference to the works of C.S. Peirce

References to C.S. Peirce's *Collected Papers* take the form of CP n.m, where n is volume number and m is paragraph number. References to his chronological *Writings* take the form CE n,m where n is volume number and m is page number. MS refers to the Charles S. Peirce Papers on microfilm and NE n:m refers to *New Elements of Mathematics*, where n is volume number and m is page number. See Bibliography for full details.

Introduction

The notion of truth has fallen from grace in some quarters of epistemology. In moral and political philosophy it perhaps did not have far to fall, the pull towards relativism and subjectivism there being what it is. And even amongst those not especially inclined towards such anti-objectivist positions, one often senses an anxiety about talking of truth and morals in the same breath. For it can appear that truth-talk encourages zeal, proselytising, and other dangerous attitudes.

In this book I shall suggest that the notion of truth is not something from which philosophers have to keep their distance. Against pragmatists of Richard Rorty's stripe, against non-cognitivists, and against some sorts of neutrality-focused liberals, I shall argue that we ought to explore the idea that moral and political deliberation aims at truth.

Not just any conception of truth, however, will do. I shall argue that the appropriate account of truth and objectivity – the appropriate epistemology – is that which is urged by a certain kind of pragmatism. That view has it that a true belief is one which would stand up to the evidence and reasons, were we to inquire as far as we could on the matter.

The founder of pragmatism, C.S. Peirce, sometimes articulated this thought by saying that a true belief is one which would be agreed upon at the hypothetical or ideal end of inquiry. We shall see in Chapter 2 that there is a better way of putting the point: a true belief is one upon which inquiry could not improve – a belief which would fit with experience and argument and which would satisfy the aims of inquiry, no matter how much the issue was subject to experiment, evaluation, and debate.

Pragmatism thus abandons the kind of metaphysics which is currently in so much disrepute – it abandons concepts which pretend to transcend experience. Truth and objectivity are matters of what is best for the community of inquirers to believe, 'best' here amounting to that which best fits with the evidence and argument. On the pragmatist view of truth, when we aim at empirical adequacy, predictive power, understanding the way things work, understanding ourselves, and the like, we aim at the truth. For a true belief is the belief which best satisfies those and other particular aims in inquiry.

My claim will be that this view of truth and objectivity is fitting for moral and political philosophy – it is a view on which it makes sense to think that our moral and political debates aim at truth. The pragmatist idea has struck many as being especially valuable here, for a competing epistemology – let's call it realism – stacks the deck against objectivity in morals and politics. The realist I have in mind holds that a proposition (or a statement or a sentence) is true if and only if it corresponds to something like a fact in the believer-independent world. Since truth and objectivity in morals and politics cannot be anything like that, realism seems to lead directly to moral relativism and non-cognitivism. It seems to lead directly to the conclusion that moral and political judgements cannot fall within our cognitive scope – within the scope of truth and knowledge.

I shall suggest that a plausible epistemology – pragmatism – is available for science, mathematics, *and* morals. We shall see that some of those who are attracted to pragmatism in morals think that other discourses have more robust truth-predicates. I shall argue against this kind of pluralism about truth. Judgements about what ought to be done, what is good, and what is just can be true or false. Truth here will be as the pragmatist sees it, but it is not for that reason second-rate. There is nothing more independent or more certain with which to contrast it. I suppose, however, that it is open to the reader to go against my advice, sweep the general arguments aside, and take the view of truth offered here as a view good only for the likes of moral judgement.

It is almost a philosophical commonplace these days to reject the idea that we might find a foundation for our principles of right belief and of right action in some infallible source – from God, from some special faculty of intuition, or from what is given to us with certainty by experience. But once this anti-foundationalist move is made, it might seem that the source for, and the status of, our judgements, theories, and principles is altogether human and therefore arbitrary.

It will not be good enough to say, with the Rortian kind of pragmatist, that here we must simply reject the dichotomy between an utterly secure grounding and an arbitrary grounding. For we must also replace the dichotomy with a positive view which really does help us think through the problems which arise naturally in our lives as deliberators, actors, and deciders. So while I too want to make the anti-foundationalist move, I do not want to scoff at the project of trying to show that this or that belief is objectively justified and is likely to be true.

My suggestion is that truth is not at the mercy of the vagaries of individuals, as some suppose it to be, nor is it a matter of getting right the believer-independent world, as others suppose. It has, I shall argue, enough marks of the objective to be deserving of that label, suitably qualified. I shall try, that is, to present a view of truth and objectivity which undermines the usual all-or-nothing dichotomies and which gives us everything we could reasonably want.

It is important to see that the first step in such a project should be to examine the aspirations of our moral inquiries and see whether those aspirations can be met. This means that we should begin by exploring the prospects for cognitivism. For it seems that when we make moral judgements and when we act in the ways which we think are morally right, we take ourselves to be aiming at something objective – at the truth or at getting things right, where 'right' does not mean merely 'right by the lights of my group'. We distinguish between thinking, on the one hand, that one (or one's culture) is right and, on the other hand, being right. We attribute moral beliefs to ourselves and to others, we use such beliefs in inferences, and we think that they can conflict and compete with each other. We think that we can discover that something is right or wrong – that we can improve our views. We want not the illusion that our projects, plans, ambitions, and relationships are worthwhile – we want good reason to think that they are worthwhile. We think that it is appropriate, or even required, that we give reasons and arguments for our beliefs, that 'rational' persuasion, not browbeating or force, is the appropriate means of getting someone to agree with us. Indeed, we want people to *agree* with, or at least respect, our judgements, as opposed to merely mouthing them, or falling in line with them. And we criticise the beliefs, actions, and even the final ends and desires of others, as false, vicious, immoral, or irrational. The fact that our moral judgements come under such internal discipline is a mark of their objectivity. The above phenomena are indications that moral inquiry aims at truth. They are indications that the relativist or non-cognitivist thought is not the thought which should stand at the start of our moral theory.

Moral and political theory must, the pragmatist suggests, take the phenomenology of inquiry in stride. It must try to save the phenomena, or at least enough of them, so that our moral lives and explorations are still recognisable as being that and not something else. Thus, it should, at least initially, make the attempt at showing how it makes sense to think of moral discourse as aiming at truth or as being truth-apt. Philosophy must try to leave the business of inquiry intact, no matter how much fun destruction and deconstruction might be.

We shall see that it is not that moral and political theory must be a slave to the picture that morals and politics has of itself, or to the picture that this or that moral deliberator has of the business. Rather, the requirement will be that the theorist give principled reasons when her theory is revisionist about the practice of inquiry. The presumption that our epistemological and moral theory should preserve our deeply held convictions and our ways of inquiring into various subject matters is defeasible, but it is nonetheless something that we must do our best to respect. A theory of *x*, in order to remain a theory of *x*, must try to preserve at least some of the features of *x*; it must try to preserve at least some of the phenomena that it is a theory *of*. Wanting to maintain the way we go about moral deliberation is not a recommendation of conservativism or the preservation of the *status quo*. It is not a recommendation of anything, but an acknowledgement of the necessary rootedness of a theory in practice.

Not only is there the above reason in favour of taking seriously our practice of moral deliberation, but the following as well. Those practices have real weight and importance in our lives and for our conception of ourselves. If we gave them up (if indeed we really could), we would give up something of enormous importance – we would give up on a large part of the point and meaning to our lives.

Many will think that a disturbing question presses here. Is the pragmatist taking what *is* the case by way of our human methods of deliberation to be the source of what we *ought* to believe and do? The answer is a qualified 'yes'. The pragmatist tries to make sense of our having to start from where we are in the philosophical project of characterising the notions of truth and objectivity. That is, the pragmatist tries to make sense of the idea that our concepts, standards of inquiry, and our conception of ourselves and the world are conditioned by the fact that we are cultured and social animals in the natural world. But she does so without giving up on a robust conception of objectivity and without dumping everything into a sea of post-modern incommensurable standpoints and irreconcilable differences of value.

Again, the need for a replacement for that all-or-nothing dichotomy cries out. While many might applaud the move away from the search for infallible and secure foundations, it is not so easy to find it made in a satisfactory way. A difficult set of questions immediately arise. If we must think about the standards for truth and objectivity from within human practice – from the way in which we actually go about the business of inquiry and debate and from what we already in fact believe – what reason do we have for thinking that we are on the right track? What reason do we have for resisting the thought that, from an inadequate set of practices and beliefs, we merely perpetuate the inadequacy? Is there any room at all for recognisable notions of objectivity and truth in such a view? Is there any possibility of genuine criticism of our beliefs if we think that inquiry into the right principles of belief and action must be based on the principles we already have?

I shall try to answer these questions in the pages that follow. We shall see that the phenomenology of moral and political inquiry is not that it is a straightforwardly objective matter. We are in fact frequently moved to wonder whether there are indeed standards by which we can criticise a particular way of life, a value, or a practice as being bad, unjust, or immoral. We are sometimes drawn to the idea that a particular judgement that something is wrong amounts to the claim that my like-minded friends and I dislike it, either because we were brought up that way or for reasons which have no more weight than the reasons of those who judge that it is right. We often find issues to be thorny and intractable. The challenge is to say how all of this can be so and yet maintain that moral deliberation is not entirely unprincipled.

I have suggested that the central insight of pragmatism is that there is a connection between truth and inquiry – that philosophical theory must keep in touch with the practical business of inquiry. In the moral and political domain the connection is between deliberation, agreement, debate, and reflection, on the one hand, and, on the other, the reasonableness and truth of our judgements and the legitimacy of law, government, and policies. The view thus seems to have affinities with positions such as 'deliberative democracy' and Habermas' communicative ethics.

The idea of basing justification and legitimacy on public deliberation is an attractive one to democrats. But the reasons for its attractiveness might seem a bit too obvious. For it might seem that the view of legitimation which centres around the notion of public reason is just a restatement of a principle which the democrat holds dear – the principle that everyone has a right to participate in discussion of social policy. If that were all that could be said in favour of the idea of deliberation or public reason, it could not provide any support for the democrat, only a nice way, perhaps, of putting the democrat's position.

I shall argue in Chapter 1 that this first impression is correct of some deliberative democrats and others who take the notion of agreement to be at the centre of moral and political philosophy. This chapter sets the stage for distinguishing the way in which I think agreement is important from the ways of some others. The chapter can be thought of as a partial survey of current thought about the connection between agreement and truth.

My claim shall be that there has been a failure to offer a non-circular or non-question-begging justification of the view that we ought to arrange moral and political decision-making around open and free debate with agreement as its aim. That is, there has been a failure to provide a justification of why discussion should be a central notion in politics rather than say, private decision-making and then voting, or the elimination of those who disagree with us.

Many will respond with the anti-foundationalist claim that the idea of providing a non-circular justification is rightly out of fashion. Arguments have been advanced by Rorty and others as to why such a justification cannot be had. Even Rawls, who initially seemed to make the full justificatory attempt, appears to accept the folly of the move and is content to merely show how his view fits with things we find important.

It will be clear by now that I have some sympathy with this response. Indeed, I shall join forces with it to some extent when I argue in Chapter 1 that quests for a certain kind of strong justification of deliberative democracy are misguided. And some of the justifications I shall criticise as being too weak, such as various attempts at showing how deliberative democracy fits well with many things we take to be important, are not to be sneered at. Perhaps this sort of work is most of the task of showing a view to be the right view.

Nonetheless, I think that something must be said about what response the advocates of deliberation can make to those who do not share their thoughts about what is important. More of a claim must be made than the existentialist 'Here I stand, I can do no other'.

Something must be said about whether the view has an independent justification. This need not be the kind of foundationalist justification which I shall join in eschewing. Seeking a justification of our deeply held moral convictions or seeking something to say against those who see no point at all to them, is not the same thing as seeking a foundation of indubitable, provable convictions.

This problem, which we have now approached from a number of angles, is of immediate concern for the pragmatist. If truth is what is best for the community of inquirers to believe, then the fact that different inquirers find different things best to believe seems to undermine the possibility of agreement and of truth. Can we criticise others – flat-earthers or neo-Nazis – as holding beliefs which are likely to be wrong? Or must we, like Rorty's pragmatist, abandon the notions of truth and objectivity and somehow find it good enough to say that one belief happens to be best for us and an incompatible belief happens to be best for others? This issue arises in any domain of inquiry, but it shouts for our attention in morals and politics. For there we seem to run into deep disagreement everywhere.

I have announced my intention to avoid the kind of view which gives us no standpoint from which to criticise. Fortunately, we are not in the position where this view, in whatever guise it takes, is forced upon us. A methodology can be justified by the pragmatist and some moral beliefs and some conceptions of the good life can be criticised.

I shall argue that a methodological requirement falls out of the idea that a true belief would be the best belief, were inquiry to be pursued as far as it could fruitfully go. That methodological principle is that the experience of others must be taken seriously. In the moral and political realm, this requires that everyone be given the chance to contribute to debate. It requires a democracy in inquiry.

I shall not, however, be making too much of this point. For one thing, we shall see that although the methodological principle gives us something to say to those who denigrate the experience of others, it provides nothing like a knock-down argument against them. It mostly gives us something to say to ourselves about why they are mistaken.

In addition, it is not my intention to try to show how we can derive all of morality and politics, or even the basic principles of justice, from the methodological principle. We do not need, and should not want, to try to derive most or all of our moral values from some foundational principle. Nor need we point to an equivalence between justice on the one hand and something like impartiality, equality, mutual advantage, or fair reciprocity on the other. Each of these concepts, we shall see, plays a role in determining what is just and unjust, but there will be no such *theory* of justice, of what justice *is*, offered here.

Philosophy, that is, has something to say about how we should arrive at answers to our moral and political questions, but it does not have everything to say. We shall see that, on the pragmatist view, our local deliberations will continue to be conducted much as they are already conducted – with a variety of thoughts which support our actions and with a variety of arguments and appeals. My project here is not to try to say what the upshot of those inquiries will be, or must be. My project, rather, is meta-ethical. It is an exploration of how morality and politics fit into our world-view. It is an argument about why our substantial debates in morals and politics have the shape they do. It is an argument which starts from some general thoughts about the nature of truth, belief, and assertion and proceeds to the conclusion that we can see moral deliberation and deliberation about how best to live our lives as being truth-apt.

So, in the course of Chapter 3 when I make substantive points about what kinds of institutional and educational reforms might be needed to make possible and encourage debate which is open and accessible to all, my intention is not to provide a blueprint for how society ought to structure itself. All of these are mere suggestions, themselves open to debate, about what best promotes moral inquiry and the search for truth.

I shall, that is, offer only a guiding methodological principle for inquiry, one which insists upon the inclusion of those who are or might be excluded in deliberation. This principle will lead to a justification of democracy, in its broadest sense. It will not suggest that the outcomes of a deliberative democratic process are true, but it will suggest that such outcomes are legitimate.

We shall see that one point to make with respect to any democratic deliberation is that, in principle, one can learn from others. With respect to deliberation about what is valuable, this means that personal conceptions of the good, if you like, aren't entirely personal. This is not the claim that in fact I have to be able to successfully defend my conception of the good against other people, only that, in virtue of having beliefs and assertions that aim at truth, I am committed to being prepared to make the attempt. It is also not the claim that, in order to live on morally acceptable terms with others, I must present to them reasons which they can accept. That is a claim which rests on the prior acceptance of an idea like equality or respect for persons, ideas which we shall see we cannot take for granted.

Those readers who already see the need to provide a non-foundationalist account of objective justification which does not beg the question against anti-democrats can proceed directly to Chapters 2 and 3 without much trouble. For Chapter 1 is concerned with showing the need for that kind of theory of justification. It is concerned with displaying a problem about truth which plagues moral and political theory – the anxiety which arises from not wanting anything to do with dogmatism in moral philosophy but then not having anything much to say about truth and justification.

Those concerned primarily with moral epistemology – questions about objectivity and truth – will find Chapter 2 more pertinent. Those concerned with political philosophy – questions about neutrality, conflict, and the politics of difference – might want to focus on Chapter 3. The different styles of these last two chapters is, I think, unavoidable for those who want to link 'analytic' discussions of moral epistemology with debates about the nature of and prospects for democracy and liberalism. But understanding that link need not require being as interested in one part of it as the other.

1 The problem of justification

Carl Schmitt and the aim of substantive homogeneity

Colonialisation, immigration, war, movement of refugees, redrawing of boundaries, and increased mobility and communication have made contemporary society highly pluralistic. Within any nation state, there are competing conceptions about how best to live a life, about what is good, and about appropriate religious, educational, and moral values. These differences may be magnified where there is civil strife or war, or between nations states where there is competition for territory or for dominance. Often disagreements become intractable and turn violent. Indeed, the liberal democratic hope for a peaceful future might seem these days rather naive. Michael Ignatieff captures the disappointment nicely:

> With blithe lightness of mind, we assumed that the world was moving irrevocably beyond nationalism, beyond tribalism, beyond the provincial confines of the identities inscribed in our passports, towards a global market culture which was to be our new home. In retrospect, we were whistling in the dark. The repressed has returned, and its name is nationalism.
>
> (1993: 2)

Of course, pluralism has been around for a long time and the need for moral and political philosophers to respond to it is not new. In this chapter I shall articulate some responses to the fact that values conflict and I shall display the anxiety about truth that often accompanies such responses. It appears to many that it is so difficult, and so dangerous, to maintain that there is one and only one truth that we ought to stay away from truth-talk in morals and politics.

One way philosophers and political theorists have responded to the fact of pluralism has been to try to set out some universally applicable, categorical standards which will, in principle at least, objectively resolve the conflicts which arise. But, on inspection, none of the proposed standards really is universal and none of the proposed systems really does justice to the situations in which we find ourselves. Indeed, it has been argued that the proposed standards are simply those thought best by a particular group – usually comfortable white liberal male theorists.

I shall nod in the direction of some of these arguments against the standard-setting liberal later on. Here I want to examine an alternative liberal response to the fact of pluralism. For it leads quickly to a disturbing problem, one which we will encounter again and again in the pages to come.

A second way liberal political theorists try to cope with the fact that there are many competing moral ideals or conceptions of the good life is to take a hands-off attitude. It is urged that the state be neutral about what is worthwhile and what is not. This kind of liberal is a sceptic about objectively right standards – we cannot know what is good and what is not.[1] If we cannot adjudicate between competing conceptions of the good, then we should tolerate them all or treat them all as equally worthy. This requires us to refrain from supporting laws or policies on the basis of our conception of the good.

A problem which is supposed to arise for this view is the problem of relativism, of having to say that rightness is always a matter of merely being right-for-us. There is supposed to be an air of inconsistency here, for the relativist seems to want to make one non-relative claim – that relativism is correct. We shall see, when we turn to Richard Rorty's view, that this sort of charge is easy enough for the hands-off liberal to sidestep. And this way of putting the problem for the hands-off view fails, I think, to get the heart of the matter.

To see what is at issue here, let us not insist that there is something incoherent about relativism. Let us assume, for the sake of argument, that moral and political judgements can be right-for-us and wrong-for-others. One response to this thought is the liberal-designed response. If there is no way of determining which set of beliefs, which way of life, is best, then everyone must tolerate the ways of life which differ from his or her own. But another, all too frequent, response to the relativist idea is that which was most famously and most frighteningly put by the philosopher of fascism, Carl Schmitt.[2]

Schmitt was a Weimar legal scholar who found the Nazi bandwagon so congenial to his view that he for a time jumped aboard it. He held that there is no truth or rational adjudication in post-Enlightenment ethics and politics. Rather, politics is a matter of conviction, akin to theological fervour. He concluded, not that the beliefs of all must be respected, but that politics is a battleground between self-defined friends and enemies where the strongest will win:

> ... each has to decide for himself whether in the concrete situation the otherness of the stranger signifies the negation of his own way of life so that he has to be fended off and fought in order to preserve the way of life that is existentially important.
>
> (Schmitt [1932](1976): 27)

Of course, a way of life can lose out in a political battle. Schmitt argued that a mark of the political is intensity and 'the real possibility of physical killing … the existential negation of the enemy'. ([1932](1976): 33) He seems to have seen no moral problem here:

> When a people no longer has the power or the will to maintain itself in the political sphere, so politics does not disappear from the world. All that disappears is a weak people.
>
> ([1932](1976): 53–4)

The way of life Schmitt favoured was fascism or a right wing nationalism. He argued, moreover, that liberals are bound to lose the battle against such nationalism. Liberalism is an ideology which supposedly does not carry with it a conviction of its truth, for it claims to be neutral between or tolerant of all ideologies. And here Schmitt saw a tension at liberalism's centre. Liberalism is an ideology based on the conviction that a neutral state is best, while at the same time claiming that the pluralism of ideologies is to be tolerated. Liberalism's institutions try to prevent any one of those ideologies from dominating the others. In fact, however, the ideology of liberal neutrality then dominates the others.

It is this tension, Schmitt argued, which makes liberalism sow the seeds of its own destruction. Liberalism attempts to institutionalise neutrality by giving the individual certain rights against the state. These rights, however, enable the individual to get together with like-minded sorts and try to establish the particular conception of the good which he or she believes to be true. Liberalism thus opens its door to crises and power struggles. Because it survives only if no particular group wins the battle, liberalism poses a great threat to itself. It can deal with the threat only if the pluralism within society is watery; only if there is a good deal of taken-for-granted homogeneity. As soon as pluralism thickens, liberalism is in serious trouble.

The authoritarian solution to this dilemma, Schmitt argued, is irresistible. A sovereign decision must end the continual crisis of liberal democracy. 'Substantive homogeneity' amongst the population is what is to be strived for. The best political arrangement is one where a strong, centralised, authoritarian state is recognised as the source of political legitimacy.

There is a lot more to Schmitt than this. But the little I have said is enough to make his views sound familiar in today's resurgence of nationalism (indeed, Schmitt is still very popular in Germany and attracting interest in the United States, France, Italy, and Spain[3]) and it is enough to set the problem.

We can put it this way. If there is no objective right or wrong in moral matters, then what prevents one from adopting Schmitt's line rather than the line of tolerance? What can the hands-off liberal say to the Schmittian? If nothing can be said, then that is an indictment of that kind of liberalism. For the problem which presses at us from all sides is that the response to pluralism and to the absence of a universal basis of adjudication has too often been intolerance, an intolerance which has sometimes culminated in genocide. A political or moral theory cannot simply ignore such responses. It must have resources to deal with them; it must have something to say about why it is that such responses are mistaken. It must have some way of engaging the illiberal's arguments.

This problem for political philosophy has a parallel in moral philosophy, insofar as a distinction between the two can be drawn. The non-cognitivist in morals thinks that statements about what is right and wrong are not true or false. They merely express preferences.[4] But the non-cognitivist, like the hands-off liberal, also seems unable to say anything much against actions and views which she thinks abhorrent. What she can say is that torture or gratuitous cruelty to children is something which she has been brought up to react against. But her reasons for so reacting will be reasons which can only be local to her and those brought up like her.

The view of truth and justification I elaborate in the next two chapters will try to resolve this conundrum for political theory and moral philosophy. For the pragmatism one finds there does not give up altogether on a universal conception of truth. It is a view on which moral and political judgements can be true or false, despite the fact that people, within specific cultures and contexts, bring moral and political principles into being. And it is a view which offers a justification of tolerance and democracy which bypasses the principle of neutrality.

But before that view is set out, I want to try to show, by example, just how difficult it is to get such matters right.

Rorty and the abandonment of justification

Richard Rorty has campaigned over the last two decades to explode an old philosophical picture of truth and objectivity and replace it with his version of pragmatism. In some quarters he has been so successful that the first task for any other kind of pragmatist is to wrest the label from him.

Many of Rorty's negative points are well within what I take to be the real spirit of pragmatism. We must, he urges, cease thinking of the mind as a 'great mirror, containing various representations' of the world. (1980: 12) For this thought requires us to attempt the impossible – to try to get outside of our own minds and see the world as it really is. And we must resist the temptation to seek answers to questions such as 'Is reality instrinsically determinate, or is its determinacy a result of our activity?' All the potential answers share presuppositions which we would be better off dropping. We cannot find solutions to insoluble problems – problems which are mischaracterised and which take us down ill-chosen paths.

It is Rorty's positive arguments which, upon scrutiny, break with the pragmatist aim of elucidating the notions of truth and knowledge in human terms. Rorty thinks that the philosopher should happily jettison the notion of truth altogether and speak rather of justification relative to one group of inquirers or another. Truth, right reason, rationality, validity, and the like are myths. Truth is merely what passes for good belief; it 'is not the sort of thing one should expect to have a philosophically interesting theory about'. (1982: xiii) Indeed, Rorty is generally dismissive of theory. We must simply describe practice as we find it.

Were we to hold on to the term 'truth', against Rorty's advice, we would have to take it to mean that beliefs which are currently approved of are true. The notion of objectivity must be reinterpreted to mean intersubjectivity or 'solidarity'. (1991a: 13) It is what *we* have come to take as true.

What, we might well ask, is left of philosophy? Sometimes Rorty suggests that the role left for the philosopher is to become a 'kibitzer' (1982: 73) – a kind of informal cultural critic. We must abandon the 'spirit of seriousness' and get down to some 'play'. (1991a: 193–4). At other times, he says that philosophy must lower its sights and become a genre of literature or cultural studies. (1982: xli–xliii) It is a conversation governed not by truth and reasonableness, but by convention, culture, and personal interests. And at yet other times, he says that the philosopher's job is to produce generations of 'nice' liberal students (1993: 127).

Of course, if truth is as Rorty describes, philosophy is not the only area of inquiry which must face up to the fact. Even in science, on his view, we can identify no standards over and beyond the ones we happen to find ourselves with. Rorty thinks that it has been a pernicious mistake for humanists (philosophers, historians, literary critics, etc.) to take the 'objectivity' of science for their model, for there is there no objectivity there either (see 1991a: 36).

And in politics, morals, and political philosophy, we should not expect to find a rational justification of democracy or liberalism, or of this or that conception of the good, for nowhere are rational justifications to be had. What we have is the ongoing conversation in which we must make our decisions, form our policies, and live our lives. Here, as everywhere, we are to 'substitute the idea of "unforced agreement" for that of "objectivity"' (1991a: 38).

Rorty is a democrat and a liberal. The fact that he has given up the search for foundations does not, of course, lead him to give up his beliefs. But how, we will want to ask, can he assert that democracy, liberalism, and unforced agreement are best, if what is best is simply what is taken by some group to be best? It turns out that the 'we' in his claim that truth is what we take to be true is spelled out as follows: 'us twentieth-century Western social democrats' (1991a: 214), 'Western liberal intellectuals' (1982: 44), 'us post-modernist bourgeois liberals' (1991a: 199). What is best to believe is what democrats and liberals take to be best to believe.

To see just how Rorty thinks he can maintain that liberalism is the best view, while at the same time holding that there are no objective standards of reasonableness, let us turn to some familiar and related criticisms of his position.

First, it has seemed to many that Rorty's liberalism is especially smug and clubby – it seems that we are to determine what we are to believe and do by engaging in a playful, ironic conversation amongst those who agree with us. But of course, to the disenfranchised and the marginalised, it looks as if the powerful have simply formed an elite from which they are excluded. The deliberation that will issue in what 'we' take to be justified leaves out the voices of many.

A second charge, or set of charges, that Rorty has had to face is that his view results in a relativism where any view is as good as any other. This is then said to be an incoherent doctrine, or incompatible with Rorty's own commitment to democratic liberalism, or incompatible with Rorty's doing philosophy at all.

One of Rorty's responses to this clutch of criticisms is to say that he does not assert the bankrupt doctrine of relativism. Once we drop the vocabulary of truth, right reason, and objectivity, he thinks that we shall see that both realism and relativism are spurious. The very notion of a claim's being relative or having relative validity only makes sense if we have something with which to contrast it – something like absolute or objective validity. (1989: 47) Rorty is not putting forward any theory of truth, hence he is not putting forward a relativist theory (1991a: 24, 1989: 53).

But the dangers associated with relativism do not go away so easily. Calling for the dissolution of a dualism such as that between absolutism and relativism does not guarantee that one succeeds in escaping the pitfalls of one of the two positions. That is, after the call for an abandonment of a way of looking at things, that way must be replaced by another which *really does* undercut the old way. Rorty, like Schmitt, inveighs against the appeal to anything absolute, to criteria which pretend to be objective or neutral, and takes the only alternative to be to think that there are no criteria at all. But this is just to reproduce the dichotomy which he is set against.[5] The point of pragmatism, I shall argue, is to do something different – to put forward some modestly justified criteria, never pretending that they are neutral or that they mirror a reality which is utterly independent of what we think about it.

The best kind of pragmatist, that is, offers us a different way of looking at truth and objectivity. The best kind of pragmatist replaces the old dichotomy between neutral standards and no-standards-at-all with a substantive, low profile, conception of truth and objectivity, a conception which nonetheless can guide us in inquiry.

Another of Rorty's responses to the above set of problems is a response to the objection that someone who rejects philosophy cannot wield a philosophical theory to declare philosophical theorising spurious. Rorty argues that if one has a 'taste' for philosophy, as he does, then one will play with notions such as the 'self', 'language', 'knowledge', etc. and he commends his own picture 'to those with similar tastes' (1991a: 192). He is not going to *argue*, in the usual philosopher's way, for his position. Rather, he will try to make the vocabulary he favours 'look attractive by showing how it may be used to describe a variety of topics' (1989: 9).

But as Bernstein (1991) suggests, this defence is not convincing. Rorty does more than commend his view – he argues against absolutism and other associated philosophical positions. The standards of reasoning he uses in these arguments are ones he believes are good, not merely ones which he happens to have picked up and developed a fondness for.

Rorty does, however, think that in one respect his set of standards, what he plugs for, really is better than others. The 'ironic liberalism' he recommends has a strategy for 'avoiding the disadvantage of ethnocentrism' – it distrusts ethnocentrism by being open to other cultures (1991a: 2). The thought is that we are always trying to enlarge the scope of our community 'by regarding other people, or cultures, as members of the same community of inquiry as ourselves' (1991a: 38). 'What we cannot do is to rise above all human communities, actual and possible' (1991a: 38).

In this last remark, Rorty brushes up against the kind of pragmatism which I articulate. But, even if we were to grant that this enlargement of the community of inquirers is what liberals in fact do, it is far from clear that Rorty can claim that it is the right thing to do. I shall argue in Chapter 2 that the pragmatist should think it is the right thing to do because her view of truth and its accompanying methodology requires it. In the absence of such an account of truth, the Rortian pragmatist cannot help himself to the idea that we should try to take all cultures into account.

Moreover, Rorty's contention that all philosophical questions and hypotheses are spurious is itself an odd turn for a pragmatist – for one who insists that theory and practice be connected. Rortian pragmatism has it that philosophical theory, vocabularies, and debates are irrelevant to practice – they are pointless (1991a: 181–4). Rorty has become popular amongst some left-wing and radical thinking people. But, as Christopher Norris has argued, his advice to turn away from theory is devastating:

> we have reached a point where theory has effectively turned against itself, generating a form of extreme epistemological scepticism which reduces everything – philosophy, politics, criticism and 'theory' alike – to a dead level of suasive or rhetorical effect where consensus-values are the last (indeed the only) court of appeal.
>
> (Norris 1990: 4)

If someone really thought that there was no truth of the matter at stake, that there was nothing to get right or wrong, why would they commit themselves to a political cause? Theory is the stuff of many a revolution. Indeed, as Michelle Moody-Adams (1997: 160f) argues, it has *shaped* our practice. The language of property rights, cultural survival, liberty, equality, etc. saturate our moral and political lives and that language comes from philosophical theorising.

Rorty is passionate about the need to be an actor, not a spectator in political life. But he bluntly denies the point that his theory disables action: 'a belief can still regulate action, can still be thought worth dying for, among people who are quite aware that this belief is caused by nothing deeper than contingent historical circumstance'.[6]

We require more here. Any theory or interpretative stance, to use a nice phrase of Sergio Sismondo's, hugs the ground of practice (1997: 228). Philosophical positions have an effect on our practices and philosophers should see to it that their theories make sense of and promote what is good in that practice. Rorty's theory, despite his intentions, is not a friend of action, but of inaction.

Another way of putting the objection is to see that what opponents of relativism are often worried about is the inability of the relativist to say anything in response to those who assert and act upon evil beliefs. We want to be able to say that the neo-Nazi, for instance, has got things wrong or is immoral and we want to be able to explain to ourselves, in a convincing manner, why we are so right to oppose him. But all it seems that Rorty can say is that the neo-Nazi believes one contingent, cultural-laden theory and we believe another. It might be the case that nothing we can say will convince the committed neo-Nazi. But to think that we just *happen* to believe that he is wrong seems a rather pitiful reason *to give to ourselves* to justify our anti-Nazi stance. We can of course, rehearse the reasons we have for our stance, reasons having to do with individual equality and equal respect. But we will then have to admit that they are merely historically conditioned reasons, no different in status or worth from the neo-Nazi's reasons based on inequality and hatred of those who are foreign.

Rorty at times acknowledges that his position leaves one with nothing much to say. In the 'post-philosophical culture' he advocates,

> when the secret police come, when the torturers violate the innocent, there is nothing to be said to them of the form 'There is something within you which you are betraying. Though you embody the practices of a totalitarian society which will endure forever, there is something beyond those practices which condemns you'.
>
> (1982: xlii)

He thinks that prophecy is all that non-violent political movements can fall back on when argument fails (1991b, 1993). Emancipatory movements must reject argument and rational persuasion and then they are left with two choices – violence or prophecy.

These ideas are troubling because they seem to play directly into Schmitt's hands. Schmitt argued that political life is a struggle in which one claims some ground for oneself. Without asserting the objective truth of that ground (for there is no such thing as objective truth, over and above what is successfully established in struggle), one then attempts to win out over others. If we give up on truth, there seems to be nothing to stand in the way of thinking of 'us' as a narrow, homogeneous group. There seems to be nothing to stand in the way of refusing to see 'the other' or the stranger as a full participant in *our* moral life.

If one wants to avoid such a view of political life and its consequences, then something must be said about why some views are better than others; something must be said about why one view is right and another wrong. Against Rorty, there has to be a truth which is over and above the deliverances of particular ways of looking at things. Rorty is right that the thought that we have no basis upon which to criticise the torturer is a 'hard thought' to live with. But he is wrong, we shall see, in insisting that one who rejects foundationalism and absolute notions of truth must live with it.

We should watch out for Rorty's rhetoric here. He argues that we must give up our 'comforting belief' that 'competing groups will always be able to reason together on the basis of plausible and neutral premises' (1991b: 234). But no one thinks that competing groups will always be able to sweetly reason together and no one thinks that the basis of reasoning with others will be grounds which strike both as entirely plausible and neutral. We shall see that moral theory can adopt a much richer, much more accurate, picture of reasoning and deliberation than that.

Indeed, to characterise the cognitivist's thought as merely a comforting belief, like some kind of addictive crutch, is rather unfair. Rorty wants us to believe that there are no options for the cognitivist but an extreme form of realism (which Rorty mocks by giving it a capital 'R'), the function of which is only to give us a deluded sense of security. In doing so, he turns his back on all that is worth pursuing in his own pragmatist tradition – he turns his back on the subtlety the pragmatist has struggled to maintain in undermining the dichotomy between realism and relativism.

We might say that, as a pragmatist, Rorty is committed to bridging the gap between theory and practice and that the way he does it is by getting rid of theory and leaving only parochial practice. His is exactly the wrong way of looking at the relationship between philosophy and the ways we have of going on. The problem comes out starkly in the following passage, where it is recommended that philosophy be drawn from local custom:

> Given the preferences that we Americans share, given the adventure on which we are embarked, what should we say about truth, knowledge, reason, virtue, human nature, and all the other traditional philosophical topics?
>
> (1998: 28)

Taking the parochial status quo as a given and then going on to philosophy seems to be a strategy which arises out of despair – out of the realisation that philosophy cannot provide us with a rock-solid, entirely universal, foundation for our beliefs. If we cannot be put 'in touch with the way things really are', Rorty thinks we are left with no general criteria for justification at all.[7] We are left with nothing but this or that way of doing things.

But surely the appropriate response to Rorty here is that philosophy need not adopt the foundationalist universalist model, nor need it abandon standards altogether. If certainty or an utterly secure grounding is what is being sought by philosophy, philosophy is not going to be of much use. We shall see that this is a point at the heart of pragmatism. But following hard on the heels of that point ought to be the insistence that philosophy need not be so useless. We shall see that there are other kinds of justifications which can go hand in hand with the requirement that philosophy be connected to practice.

We should, I think, cast our lot in with those attempts rather than abandon ship as quickly as Rorty advises. If we take inquiry as seriously, as all pragmatists, including Rorty, recommend, the notion of truth cannot simply drop out of our vocabulary. For without the idea of truth, some core practices of inquiry, belief, and assertion cannot be explained or accounted for.

We assume, for instance, that it is appropriate to criticise the beliefs and actions of others and that we can make discoveries, mistakes, and progress. All of these practices need to appeal to something which goes beyond the parochial. We also require the concept of truth to distinguish between a belief which is adequate on the evidence and argument available, and a belief which would be adequate were all the evidence and argument available. Inquirers do not usually think that they have the truth in their hands, no matter how pleased they are with their views. In order to make sense of this thought, we must appeal to something which goes beyond what is reasonable here and now – we must appeal to truth. The pragmatist is well-advised to see what can be made of the notion of truth, before he recommends what the inquirer will find impossible.

Rawls: political, not metaphysical

In *A Theory of Justice* (1971), John Rawls put forward an influential thought experiment – one whose conclusion is that certain principles of justice are justified. The reader is to imagine entering an 'original position', abstracted from all personal, physical and intellectual capacities, race, gender, religion, and class. The only things to be retained are an ability to reason, a sense of justice, and some knowledge about how characteristics and capacities tend to be distributed in society. It is from behind this 'veil of ignorance' that we ought to choose the principles of justice that will govern society. The veil is supposed to embody the idea of fairness – thus Rawls calls his position 'justice as fairness'. It is also supposed to embody the thought that the right has priority over the good. The principles of justice which set out the rights of citizens will not depend on some particular conception of the good, the conception held by Catholics, by gays, by Muslims, or by thrill-seekers, for those in the original position will not know whether they are gay or heterosexual, Catholic or Muslim, cautious or adventurous.

The notion of agreement is central here. Justice is that framework which parties with potentially different outlooks and interests can agree upon, can enter into a contract with each other upon. The justification of moral and political claims is a matter of being able to justify one's policies and actions to other people in terms they could not reasonably reject.

Rawls argued that the following two principles would be decided upon in the original position:

(a) each person is to have an equal right to the most extensive basic liberty compatible with a similar liberty for others (1971: 60)
(b) Social and economic inequalities are to be arranged so that they are both (1) to the greatest benefit of the least advantaged and (2) attached to offices and positions open to all under conditions of fair equality and opportunity (1971: 83)

The second principle, the 'difference principle', holds that inequalities are justified only when they are to the advantage of the worst off. In a society which has allocated wealth such as ours has, this principle requires redistribution and captures Rawls' egalitarian liberalism, on which the state should see to it that each person has decent education, housing, and health care.

It may look as if Rawls' thought experiment makes deliberation central to the justification of the principles of justice. The correct principles of justice are not those which are arrived at by some special faculty of intuition or by divine revelation. They are determined by a certain procedure – a discussion between ordinary people who cannot let their own ideas of the good and their knowledge of their own lot in life influence the debate.

But much of the well-rehearsed criticism which *A Theory of Justice* has attracted takes it not to be a view which brings justification down from lofty heights and returns it to the people. Some have seen the original position to be an attempt to justify the principles of justice by transcending or ignoring the particulars of people's lives.[8] Rawls says that the basis he aims to establish for liberalism rests on an 'Archimedean point' (1971: 263) and of course such a point is not one which is capable of occupation by ordinary mortals. Individuals, the objection goes, are *constituted* by their commitments and attachments and cannot be thought of, and cannot think of themselves, as divested of them. There is no conception of the self prior to an individual's aims, hopes, and attachments, no persons who might be able to think themselves into the original position.

But once it is acknowledged that those in the original position will have to take some stance, it looks as if the stance Rawls must require of them is a life of rational debate or rational choice.[9] This, one imagines, would be Schmitt's response to Rawlsian liberalism. Rawls implicitly makes assumptions about what kinds of life are best – lives where rationality, conservatism with respect to risk-taking, etc. are dominant.

It has also been argued that the position articulated in *A Theory of Justice*, although it seems at first blush to be one which holds deliberation in high esteem, in fact seems to wash away real argument and debate.[10] There will be no disagreement amongst those in the original position, because they all share the same point of view. Rawls says:

> it is clear that since the differences among the parties are unknown to them, and everyone is equally rational and similarly situated, each is convinced by the same arguments.
>
> (1971: 139)

In the original position, 'the deliberations of the parties must be similar' (1971: 139). An individual could, by herself, make the required deliberations. There is nothing which requires communication in Rawls' thought experiment. From the impartial view of the original position, one need not consult or engage with others.

Over the last fifteen years, culminating in *Political Liberalism* (1993), Rawls has elucidated the ideas of *A Theory of Justice* so as to deal with such points. He argues that he puts forward no metaphysical view of the self as a rational chooser and no ultimate justifications or foundations for principles of justice. Indeed, the principles which would be decided upon in the original position are not meant, Rawls says, to be universally applicable. They apply only to modern constitutional democracies such as that found in the United States ([1985] 1999: 11).

These thoughts are summed up in the slogan that the theory of justice is *political*, not metaphysical. It is not meant to be a comprehensive philosophical, religious, or moral way of life – a doctrine which 'covers all recognized values and virtues within one rather precisely articulated system'.[11] Unlike comprehensive liberalism, which argues for liberal political arrangements on the basis that they promote certain goods, political liberalism is not a pronouncement about what is of value in human life. (1993: 175). Rawlsian liberalism is supposed to be independent of comprehensive doctrines.

Rawls' two principles of justice survive in a modified form in his recent work (see 1993: 5–6). But their justification is different. He now argues that they ought to be accepted, not primarily because they would be agreed upon in the original position and are thus shown to be correct, but because they are the principles on whose basis politics in a pluralistic society can proceed in a stable fashion.

Rawls, that is, holds that it is not the business of the political philosopher to articulate the 'true foundation' for this or that comprehensive view (1993: xviii). Even if one comprehensive doctrine is true, we could not know with certainty that it is true and we could not convince those in the grip of different comprehensive doctrines that it is true. Rather than search for such ambitious groundings of our beliefs, we should start from where we are and work out the relationships between, and implications of, our most important beliefs. We must start with our most firmly held beliefs and in inquiry, deliberation, and experimentation, forge them again and again into what approximates a coherent and consistent whole that squares with our beliefs in other domains.

Rawls, unlike Rorty, does not inveigh against the very idea that a comprehensive doctrine might in fact be true. But he does advise us to drop truth talk from politics and from political philosophy. Political liberalism is unmetaphysical in that it does not claim any kind of truth for itself. A political conception of justice 'does without the concept of truth' (1993: 94). Truth-claims are the province of those comprehensive doctrines. Reasonableness, in what we shall see is Rawls' rather special sense of that term, not truth, is the standard of correctness for political liberalism (1993: 127).

Like Rorty, Rawls seems to see the claim that a view is true to be a very strong claim. Bringing truth into a debate brings in 'zeal' (1993: 42–3) and brings in 'the relentless struggle to win the world for the whole truth' (1997: 766). I shall argue in the chapters that follow that we need not think of truth as being like that. But it is important to see at this stage that Rawls' political liberalism is not altogether sceptical about, or indifferent to, truth. Rawls makes it clear that one route that a comprehensive doctrine might take to political liberalism involves holding political liberalism to be true (1993: 150). And a comprehensive doctrine might well be true, but its truth cannot be appealed to in politics.

If we take the pragmatist's advice and refuse to think of truth as a metaphysical, all-or-nothing concept, perhaps Rawls would be less wary of thinking that political liberalism is true. Political liberalism, it might be argued, is the best arrangement, the best way to conduct our public lives. If that is right then, on the pragmatist's view of truth, political liberalism is true. But since Rawls does not contemplate such a view of truth, I shall stick to his stated aversion to truth-talk in political theory and see where that leaves him.

The shift in Rawls' mode of justification is due to his taking the fact of pluralism very seriously: 'a plurality of reasonable yet incompatible comprehensive doctrines is the normal result of the exercise of human reason within the framework of the free institutions of a constitutional democratic regime' (1993: xvi). He agrees with the oft-expressed thought, which motivates Schmitt and Rorty, that the Reformation scuttled the hope of a homogeneous system of values. What was faced there was a plurality of religious sects, where each claimed truth and authority for itself and where 'Luther and Calvin were as dogmatic and intolerant as the Roman Church had been' (1993: xxiii). From this set of historical circumstances, irremediable pluralism arose and, with the resulting inconclusive and interminable wars of religion, liberalism was born (1993: xxiv).

The question which then became pressing and which liberalism tries to answer is this: 'How is it possible that there may exist over time a stable and just society of free and equal citizens profoundly divided by reasonable religious, philosophical, and moral doctrines?' (1993: xxv). The answer, for most liberals and for Rawls (despite some qualms) is to insist on neutrality between reasonable conceptions of the good.[12]

The way Rawls in *Political Liberalism* gets to neutrality involves his thought that if one holds something to be true, then one is tempted to try to impose that view on the world. People's conceptions of the good, he says, often have a 'transcendent element not admitting of compromise. This element forces either mortal conflict moderated only by circumstance and exhaustion, or equal liberty of conscience and freedom of thought' (1993: xxvi). The first option aims to oppress all doctrines but one. Such oppression, Rawls suggests, is the only way a single conception of the good – even a liberal conception such as Kant's or Mill's – can be maintained. Oppression is the only way pluralism and diversity can be overcome (1993: 37, 54).

He thinks that the second option is clearly better. People take their conceptions of the good to be true – their conceptions of the good have a transcendent element – and they should cope with the pluralism of such conceptions by trying to achieve a stable and just society of free and equal citizens. We should not try to overcome pluralism, but rather, we should try to live with it.

What we must aim for is an 'overlapping consensus' where citizens, whatever their comprehensive religious, philosophical and moral doctrines, affirm the same political conception of justice. This overlap will not be a mere *modus vivendi* – whatever agreement or compromise a group of people happen to find acceptable or expedient. Political liberalism does not seek a metaphysical foundation for principles of justice, but neither does it seek any old consensus about them. The challenge in maintaining such a position is, of course, the challenge of justification set out at the beginning of this chapter and it presses hard on Rawls. Let us see how he thinks it might be met.

Rawls suggests that a 'free-standing conception of justice' will be agreed upon by all (1993: 10). It will be found to be the reasonable doctrine from the perspective of those holding different and competing conceptions of the good. One's reasons for accepting this conception of justice may appeal to specific beliefs in one's comprehensive doctrine. Individuals might have different moral reasons for accepting the conception of justice (which we might as well call liberal) and its associated institutional constraints. They will be genuinely committed to the conception of justice and thus it is not an agreement caused by a perception that something would be expedient or would be the best compromise. It is *endorsed* as the best outcome, morally speaking.

Thus Rawls thinks that 'we must distinguish between a public basis of justification generally acceptable to citizens on fundamental political questions and the many non-public bases of justification belonging to the many comprehensive doctrines and acceptable only to those who affirm them'

(1993: xix). For the overlapping political conception of justice and the overlapping conception of how to arrange the basic structure of society would be shared by more or less everyone and the comprehensive doctrines are not.

Here the liberal trademark distinction between the public and the private is found in Rawls.[13] Reasoning about politics or about 'the constitutional essentials and basic questions of justice' is distinct from reasoning about 'the associational ... the personal and the familial'. In public reasoning, one must rely on principles and values which all citizens can endorse (1993: 10). If my reasons for holding a principle in fact rely on a comprehensive religious, philosophical, or moral doctrine, I must refrain from citing those reasons in the public domain – in a court of law, in parliamentary debate, in my platform when I run for public office, etc. Public reason must not appeal to any substantive view of the good. To check whether we are following public reason we might ask:

> how would our argument strike us presented in the form of a supreme court opinion? Reasonable? Outrageous?
>
> (1993: 254)

Citizens, like judges, must keep their moral and religious convictions out of their public life. Only on the basis of an overlapping public consensus can coercion be justified – one must not impose upon others the values one thinks are right (1993: 61). Even if one's beliefs about what is valuable *are* true and important, they are in the wrong epistemic class for government use. Governments, political candidates and their campaign managers, policy makers, and judges must practice epistemic abstinence with respect to such reasons.[14]

So even if, against *A Theory of Justice*, we cannot conceive of ourselves independently of our attachments and commitments, we must bracket those commitments and attachments when acting as public citizens. The veil of ignorance in the original position can be kept on as a 'representational device' – it represents or models free and equal citizens, fairly situated (1993: 24–5). For political purposes, we must be as unencumbered as the stripped-down individuals in the original position. If this methodological principle is adhered to, our institutions can gain the support of an overlapping consensus and they will be stable.

So the justification of neutrality or 'impartiality between comprehensive doctrines' (1993: xxviii) and the priority of the right over the good in Rawls' recent work is that these are the only reasonable responses to 'reasonable pluralism', to the fact that free citizens will naturally disagree, and disagree reasonably, about what is good. We want to be neutral on divisive questions about the good life because then we can live with others on terms of mutual respect. Because we cannot expect agreement about the good and because we want to treat others with equal concern and respect, liberalism must be political. It must be a conception of politics, not of the good life. It is freestanding between conceptions of the good life, even if it is justified by a variety of comprehensive positions of the good.

The point I want to make against Rawls' way of articulating his non-foundationalist political theory can be got at in a number of ways. One is to follow through on an issue which begs to be heard throughout *Political Liberalism* – the complicated and deep issue of the nature of reasonableness. It will turn out that, although Rawls might be able to rule appeals to the good out of the court, he cannot rule such appeals out of the reasonable.

Rawls thinks that the minimal conditions for a doctrine's being reasonable are that it respects the principles of logic and practical reasoning, and it is open to gradual revision in light of what it takes to be good reasons (1993: 59). If this were the sole characterisation of a reasonable doctrine, almost every doctrine, even an illiberal one such as Schmitt's, would count as reasonable.

The crucial distinction for Rawls is that between the reasonable and the rational, where the rational is about means-end reasoning, not about the 'desire to engage in fair cooperation as such' (1993: 51). Rational action is acting effectively to promote one's ends and reasonable action is interacting with others on terms of equality (1993: 50). Reasonableness is tied, that is, to the ideas of equality, fairness, and cooperation. A person is reasonable if she is ready to propose principles as fair terms of cooperation and abide by them (1993: 49–50). A doctrine is reasonable if it upholds democratic freedoms (1993: 64, n.19). Reasonableness, Rawls argues, is not an epistemological idea; 'it is part of a political ideal of democratic citizenship that includes the idea of public reason' (1993: 62). Reasonable persons are those who are able to be 'free and equal citizens in a constitutional regime, and who have an enduring desire to honour fair terms of cooperation and to be fully cooperating members of society' (1993: 55). In short, the reasonable 'is an element of the idea of society as a system of fair cooperation' (1993: 49–50).

Rawls, that is, identifies a reasonable view of the good life with the liberal democratic view: 'Political liberalism ... supposes that a reasonable comprehensive doctrine does not reject the essentials of a democratic regime' (1993: xvi). And '[t]o see reasonable pluralism as a disaster is to see the exercise of reason under the conditions of freedom itself as a disaster' (1993: xxiv–xxv). Here, we have values or truths that the political liberal seems happy to assert: democracy is reasonable, non-democratic conceptions of the good are not reasonable, and unity, cooperation, and justice are what we aim at in political theory and policy. Indeed, it is also asserted as true that justice is a fair scheme of cooperation aimed at mutual advantage.

Schmitt will argue that the exercise of free reason will end with the conclusion that pluralism is indeed a disaster. Rawls thinks that such intolerant beliefs have been weakened (1993: xxv), but a quick look at the state of politics just about anywhere makes this look optimistic indeed.

So, despite Rawls' disclaimers, there seems to be a substantive, controversial conception of the good which drives his project.[15] It is, granted, a conception of the good which happens to have the feature that it is neutral among all other conceptions of the good that are in favour of (or capable of) peaceful coexistence. But this will not impress the Schmittian, who scorns such conceptions. His point will be that Rawls does not provide us with an independent or neutral justification of the liberal or democratic virtues; he just assumes those virtues.

Rawls admits that it is a mere 'hope' that views which would suppress basic rights and liberties will not be 'strong enough to undermine the substantive justice of the regime' (1993: 65). But he has real confidence that this hope will be fulfilled, that reasonable, 'normal'[16] citizens will gradually come together around the liberal democratic set of political values.

Schmitt rejects this social ontology – the view that the deep structure of society is that it is a cooperative venture for mutual advantage. On this view of society, the reason people form the likes of tribes and towns is that they aim to get along with each other in a way that benefits all. Schmitt, of course, thinks that the only people one really wants to get along with are those who are substantially like oneself and that the idea of mutual cooperation with others as a basis for stable society is unworkable.

Rawls does not pay much attention to this possibility. He merely hopes that what he takes to be 'irrational' and 'mad' and 'aggressive' (1993: xvii, 144) views of the good will be undermined when they are exposed to the public culture in a liberal democracy. The hope is grounded in the fact that the constitution in such a democracy will be against the spirit of illiberal views (1993: 64–5).

But the Schmittian will quite plausibly press us to notice how little the empirical facts justify us in helping ourselves to the thought that there is an overarching shared political culture; how little we are justified in thinking that social organisation has to be as Rawls says it is. Given the differences between people and cultures, it seems clear that there is nothing like a nascent consensus regarding the ideals at the heart of political liberalism. As Christine Sypnowich says, 'in taming justice as fairness ... Rawls becomes guilty of an undue optimism about, not just the value of agreement on his terms, but the extent to which this agreement is in place' (1996: 301).

Illiberal views cause trouble for neutralist liberal theory because liberalism has scant resources to deal with the illiberal. It must, Rawls says, 'contain them so that they do not undermine the unity and justice of society' (1993: xvii, also 64n.19) and contain them without asserting the truth of liberal democratic principles. One feels Rawls pulled toward the unhappy solution of guaranteeing that reasonable people with different comprehensive doctrines agree on the political conception of justice – for that is what it is to be reasonable.

Another way at getting at the problem is as follows: Rawls thinks that certain features of justice are 'implicit in the public political culture of a democratic society' (1993: 13). We are to begin 'from within a certain political tradition', one whose 'fundamental idea' is that society is a fair system of cooperation between people (1993: 14). We 'start within the tradition of democratic thought' and thus 'think of citizens as free and equal persons' (1993: 18–19). That there is, or at least could be, this kind of common democratic political culture is an assumption of Rawls' project.

Now if this were just the point that we must start from where we find ourselves, a point which is dear to the heart of the pragmatist, all would be well. But Rawls suggests something stronger, something normative. On the pragmatist view, there is nothing special about our starting point. It is the body of revisable background belief that we find currently justified, for reasons we think good. We might eventually find ourselves with beliefs very different from what we believe now, indeed, that is what we should expect of many a branch of inquiry.

Rawls is more wedded to the character of the starting point – rightly seen, justice is a matter of aiming at mutual cooperation. It is not clear whether this is supposed to be an analytic or conceptual truth or whether it is supposed to be so deeply entrenched that it is pretty much shared by everyone. One would think that if Rawls wanted to make the analytic, conceptual claim, he would have made that explicit. For then his conclusions would follow without further ado.

And if the identifications of reasonableness with liberal principles and of justice with mutual cooperation are supposed to unpack the concepts of reasonableness and justice, then these assertions of conceptual truths cry out for argument. None is forthcoming. We must, I think, take him to mean that history has delivered to us a political culture which takes, as a fact beyond dispute, that justice requires finding out how to live on terms of fair cooperation with others. This situation has of course arisen because of the facts of the wars of religion in the 16th and 17th centuries and the wars of ideology in the 20th century. In this sense, it is no accident that we are where we are.

Then he hits the difficulty. He cannot say, given that it is merely where we find ourselves, that the aim of cooperation is *right*. He must mean that it is simply with us, a part of what it is to be a citizen in a modern democracy. Our society happens to be a cooperative venture for mutual advantage. In this sense, it is an accident that we are where we are.

The problem is that, even if Rawls' social ontology were right, even if such ideas were so deeply entrenched that they were shared by everyone, nothing about that fact warrants the thought that that is what we ought to aim at.[17] But the assumption that it is what we *ought* to want is crucial. Without it, as Raz says, we would not regard Rawls' theory as a theory of *justice*, but a theory of social stability (Raz 1994: 54).

Rawls sees the danger of having a conception of justice which is 'political in the wrong way' – a mere list or some kind of average of the goods valued by existing doctrines (1993: 39–40). He thinks that his reasonableness requirement ensures that political liberalism will have at its heart the values of cooperation, equality, and the like. But in the face of Schmitt, this is just a list of the goods valued by an existing doctrine – liberalism. Why must we value cooperation and equality? Why must we want to live in a harmonious stable pluralistic society, as opposed to the Schmittian homogeneous society? Schmitt undermines Rawls' conception of the social world by arguing that a strong, homogeneous subgroup should use force to destroy that world – the doomed liberal political culture. Once the 'other' is eliminated, society will become substantively homogeneous and the problem of how to live cooperatively together will disappear. It will not be a problem because no issues which raise questions of cooperation will arise. Only co-ordination problems will remain, such as fixing railway timetables.

So the Schmittian challenge is to the very assumption that underlies political liberalism – to the thought that we should aim at a society of mutual advantage. Without that assumption, Rawls has nothing normative to say to the Schmittian, except that his own comprehensive doctrine is set against Schmitt's. Rawls simply does not have the theoretical resources to cope with the Schmittian position. Indeed, he says that his view just does not address those who take politics to be about the relation between friend and foe[18] – '[p]olitical liberalism does not engage those who think this way' (1997: 766–7).

Notice that the Schmittian challenge manifests itself in a number of ways in society – in the patriarchal, racist, anti-Semitic thoughts that women, non-whites, and Jews are inferior and must be kept in a substandard place. That is, the Schmittian challenge is not confined to the sceptical challenge – to the idea that there is no truth at stake in politics. The racist, the patriarch and the anti-Semite – anyone who seeks homogeneity – pose formidable Schmittian challenges, whatever they think about the prospects for truth in politics.

Rawls might say of the Schmittian in our midst that if he is not committed to the overlapping consensus, then we ought to coerce him to conform to the standards of that consensus. Indeed, there are moments in *Political Liberalism* where Rawls allows comprehensive doctrines to assert themselves in exactly this way:

> Nevertheless, in affirming a political conception of justice we may eventually have to assert at least certain aspects of our own comprehensive religious or philosophical doctrine … This will happen whenever someone insists, for example, that certain questions are so fundamental that to insure their being rightly settled justifies civil strife. … At this point we may have no alternative but to deny this … and hence to maintain the kind of thing we had hoped to avoid.
>
> (1993: 152)

Sometimes advocates of political liberalism will say that they think that their comprehensive doctrine is true, not just something about which there is an overlapping consensus (1993: 152–4). But this seems in straightforward tension with Rawls' insistence that political liberalism does not assert its truth.[19]

We have seen that Rawls' view, despite his claims to the contrary, appears to rely on a conception of the good. In light of this problem, we might conclude that Rawls should retract his claim that public reason should exclude appeals to the good. But there is an additional reason for the retraction. The idea that the citizen should bracket her beliefs about the good seems both unrealistic and undesirable.

Rawls' refusal to allow public talk about the good threatens to establish a kind of inarticulateness in ethics, a kind of quashing of moral and political debate as we know it. While no one should like such trends as that in American politics, where a speaker has to establish his Christian credentials before going on, and while a dislike of this kind of thing fuels Rawls' insistence that conceptions of the good are not grist for the public mill, the restriction on what can be said in public is overkill.

As Seyla Benhabib (1992: 98ff) has argued, the Rawlsian restriction would rule as illegitimate the many struggles against oppression which try to redefine what is considered private into matters of public concern. Issues regarding industrial accidents and harmful effects of chemicals used in the workplace, for instance, were at one time construed by employers as private, almost secret, matters for the business or trade. It took political struggle to make these issues ones of public concern, a fact that we now take for granted.

Along a similar line, David Dyzenhaus (1996) argues that Rawls' restriction would prevent gay couples from arguing in the public forum that their way of life is just as worthy of institutional respect as the heterosexual way of life. On Rawls' view, it seems that they can only argue that the law must not make judgements about any lifestyle, in particular, negative judgements about their own. But a prominent part of the gay political platform has been to have the worth of their way positively recognised.

Michael Sandel summarises these worries when he argues that taking moral and religious controversies off the public agenda results in a society which 'cannot contain the moral energies of a vital democratic life' (1996: 24). By taking comprehensive views off the agenda for public debate about policy and law, we deprive ourselves of an important way of deliberating about the plausibility of contending comprehensive moralities. If we can stay away from proselytising, if we can stay away from thinking that we must impose our views on others,[20] the attempt to persuade others of the merits of our moral ideals and to be persuaded by others of the merits of theirs is an important part of our moral and political lives. We respect others not by ignoring their comprehensive views, but by engaging those views – by attending to their beliefs, challenging them, learning from them, and arguing with them.

In the next chapter I shall put forward the kind of position of which Benhabib, Sandel and Dyzenhaus would approve, where deliberation and debate do not restrict themselves to that upon which we can all agree. Unlike

Rawls' view, this position shall not base itself on neutrality and it shall attempt to speak directly to illiberal views.

Harmony and the virtues of deliberation

We have suspected that at the heart of Rawls' political theory of justice is the assumption, contended by many, that we want to live in harmony with those who are not like us – that we want a pluralistic, stable, society to be possible. Here, I will look at how three other political philosophers who focus on the idea of public dialogue take this assumption to be pretty much straightforward. We shall see, in an even sharper way, how we must not take the assumption to be all that is needed by way of justification for the claim that public deliberation is central to questions of justice.

The first is Bruce Ackerman, who argues that the idea of neutral dialogue is the key concept of liberalism. It would be easy to mistake him for putting forward a practice-transcending thought experiment as the justification of certain principles of justice. For he at times draws heavily upon a scenario where a spaceship circles an empty planet, the colonisers bracing themselves for a decision as to how they will divide the scarce resources when they land and settle. They must have certain kinds of discussions, Ackerman argues, discussions which abide by certain conversational constraints. No one is allowed to suggest that her conception of the good life is superior to another's and no one is allowed to make an argument based on the claim that she is intrinsically superior to others (1980: 31ff). Ackerman thinks that the following is the central principle of rationality: 'Whenever anybody questions the legitimacy of another's power, the power holder must respond not by suppressing the questioner but by giving a reason that explains why he is more entitled to the resource than the questioner is' (1980: 4).

Like Rawls, Ackerman thinks that this dialogue must be constrained by a sort of neutrality. If you and I discover that we disagree about some moral matter, we 'should simply say *nothing at all* about this disagreement and put the moral ideals that divide us off the conversational agenda of the liberal state' (1989: 16, see also 1980: 11ff).

But it turns out that the view of justice, which is the conclusion of this thought experiment, can be got to in a less fantastic way.[21] In a paper about the justification of deliberation titled 'Why Dialogue?', Ackerman is very clear that a load-bearing pillar in his argument is the idea that we want to maintain a peaceful co-existence with others who are unlike us. *If* we are to maintain such a pluralist society, we must negotiate the distribution of goods and power in our society by dialogue. It is interesting to note that here again a thought experiment that initially seems to promise to *establish* a conclusion is really just a supplementary device. The real argument is an argument about what we want and what we need to do if we are to get what we want.

Once we see this, we can also see that Ackerman's recommendation that we must resolve our differences by talking to one another in this limited way will be attractive only if we accept what he calls the liberal problematic. It makes sense to resolve differences by democratic dialogue only if we want to find out 'how people who disagree about the moral truth might nonetheless reasonably solve their ongoing problem of living together' (1989: 8). Ackerman's 'supreme pragmatic imperative' is that '[i]f you and I disagree about the moral truth, the only way we stand half a chance of solving our problems in coexistence in a way both of us find reasonable is by talking to one another about them' (1989: 10). In order to live together, 'citizens of a liberal state must learn to talk to one another in a way that enables each of them to avoid condemning their own personal morality as evil or false' (1989: 12).

Ackerman is perfectly aware of the fact that his argument 'will not convince people who reject the underlying liberal problematic' (1989: 8). His aim is to convince one group in the liberal camp – those who think that disagreements are best solved in the economic marketplace – that dialogue is better.

It will by now be clear that I think this is not quite good enough. We need to search for an argument which will, if not convince, at least engage, those who reject the liberal problematic. It would seem that what Ackerman has to say about such people is that they are 'disqualified from the liberal project' (1989: 10). A person 'cannot think of herself as a participant in a *liberal* state unless she is willing to participate … in this ongoing conversation' with those with whom she disagrees (1989: 10).

But of course non-liberals will be happy to disqualify themselves from what they see as the bankrupt liberal project. The Schmittian does not want to live peacefully with those who do not share his conception of the good. He will turn rather to the project of securing substantive homogeneity in a nation, by violent means if necessary. Something more needs to be said. Repeating Schmitt's claim that he is not a liberal and does not want to participate in liberal democracy goes nowhere at all.

Let us also register a complaint about Ackerman's suggestion that liberals should not want to condemn the moral views of their fellow citizens as being evil or false. Surely we *do* want publically and morally to condemn the neo-Nazi amongst us, however inactive he might be and whatever we think about the issue of curbing his freedom of speech. The least, or in some cases the most, we need to do is to voice our moral approbation.

Not only do we need that approbation *heard*, but we need to think of it as having a particular status. If our moral condemnation of the racist who advocates genocide is to be made merely from within the privacy of our own conception of how we are to live, then the condemnation begs to be seen as not quite above board. It begs to be seen as having the same status as an aesthetic condemnation of the neo-Nazi, such as 'They're a tacky and unsavoury bunch'. Both kinds of judgement will seem to be made from within a parochial system of values, no better than any other system. What one wants is a moral judgement of larger scope – a judgement which has the neo-Nazi rightly condemned on moral grounds. I shall try to suggest how this might be possible in the next chapter.

Mark Kingwell also argues that just principles are the product of a kind of dialogue. And like Rawls and Ackerman, he thinks that when I don my role of citizen, I 'voluntarily screen off a host of (perhaps true) locutions I might utter in various other contexts' (1995: 89). One refrains, for instance, from making arguments based on one's Catholic or feminist beliefs (1995: 84). 'This is what it means to be a citizen'. (1995: 89) Society is always going to involve compromise (1995: 46). We do not, as citizens, aim at truth, but at civil goals – at getting along with others (1995: 218). Kingwell sees, and explicitly asserts, that a corollary of demoting truth as the goal of public deliberation is that we must also embrace a 'principled moral non-cognitivism' (1995: 218). Statements about what is right or wrong, just or unjust, do not fall within the scope of knowledge, for they are not the sort of statements that are true or false.

Kingwell's focus is on the constraint of civility in deliberation. It demands that we sometimes restrain ourselves from saying things which we think are true, but which are also irrelevant, inappropriate, or hurtful. There is much that is important in this point. That we try to be civil and careful of the sensibilities of others is necessary grease for the wheels of society. Indeed we might expand the point and argue, with Philip Pettit, that the law alone is not enough to establish freedom from arbitrary domination (1997: 246ff). If there are socially established norms in place which support freedom, then inclination, not law, will lead people to respect others. We might say that it is much better to be the kind of society where individuals are inclined, by way of acculturation, to respect others, not forced, by pain of sanction, to do so.

But even if acting civilly in deliberation required us to always withold our moral judgements and even if civility were the only way that our talk ought to be self-regulated (and of course, neither of these can be the case), the problem of justification would loom large for this view. The value of civility must be *justified* by the political theorist if he is going to take it as such an important constraint on dialogue. For civility is not thought by everyone to be a virtue.

Kingwell rests his justification of the value of civility on that now-familiar thought that we want to live in a peaceful and harmonious pluralistic society. We must be civil in order to 'show the minimal good faith necessary for a society to hold itself together' (1995: 45). We must engage in civil dialogue because of a *'political-pragmatic commitment'* to share and support common social space (1995: 178). Kingwell suggests that this commitment is not necessary, but rather, it is something that one finds in this society or that – in Canada, or Britain, or the United States.

But the difficulty for such views, we have seen, is what one might say to those who do not think it wise or desirable to try to hold our pluralistic society together, to those who think there is nothing good about sharing a society with those who are defined as 'others'. Those who believe that sharing a society is something which is alterable by force or by ethnic cleansing, or by marginalisation of the outsider will simply stand apart from Kingwell's audience. Kingwell argues that '[u]ntil we actually cease to share those goals – until we in fact go our own ways – this debate is the only kind of justice we can either desire or defend' (1995: 48). But the danger lies not only in going our own ways – in dissolving pluralistic society. The danger lies with those who would go their own way and block the way of others, or eliminate others altogether. Kingwell's position invites a kind of Schmittian battle: I will talk civilly to my friends, but if it turns out that we cease to share goals, we shall go our own ways, and those friends will become enemies.

Let us look at one more political theorist who rests his case on such assumptions about the value of harmony. Joshua Cohen, in 'Deliberation and Democratic Legitimacy', is also concerned with justifying the thought that the outcomes of a free and reasoned debate are legitimate. He sees that we need to explain why the features of the democratic ideal are important (1989: 17), and that our explanation must not be 'indirect and instrumental' (1989: 20). But he criticises Rawls' initial attempt at a full justification – the suggestion that the principles of justice mirror the choices that would be made by those in the original position. Cohen suggests that other political arrangements could just have well been 'derived' from the original position. A conception of democratic politics as a market system of bargaining with fair representation might just as well mirror Rawls' ideal of fairness (1989: 20). And justice based on bargaining – on the exchange of threats and promises[22] – is not what Rawls or Cohen wants to champion.

Cohen replaces Rawls' veil of ignorance model for our political institutions with a model of his own. We should not take the notion of fairness to be fundamental and then try to get to debate about the common good. Rather, we should start with the notion of ideal deliberation and try to mirror that in our institutions (1989: 20). We must start with an 'intuitive ideal of a democratic association'. On this ideal, the main principle is that outcomes of a decision-making procedure are 'democratically legitimate if and only if they could be the object of a free and reasoned agreement among equals' (1989: 22).

By way of elucidation, Cohen specifies that deliberation must be free insofar as the participants see themselves as bound only by the results and preconditions of the deliberation and they can act on those results (1989: 22). Deliberation must be reasoned insofar as the participants must state reasons with the expectation that those reasons will provide whatever persuasive force there will be (1989: 22). Participants in deliberation must be formally and substantially equal in that each can make proposals, offer reasons for or against proposals, etc. (1989: 22–3). And finally, the aim of deliberation is to 'arrive at rationally motivated *consensus* – to find reasons that are persuasive to all who are committed to acting on the results of a free and reasoned assessment of alternatives by equals' (1989: 23). If no consensus is reached, deliberation concludes with a vote. These are 'the conditions that should obtain if the social order is to be manifestly regulated by deliberative forms of collective choice' (1989: 21–2).

But of course this is a rather big 'if'. The question of justification is the question of why we should think that the social order should be regulated by deliberation. Cohen thinks that this ideal is intuitive, but he must spell out what stands behind his intuition. What justifies this model as opposed to another? Why should we mirror our institutions on the ideal of deliberative democracy rather than on some other ideal?

Cohen sees the justification of deliberative democracy in a set of its features. Deliberative procedures help 'to account for some familiar judgements about collective decision-making, in particular about the ways that collective decision-making ought to be different from bargaining, contracting and other market-type interactions' (1989: 17). A second virtuous feature of deliberative democracy is that it 'accounts for the common view that the notion of democratic association is tied to notions of autonomy and the common good' (1989: 17). Because everyone aims at getting results which are acceptable to all, deliberation is focused on the common good (1989: 23–4). A third virtue is that the theory 'provides a distinctive structure for addressing institutional questions' (1989: 17–18).

But the problem of justification reappears in the list of virtues. Why should participants in deliberation not reject the common good and aim at maximising their personal advantages? Why should we be committed to consensus and to collective decision-making and what do we think and do about those who are not so committed? What do we say about competing distinctive structures for addressing institutional questions?

We shall see in what follows that Habermas' and Apel's answer to these questions is that people necessarily are committed to free and equal deliberation as soon as they open their mouths to speak. But we shall also see that this kind of answer is far too ambitious. Cohen, like Ackerman and Kingwell, does not make that mistake, but rather, sets his sights too low.

His first response to the issue of justification is to acknowledge that thus far he has *stipulated* that the commitment to consensus and the common good exists (1989: 24). His second response 'rests on a claim about the effects of deliberation on the motivations of deliberators' (1989: 24). His answer to the question 'why should we be committed to deliberation?' is to show what good things follow from the commitment for deliberators.[23] Cohen's way of justifying the principles of deliberative democracy is to outline some more laudable features of such an ideal procedure of collective decision-making.

The thought is that '[w]hile I may take my preferences as a sufficient reason for advancing a proposal, deliberation under conditions of pluralism requires that I find reasons that make the proposal acceptable to others who cannot be expected to regard my preferences as sufficient reasons for

agreeing' (1989: 24). When I deliberate with others, I cannot take my preferences, as they stand, to be conclusive reasons. For those preferences are not
likely to be shared. In this way, the adoption of the deliberative attitude has
beneficial and transformative effects on our preferences. Someone who is
committed to the ideal of deliberation, as opposed to aggregate voting on
one's own preferences, will be willing to revise her understanding of her own
preferences and convictions (1989: 23). The need to advance reasons aimed
at a consensus, Cohen suggests, will increase the likelihood of a sincere
representation of preferences and convictions and decrease the likelihood of
their strategic misrepresentation (1989: 24).

Further, the commitment to deliberation will 'shape the content of preferences and convictions' (1989: 24). For 'the discovery that I can offer no
persuasive reasons on behalf of a proposal of mine may transform the preferences that motivate the proposal' (1989: 24). If, for instance, I desire to be
wealthy, and if I am committed to deliberation, I must find some independent justification for the policies which might make me wealthier. I cannot
appeal to my preference for wealth in the deliberation. I must appeal to the
common good and, when I have to be self-conscious of doing that, my preference for wealth might be transformed.

The voices of many others who think that the transformative effects of
the practices of deliberation contribute to the justification of those practices
can be added to Cohen's. Mark Warren argues that there are good effects on
self-development and self-realisation. Democratic experience produces
better people; making oneself in democracy is a good way of making oneself
(1995: 169).[24] Carlos Santiago Nino points out that having to justify yourself in front of others expands your knowledge and reveals defects in your
reasoning (1996: 113). It is also the best way to find out about the interests
of others, since an individual has trouble vividly representing the interests of
those he finds very different from himself.[25] James Bohman (1996: 27)
argues that open deliberation is justified because it is likely to improve the
quality of the reasons and arguments that get made. Public opinion is more
likely to be formed on the basis of all relevant perspectives, interests, and
information.

While it seems right that these things can flow from the practice of
advancing reasons while aiming at consensus, and while I agree that they are
good things, the question at issue remains unanswered. What do I say to
someone who does not value these things? What arguments can be given as
to why one should value them? I have been at pains in this chapter to point
to the fact that many reject the aim of getting along with those who are
different. It will be my contention in the next chapter that, contrary to the
non-cognitivist spirit of the views we have canvassed thus far, it is extremely
difficult, if not impossible, to abandon the aim of truth in political and
moral deliberation. I shall then argue that once those who reject the aim of
getting along peacefully see that they are committed to aiming at the truth,
an avenue is opened for the justification of the principles of freedom and

equality and for criticism of views which are set against those principles. That is, once we reinstate talk of truth, the problem of justification becomes less intractable.

One wonders whether a similar sort of argument might not lie behind the conditional justifications of deliberation we have just examined. Perhaps waiting in the wings is a suggestion that we constitute one and only one cognitive community.

Onora O'Neill, for instance, makes such a point in articulating a Kantian position. We can tell that there are shared standards of reasoning, that we share a tremendous amount with other, apparently very different, people because we encounter disagreement rather than disorientation. She says: 'If there were no standards of reasoning, the mutual (even if partial) comprehension on which disagreement rests would be impossible' (1989: 23). As Donald Davidson (1974) puts the point, the fact that we can understand and translate the utterances of 'foreigners' entails that we do not occupy different or incommensurable conceptual schemes.

Whether this kind of argument underpins the conditional justifications offered by Kingwell, Ackerman and Cohen is a matter of speculation. In the next chapter I shall offer my own version of it. But before I can do that, we must make ourselves aware of some rather serious pitfalls that can lie in store for such justifications of a deliberative conception of moral cognitivism. These pitfalls are illustrated best by an argument put forward by Karl Otto Apel and Jürgen Habermas and the pragmatist must do her best to avoid them. Apel and Habermas feel the full force of the justificatory demand and we will see from the difficulties they face in the attempt to meet it just why Rawls, Ackerman, Kingwell, and Cohen are tempted to ignore the call for justification.

Habermas, Apel, and the transcendental argument

Jürgen Habermas' reputation as one of the most important post-war political and social theorists rests in large part on his claim to deliver a philosophically unassailable argument for democracy. The details of that argument put Habermas squarely in the pragmatist tradition. He argues that the notions of validity, justification, and objectivity are inextricably linked to the human practices of communication and inquiry. Validity or truth is identified with what could be agreeable to all in an unconstrained communication or inquiry. [26]

Habermas' view does not face the difficulty encountered by those we have canvassed above – the difficulty of having nothing at all to say to the likes of the Schmittian. He speaks directly to Carl Schmitt. Germany's past and the current neo-Nazi threat are the heartbeat of Habermas' complex theoretical structure.[27] He is a champion of democracy and, in his 'discourse ethics', he claims to have found a justification of it.

We shall see that he thinks that he can prove, with a transcendental argument, that a moral judgement is right or valid if it could be accepted by all in an unconstrained discussion or ideal discourse. Furthermore, he thinks that he can prove that we can know that specific principles of inquiry are in fact valid, including: everyone has a right to participate in the discourse, every participant must try to assume the perspective of all others, every participant has an equal right to make his views known, to challenge other views, express his attitudes, needs, desires, etc. I shall call these the democratic principles.

Notice the strength of this view. If his arguments are sound, Habermas will have shown not only that there are right and wrong answers to our moral questions, but also that we can know that we are right about certain democratic methodological principles. And he will have shown that a valid or true statement is one which would be agreed upon under certain conditions of inquiry – i.e. that something like the pragmatic account of truth is right.

We shall see, however, that there are two instructive flaws in Habermas' attempt to make the full justificatory case. First, his proposed justification is too ambitious – it tries to show that the pragmatic account of truth and the democratic principles are necessarily true. But pragmatism, we shall see, should stick to a justification with a lower profile.[28] Second, Habermas' attempt to derive democracy from the conditions of communication works only if we adopt a strained and false-sounding definition of communication. Pragmatism must characterise the central concepts in a more intuitive, less contentious, way.

Before I can get to the details of Habermas' view, two interpretative issues must be settled. First, the transcendental argument in which I am interested is a product of both Habermas and his Frankfurt colleague Karl-Otto Apel. In the 1970s, both began to explore the idea that a presupposition of argument and communication is that a community of inquirers exists which could validate the claims made by speakers. Apel, who made the point in more detail,[29] saw himself as following in Peirce's footsteps. In 1990 Apel put forward, and Habermas seemed to endorse, a revamped version of the argument, claiming to have once and for all grounded the principles of discourse ethics 'in an undisputably valid manner'.[30] It is this argument which will be the focus of what I have to say.

Habermas has become reluctant to wholeheartedly embrace the transcendental argument. I shall argue below that his attempt to put some distance between his view and Apel's fails. Those who remain unconvinced or those who think that the other differences in the general philosophical pictures of these two philosophers are significant, can take my points to be against Apel only. I want to register an objection to the transcendental argument, unequivocally held by Apel and equivocally held by Habermas. Whether it remains Habermas' considered view is a side issue here, for it is the perils of the idea, whoever holds it, that concern me.

The second interpretative issue concerns Habermas' tendency to demarcate domains of inquiry with various sets of distinctions. First there is the purported difference between the natural sciences (the statements of which can be true or false) and morals (the statements of which can be valid or invalid). He initially spelled out the distinction with the positivist thought that only the natural sciences are formalisable. (1971: 161) Now, he says, still within the bounds of positivism, although he officially scorns that position, that the natural sciences are something we can form an 'objectivating attitude' toward (1990c: 60, 1990b: 24, 26). They are about states of affairs which 'exist independently of whether we formulate them by means of true propositions or not' (1990c: 61).

Compared to that, validity in morals, I suggest, has to look like a second-rate kind of thing. The would-be cognitivist who suggests that there is a plurality of truth predicates pays a heavy price. Moral truth, on that view, looks like truth's poor relation – warranted assertibility, unforced agreement, or whatever. These notions cannot be the notion of truth, if we have as a contrast to them something more robust, something more like the truth predicate the correspondence theorist has always sought. For in the presence of that more robust concept, a gap opens between warranted assertibility or unforced agreement on the one hand, and truth on the other. We can always ask whether a belief which is warranted or agreed upon is *really* true.

This kind of position might please the realist who wants to salvage *something* from what Quine thinks of as the wasteland of moral and political judgements (1987: 5, 1981a: 63). A realist might well be loath to give up on the thought that our moral judgements can be criticised and praised in a rational way; she might want to hold on to the idea that some moral judgements are right and others wrong. On the correspondence account of truth and objectivity, these thoughts make no good sense. A moral belief cannot mirror a believer-independent fact. The realist might thus be tempted to append to her epistemology and metaphysics an altogether different sort of objectivity for morals and politics – one which starts from the thought that morals and politics are tied to the human condition in a way that judgements about the physical world are not. In morals we can have a sort of second-best objectivity and legitimacy – that which would be agreed upon at the end of an open public deliberation.

I shall argue in the next chapter that this would be a mistake. The view of truth and objectivity which the pragmatist and Habermas share should not be intended to fit only moral and political deliberation. We shall see that the strongest arguments in its favour are entirely general – they do not turn on some special feature of moral inquiry. So I shall ignore Habermas' distinction between morals and science and use 'truth', 'validity' and 'rightness' interchangeably and of any domain of inquiry.

Habermas also distinguishes morals and politics,[31] arguing that only in morals can we have universalisability – one answer which is correct for all. In politics, bargaining and compromise get in the way of genuine communication. Politics is supposed to be about what is reasonable in certain political contexts and circumstances, whereas morals is about what is right and wrong, whatever the particular circumstances an agent happens to find herself in.

But on a pragmatist theory of morality, context and circumstance are brought to the fore, so such a distinction between morality and politics cannot be sharply drawn. We can easily rephrase questions about what compromise to adopt. The apparently circumstance-laden compromise 'in this context, we ought to do *x*' becomes the ordinary truth 'it is right to do *x* in this context'.

Finally, Habermas distinguishes moral questions from ethical questions. The moral is that which can be decided in rational deliberation (1990c: 108); it is the set of principles which govern collective life. Ethics is the set of values that govern individual decisions about the good. This, despite Habermas' best intentions, entrenches the distinction between public and private which I shall argue against in Chapter 3. And I shall also argue that statements about the good life can be true or false.[32]

On to the heart of the matter. We immediately encounter the problem of justification in Habermas' position. His view is that a judgement is valid if it could be agreed upon in an open, unconstrained public discussion; i.e. a democratic discussion. But the principles which turn out to be valid in such a discussion are the very principles which reiterate the idea of democracy: everyone must have an equal say, everyone has a right to be heard, etc. Something like a circle appears.

Habermas is keenly aware of the need to offer an independent justification of his view of validity – of the view that a valid judgement is what results from a certain kind of public deliberation. And he is keenly aware of the need to provide a non-circular justification for the principles of democratic inquiry. For only then will he be able to say to the neo-Nazi that he has *shown* that view to be wrong. His is not an account of moral validity which applies only to one culture, say a culture like ours which thinks well of argumentation. He wants to arrive at some principles which will allow him to criticise non-democrats. He wants to 'prove that [his] moral principle is not just a reflection of the prejudices of adult, white, well-educated Western males of today' (1990d: 197). So he sets out to develop an ambitious grounding of those democratic deliberative principles.

This grounding takes the form of a 'transcendental' argument. Such an argument, as it is usually conceived, aims at showing how some principle is true by showing that it is a necessary condition for the very possibility of some undeniable fact or for some capacity which we undeniably have. Accordingly, Habermas and Apel claim to have uncovered the universal, necessary, non-contingent preconditions of communication – the conditions of the very possibility of communication.[33] The justification of the pragmatic account of truth and the principles underlying discourse ethics is that if communication is possible, that account of truth and those principles must be correct. In Habermas' words, 'anyone who seriously undertakes to participate in argumentation implicitly accepts by that very undertaking general pragmatic presuppositions that have a normative content' (1990d: 197–8). Anyone who would argue against Habermas, or for that matter, make any assertion at all, commits herself to Habermas' conclusions: to the view that validity is that which would be the result of unconstrained argument,[34] to the claim that those results hold for everyone, and to the democratic principles of inquiry.

Let us look at Apel's way of setting out the argument. He takes the problem of justification to be captured by the idea that any proposed justification will be caught on one of the horns of a trilemma.

The first horn is that one can offer a justification which turns on statements which themselves need to be justified. An infinite regress will be the result. The second horn is simply to refuse to try to justify the principles any further. But to state that the rock bottom has been reached is just to dogmatically accept something like a first axiom. The third possibility is a kind of circular justification. One could appeal to a further principle which presupposes the principles which are in need of justification.

Apel's way out of the trilemma involves rethinking the third horn. He wants to argue that the principles in question are presupposed in any argument. This justification (being an argument itself) presupposes the principles and thus the justification appears to be circular. But a circular justification, Apel argues, is inadequate only on a view which identifies justification with a deductive proof, where justification means deriving a principle from something already established.[35] This view of justification, he suggests, stands in direct competition with the transcendentalist view, which holds that to justify *A* is exactly to show how *A* is always presupposed. The third horn of the trilemma is just not problematic for the transcendentalist.

That is, in Apel's transcendental proof, the capacity which we undeniably have is exercised in the very assertion of the proof. This is supposed to show that the principles are indeed unavoidable. The argument is not viciously circular in that it relies on its conclusion as a premise in the following way: *A*, *B*, therefore *A*. Rather, it proceeds like this: *A*, *B*, therefore *C* and *C* is required to even formulate *A* and *B*.

So circularity is not what is wrong with Apel's justification. To see what *is* wrong, we need to see how Apel compares his strategy with Descartes' attempt to show that 'I exist' is necessarily true. Apel claims that:

1 'I hereby assert that I do not exist'
   has the same status as
2 'I hereby assert as true (i.e., intersubjectively valid), that a consensus regarding that which I assert cannot be expected in principle' and the same status as
3 'I hereby assert as true that I am not obliged *in principle* to recognize all possible members of the unlimited community of argumentation as having equal rights'.

(Apel 1990: 43)

The claim is that the denial of the expectation of a consensus (i.e. 2) and the denial of the democratic principles of discourse ethics (i.e. 3) are, like 'I do not exist', self-contradictory, pragmatically contradictory, or performatively self-defeating.

It is this version of the transcendental argument which Habermas seems to have reservations about. Nonetheless, he approves of Apel's central point:

> ... Apel uncovers a performative contradiction in the objection raised by the ... ethical skeptic [who] denies the possibility of grounding moral principles and presents the above-mentioned trilemma ... in making his argument, he has to make assumptions that are inevitable in *any* argumentation game ...
>
> (1990c: 80–1)

Habermas claims that Apel has 'refuted the objection from the logical trilemma' (1990c: 79) and that the discourse ethics which they both champion 'uses transcendental arguments to demonstrate that certain conditions are unavoidable'. (1990c: 129) And in his most recent work he refers to the transcendental justification as if it were a rather straightforward result (1995: 4ff).

Habermas would do better, I suggest, to stand firm with his reservations. For Apel's argument is not very good. While we can see the tension in the performance of the assertion 'I do not exist', it is much more difficult to see it in Apel's two cases. First, (2) exhibits tension *only because* truth is identified with what is intersubjectively valid. That is, the tension arises in (2) only if we read it in the following way: It is intersubjectively valid (i.e. there would be a consensus about it) that I can never expect a consensus about what I assert. The tension fails to arise in the following assertion: It is true that I can never expect a consensus about what I assert.[36] Only if '*P* is true' is equated with 'there would be a consensus about *P*' is there any performative tension and of course this begs the question rather grandly. Apel's sceptical opponent and his realist opponent will have no problem asserting that no consensus can be expected about anything. The sceptic, who thinks that there is no truth to be had, will simply say that it is likely that people will never come to agree. The realist will say that, even if people were to come to agree, that would not guarantee the truth of their beliefs – it would not guarantee that their beliefs got the believer-independent world right.

Now if there is a convincing independent argument for the deliberative or pragmatic account of truth, one might go ahead and argue for a tension in 2. But since the transcendental argument is intended to be the argument for the pragmatic theory of truth, Apel cannot escape the charge of begging the question. And it is important to see that the transcendental argument cannot get off the ground if the question is begged here. For the transcendental argument needs to start with something non-contentious, such as 'everyone makes assertions' or 'everyone communicates'. It cannot rest on a claim which needs further argumentation such as 'truth is what is intersubjectively valid'.

There is another, related, reason why Apel's (2), and (3) as well, should not strike us as being in the same performative straits as Descartes' (1). We are supposed to see that one cannot engage in argumentation without adopting the pragmatic account of truth and the democratic norms. We are supposed to see that it is

> always already presupposed a priori by every person who seriously argues ... that discourse is not merely one possible 'language game' among others but rather, as the only conceivable instance of justification and legitimization, is applicable to disputed claims to validity in all possible language games.
>
> (Apel 1990: 45)

This claim can be seen as a corollary of Habermas' definition of communicative action: communicative action is non-strategic action aimed only at consensus and mutual understanding, not at influencing others.[37] Nothing else counts as communication.

But, on the face of it, it seems that some people do communicate – do speak and utter statements to others – without presupposing the things Habermas and Apel insist are undeniable. Those very people to whom Habermas is so rightly opposed, those who think that only people of a certain genetic character are worthy of rights and participation in the community, simply refuse to adopt Habermas' norms. The criticism that Habermas and Apel want to make of these people is that the tension manifested in this stance is so severe that they *must*, on pain of ceasing to be a communicator, adopt the democratic norms.

Here Habermas sometimes has rather strong things to say. Of a person who might refuse to enter into argumentation, Habermas asserts that he 'voluntarily terminates his membership in the community of beings who argue' and '[b]y refusing to argue ... he cannot, even indirectly, deny that he moves in a shared socio-cultural form of life, that he grew up in a web of communicative action and that he reproduces himself in that web'.[38] He cannot reject these

> life circumstances in which he spends his waking hours, not unless he is willing to take refuge in suicide or serious mental illness. In other words, he cannot extricate himself from the communicative practice of everyday life in which he is continually forced to take a position by responding yes or no. As long as he is still alive *at all*, a Robinson Crusoe existence through which the sceptic demonstrates mutely and impressively that he has dropped out of communicative action is inconceivable, even as a thought experiment.
>
> (Habermas 1990c: 100)

Habermas, from the beginning, has stressed the importance of the notion of communication. Truth, inquiry, and the very identity of an individual have communication at their centre.[39] Communication is not merely an important feature of our lives – it constitutes our very selves. This philosophical anthropology drives the entire project – it is why people 'do not have the option of a long-term absence from contexts of action oriented toward reaching an understanding' (1990c: 102). Such an option leads to 'schizophrenia and suicide' – to an 'existential dead end' (1990c: 102). Habermas thinks that being an indentifiable live individual entails engaging in communication.

But then he makes a further claim about what communication is. And the further claim seems either simply to be false or purely a matter of stipulation. Habermas' opponents straightforwardly engage in undemocratic, strategic, nasty communication.[40] It appears that Habermas and Apel want to stipulate them out of the game by defining the game in a way that precludes them. Being a communicator seems to mean arguing in the way Habermas and Apel advocate.

But, of course, it is just not the case that being alive or being an identifiable individual or being sane requires the adoption of the democratic principles.[41] While it might be plausible that communication is at the centre of the notions of truth, objectivity and personhood, it seems simply wrong to define communication in the restrictive way in which Habermas does. And one must ask whether a theory which starts off with such a strained characterisation of what it is to be identifiable, alive, and sane is going to be able to have any political bite; one must ask whether the theory can be of any political interest. We need other ways of criticising anti-democrats and indeed, non-cognitivists and sceptics about morality.[42]

It is not, however, to this matter that Habermas' words of warning about Apel's argument are addressed. It is the strength of the transcendental argument about which he worries. He says that he offers a 'more cautious version' of the argument (1990c: 76), a 'weak transcendental' argument (1990b: 32), or an argument for 'quasi-transcendental necessity' (1990d: 203). He wants to modify Apel's argument 'so as to give up any claim to "ultimate justification", without damage to the argument' (1990c: 77). The conclusion of his weaker argument is still that the democratic principles are unavoidable (1990c: 79,129).

But, on the surface, a transcendental argument is an all or nothing affair – it either proves that something is a precondition for a capacity we have or it fails to do so. It is not clear what a 'weak' or 'quasi' transcendental argument might aim at and it is not clear that the strength of the conclusion can be altered without doing damage to the argument.

One way in which Habermas tries to modify the strong transcendental view is to suggest that he does not want to show that denying each one of the substantive democratic principles places the arguer in a pragmatic contradiction. Rather, Habermas takes the principle which requires and which receives transcendental justification to be a general claim of universalisability:

> [U] For a norm to be valid, the consequences and side effects of its general observance for the satisfaction of each person's particular interests must be acceptable to all.
>
> (1990d: 197)

[U] is a 'rule of argumentation' which is 'implied by the presuppositions of argumentation in general' (1990c: 86). That is its justification.

The reason Habermas suggests that only [U] (not the principles of discourse ethics) is transcendentally justified is that he thinks that Apel fails to show that the principles of discourse ethics are justified outside of the context of actual discourse. Apel's argument seeks to show that when one is participating in an argument, one must accept the principles – to fail to recognise their validity places one in a tension with the business of arguing. But once the argument is over, as it were, the principles could be abandoned: participants can 'shake off this transcendental-pragmatic compulsion when they leave the field of argumentation' (1990c: 86). Thus, the 'necessity of making such presuppositions is not transferred directly from discourse to action'.

But Habermas thinks that 'once it has been shown that [U] can be grounded upon the presuppositions of argumentation through a transcendental derivation, the substantive norms of discourse ethics itself can be formulated in terms of the principle of discourse ethics [D]' (1990c: 93). [D] states that this or that ethical norm is valid only if all who might be affected by it reach (or could reach), *as participants in a practical discourse*, agreement that it is valid. What distinguishes [D] from [U] is that [D] is a principle of validity that may be asserted only after the possibility of justifying norms of action (transcendentally) has already been established (1990c: 66, 93). The upshot seems to be that if the democratic ethical norms cannot be derived directly from considerations about argumentation, they can be derived in a slightly more roundabout way. They can be derived from the presuppositions of practical discourses, for such discourses make use of the principle of argumentation.

It is not really clear how this weakens the transcendentalism of the argument. Given that the democratic principles are derived from a principle that has supposedly been shown to be necessarily valid by a transcendental argument, they too will be justified in this strong sense. Habermas, it seems, merely distinguishes different levels of generality of the principles of communicative ethics, and then has the justification flowing down from the most general to the more specific. But the justification is not watered down in the process. The 'idea of impartiality', for instance, is still 'rooted *in* the structures of argumentation *themselves*' (1990c: 75–6).

The second way in which Habermas tries to weaken the transcendental argument is to say that 'the assertion that there is no alternative to a given presupposition, that it is one of the inescapable (i.e. necessary and general) presuppositions, has the status of an assumption. Like a lawlike hypothesis, it must be checked against individual cases' (1990c: 97). The theory of communicative action is not a transcendental *a priori* theory, but a scientific-philosophical 'reconstructive theory' – like that of Chomsky, Piaget and Kohlberg (1990a: 15ff). Such a theory tries to 'explain the presumably universal bases' of some capacity, such as experience, judgement, action and linguistic communication (1990a: 16).

So the reconstructions of the presuppositions of argumentation are fallible and must be up for discussion themselves. We must 'cease striving for the foundationalism of traditional transcendental philosophy' (1990c: 98) and 'deny that the transcendental-pragmatic justification constitutes an ulti-mate justification' (1990c: 98).

His suggestion is that the principles of argumentation can be tested, 'where "test" means to investigate whether different pieces of theory are complementary and fit into the same pattern' (1990b: 39). The principles might, for instance, 'prove to be unusable in the context of application within the empirical theory', a theory such as Kohlberg's theory of moral development (1990b: 39).

This is an unusual sense of 'testing', where a theory is tested by its ability to cohere with other bits of theory. If Habermas means also to suggest that theories must fit our experiences and considered judgements, we have some-thing like a theory being tested by experience or data. I shall argue in the next chapter that this is indeed part of the method by which we justify ordi-nary moral judgements.

But it is not clear how Habermas can make the suggestion with respect to the democratic principles if he holds on to the idea that they are unavoid-able. How can fallibility be squared with his argument that one is not really alive if one does not presuppose the principles or norms in question? The claim that we must 'necessarily' presume something has a clear non-falsifi-able ring to it. It is Habermas' argument, call it transcendental or not, that the principles are *unavoidable* which jars with the claim that the principles are revisable.[43]

That is, we must ask whether Habermas' reconstructions of the principles of discourse can *really* be falsifiable hypotheses up for confirmation or disconfirmation. The thing to keep in mind is that he is not merely putting forward hypotheses about what is good, right, and just. He is putting forward hypotheses about what the unavoidable presuppositions of commu-nication are. And it is not clear what evidence could confirm or disconfirm principles such as '[i]t is a presupposition of discourse that everyone is allowed to introduce any assertion whatever into the discourse' (1990c: 89). A reconstruction of the principles which are presupposed by or built into discourse does not fall easily into the mould of a scientific hypothesis. It has more the flavour of a conceptual analysis.

Indeed, we have seen that the above principle seems blatantly false in that many people assert and argue without thinking that anyone has the right to freely speak or to have his say. Habermas, in ignoring this thought, betrays the fact that he takes the principles to have a special status. If it were the case that they were ordinary falsifiable hypotheses, one would think they would be falsified by the empirical fact that they are often absent or not presupposed in communication and argumentation.

In addition, Habermas' antipathy to the likes of Schmitt is such that he should not want to say that the principles are revisable. *Some* principles of inquiry must be really justified if we are to block claims from the neo-Nazi and misogynist that *their* principles are the best. Habermas wants the principles of discourse ethics to play this role and this is why he comes up with such a strong justification of them – they *must* be accepted on pain of cognitive suicide. If the claims are falsifiable, then the neo-Nazi will have the space to assert that they are in fact false. And Habermas wants to make that space unavailable.

I do not wish to conclude from the clutch of difficulties that face the transcendental argument that the account of truth which Habermas and Apel more or less share with the pragmatist (and the democratic principles of ethics which go along with it) cannot be justified. In the next chapter I shall try to get going a cognitivist view which incorporates the democratic principles Habermas and the others we have canvassed in this chapter are keen on. But I shall try to get them going from a less controversial starting position than that chosen by Habermas and Apel.

Any attempt to tie principles of morality or legitimacy to the very idea of communication, or language, or intersubjective meaning tries to get at the point that our humanity is bound up with that of others.[44] We need to make this kind of point without adding all of that 'necessarily' or 'non-contingent' talk which seems to draw attention away from what is important to us as human beings and toward some kind of metaphysical truth. I shall try to make these points in the right kind of way in the next two chapters.

Here we need to note how odd it is for one with pragmatist leanings to look to transcendentalism to overcome challenges of justification. The quest for necessary truths stands in tension with pragmatism itself. We would do better to abandon the quest for a first philosophy and hook up with the fallibilist[45] who gives up on such a lofty aim. Peirce, the founder of pragmatism, advises that:

> I am neither addressing absolute sceptics, nor men in any fictitious doubt whatever. I require the reader to be candid; and if he becomes convinced of a conclusion, to admit it … If you, the reader, actually find that my arguments have a convincing force with you, it is a mere pretence to call them illogical …
>
> (CE 2, 243)

Unlike Habermas, who in *Discourse Ethics* is explicitly putting forward his justification of that ethics in response to absolute sceptics, Peirce sees that to engage with them on their own turf is to prejudice the debate from the start. We must decline to assume the burden of proof the absolute sceptic tries to foist on the pragmatist, a burden which Apel and Habermas so willingly take on. The correct response to the sceptic is not to manoeuvre to *prove* pragmatism.

This is not to say that we should decline to address the sceptic's position. Indeed, I have argued in this chapter that we must be able to say something to the likes of the Schmittian, who argues that there are no right answers to our moral and political questions, only allegiance to the convictions we have decided to make our stand upon. I have argued that we must be able to give ourselves a reason, which is not portrayed as a reason which we just happen to have, against this Schmittian view. But that reason need not be necessarily true. We do not have to provide a knock-down argument that the sceptic is wrong.

The place to begin, I suggest, is with the idea of belief. We shall see that it is such that it is aimed at truth. The argument against the realist correspondence theorist is then off the ground (she posits an unbridgeable gap between truth and what we find valuable in the way of belief: a belief which is as good as it could be might still be false). And so, we shall see, are the arguments for pragmatism and for the democratic principles of inquiry.

I shall not assume that everyone wants to get along with those who are different; or that the principles of justice are the principles which best promote cooperation and equality; or that communication is always aimed at mutual understanding. What I shall be concerned with is the nature of belief and truth-seeking. And having a belief which is aimed at the truth is something that we can assume of our opponents. Once the acknowledgement is made (as it *is* made by the flat-earther, the Nazi, etc.) that one aims at getting the right belief, then one is open to a certain sort of criticism. The way is paved for the justification of the democratic principles of inquiry. Once it is acknowledged that we have beliefs, then we can say that *qua believers*, we must abide by certain principles.

The point that those who have beliefs which are aimed at the truth commit themselves to certain principles will be clear enough and plausible enough as it stands. There will be no need to dress it up with talk of a '*philosophical final justification* of the principles of ethics'. (Apel 1990: 43, his emphasis) This is too grand a claim for the humble point that those who want true belief undertake certain commitments.

Thus Rorty[46] is right in suggesting that Habermas, despite his proclamations to the contrary, attempts to build yet another misguided foundation for truth and knowledge. He is right to say that Habermas still strives for philosophy with a capital *P*: for necessary truths about truth and knowledge. Where Rorty is wrong is in his claim that *any* account of truth must have such an aim. For we shall see that the Peircean position does not. We need a justification of the principles of democracy which is, if you like, not as strong as that found in Habermas and Apel, but not as weak as that found in Rorty, Rawls, Cohen and Ackerman.

2 Truth, inquiry, and experience: a pragmatist epistemology

Peirce, truth, and the end of inquiry

The pragmatism I shall articulate and defend has its pedigree in the work of the founder of pragmatism and one of the brightest intellectual lights of the turn of the century – C.S. Peirce. His orneriness and the poor judgement of Harvard and Johns Hopkins universities combined to thwart his attempts to obtain a permanent post. He died a hungry oddity on the fringes of academia, leaving piles of manuscripts and fragments on a wide range of topics. Some of the thoughts one finds there are in tension with each other and many must be rejected. But there is a strand in Peirce's work that I think presents a sustainable view of truth and objectivity, not bettered by any subsequent pragmatist.

Peirce, however, was no path-breaker in moral and political philosophy. He was even more enthusiastic than some of those we have canvassed in Chapter 1 to downgrade the aspirations of moral and political inquiry. He argued that in 'vital matters' we should not aim at truth, but rather, we should simply follow instinct. The effect is a conservative upholding of the status quo, which suited Peirce's politics just fine. He did not, for instance, think slavery such a bad thing.[1]

This stance is odd for an unrelenting experimentalist such as Peirce. And there is nothing in his view of truth and objectivity which encourages, let alone warrants, such hesitancy about including morals in the domain of serious inquiry or in what Sellars called the logical 'space of giving reasons' (1963: 169). Peirce himself occasionally saw this and said that the idea of truth must be extended to vital matters.[2] What I shall do in the pages that follow is to set out what I take to be the best interpretation of Peirce's view of truth, objectivity, and inquiry. Then I shall use this interpretation as a basis for my own pragmatist argument about moral judgement. We shall see that we have good reason to see moral and political judgements as aspiring to truth. And the broadened pragmatism I shall extract from Peirce's work allows us to take morality as aiming at truth in a way that does not make a mockery of other kinds of inquiry. We shall not get a notion of moral and political truth at the expense of ordinary truth in science and mathematics.

Neither shall we make moral inquiry something too narrow. While it might appear, at this point, that the pragmatist must take our moral lives to be exhausted by deliberation – by a search for the right answers to our questions – we shall see in Chapter 3 that not all moral thought has this character. I might, rather, explore the contours of my own moral sensibility and that of others, or I might get a better grip on someone's character, or I might get a better grip on what something such as compassion amounts to. Or perhaps moral knowledge is, as Blackburn (1996) argues, often a knowing how rather than a knowing that (we can easily imagine, for instance, an inarticulate good person). At this stage it might look as if the pragmatist must confine herself to propositional knowledge and to propositional knowledge of the sort that aims at getting some unique answer to a question. But again, in Chapter 3 we will see that the pragmatist can be much more subtle than that.

So moral thought is not of one uniform kind and starting our moral philosophy from the idea that we aim at truth will not force us to think that. We will not be forced to think of moral inquiry as the active testing of hypotheses. Rather, we will think of moral inquiry as part of the enterprise of giving reasons. And reason here does not have to be a cold thing – a thing which stands apart from cultural meanings, from passion, and from emotion.

The core of the pragmatist conception of truth is that a true belief would be the best belief, were we to inquire as far as we could on the matter. We shall see that 'best' here amounts to 'best fits with all experience and argument', not the kind of 'best' that other pragmatists, James and Rorty, for instance, have flirted with – consoling, best for our lives, or most comfortable. A true belief, rather, is a belief that could not be improved upon, a belief that would forever meet the challenges of reasons, argument, and evidence.

Pragmatists sometimes put this idea in the following unhelpful way: a true belief is one which would be agreed upon at the hypothetical end of inquiry. But a better characterisation is that a true belief is one that would withstand doubt, were we to inquire as far as we fruitfully could on the matter. A true belief is such that, no matter how much further we were to investigate and debate, that belief would not be overturned by recalcitrant experience and argument.

Like the unhelpful formulation, this one captures what is important in pragmatism – the idea that a true belief is one which could not be improved upon. But the new formulation is much better.[3]

First, it does not run up against the possibility that inquiry might end prematurely, with, say, the destruction of life on earth. On the unhelpful formulation, it looks as if the beliefs which would be held then must be true, which is a crazy thing for a philosopher to suggest.

Second, the new formulation does not require the pragmatist to attempt the doomed task of saying just what is meant by the hypothetical end of inquiry, cognitively ideal conditions, or perfect evidence, whatever these might be. Any attempt at articulating such notions will have to face the objection that it is a mere glorification of what we presently take to be good.[4]

And, finally, the new formulation does not mislead one into thinking that the pragmatist is a contractarian or a certain kind of deliberative democrat – someone who thinks that what is important is *agreement*, rather than being the best a belief could be.

When the new formulation is unpacked, we shall see that there is a version of pragmatism on which truth is not as fickle as Rorty supposes. A belief is not true for one culture and false for another; and a belief is not true at one time and false at another. Beliefs do not, as William James suggested, 'become' true and then 'become' false, as the evidence for or against them comes to light.[5]

But truth, on the best version of pragmatism, is also not quite as objective as the correspondence theorist supposes. It is not, for instance, a property that holds regardless of the possibilities for human inquiry. Since philosophy is concerned with understanding our place in the world and with understanding the status of our beliefs, this seems to me an unobjectionable feature of pragmatism. But, of course, to properly argue for this picture of philosophy would be a large undertaking in itself. Some of the points in its favour will come out below, but the reader will have to turn to Misak (1991) and (1995) for more sustained arguments.

I shall argue that when this view of truth and knowledge is brought to moral philosophy, we can see moral judgements as being candidates for truth. Truth here is as the pragmatist sees it – a property of the beliefs which would be the best beliefs for us to have. This does not, I shall argue, make such truth and knowledge second-rate. For we shall not follow Habermas in thinking that there is something higher or better with which to contrast it.

If you like, the task before us is to say how objectivity and subjectivity can both be characteristic of our judgements. We are pulled to think that there is truth and objectivity, even if what is objectively true – belief – is a product of our deliberation and investigation. Thus, on the meta-ethical view of pragmatism, the semantic issue of whether ethical discourse is truth-apt becomes an epistemological issue about whether we can have knowledge in ethics. The question to be answered is whether our ethical beliefs have the same sorts of legitimate aspirations as our beliefs in science, mathematics, and discourse about ordinary, middle-sized objects.

This, of course, is an old and venerable problem, a problem which seems not to go away, despite our best philosophical efforts. We have seen it hound the views of the philosophers canvassed in the last chapter. How can we resolve the tension between the facts of, on the one hand, pluralism and disagreement and, on the other, the ideal of consensus and the aim of getting the right answers to our questions? What I offer here is a position which is as much of an attempt to expose the deep and pressing difficulties as an attempt to solve them.

Philosophy, practice, and correspondence

The central thought of pragmatism is that our philosophical theories must be connected to experience and practice. A belief, hypothesis, or theory which pretends to be above experience, which thinks so well of itself that it pretends to be immune from recalcitrant experience, is spurious. I have tried elsewhere to elucidate both the semantic and the epistemological arguments in this thought's favour[6], and here I will briefly rehearse some of the reasons why we might think that a belief must be linked to experience. For this requirement will shape our theory of truth, objectivity, and morality.

One point is about the demands of inquiry. Hypotheses, Peirce argued, ought not to block the path of inquiry. A hypothesis that had no consequences, that was severed from experience, that provided nothing on to which to latch, would be useless for inquiry. It would be, as Wittgenstein put it, a cog upon which nothing turned. Investigation into such hypotheses is bound to be barren and to direct attention away from worthwhile pursuits.

Another is a point about belief, a point made nicely by David Wiggins. A belief aims at truth[7] – if I believe *p*, I believe it to be true. But if this is right, then the belief that *p* must be sensitive to something – something must be able to speak for or against it. If beliefs need not be sensitive to something,

> then we could not interpret beliefs by asking: How do things have to be for *this* state of mind to succeed in its aim or be correct? What does this state of mind have, *qua* the belief it is, to be differentially sensitive to?[8]

If there was nothing a belief had to be sensitive to, then we could not individuate it; we could not tell it from another. A belief has a distinguishable content only if we can 'envisage finding the right sort of licence to project upon subjects' (Wiggins 1991b: 151). I can interpret or come to understand a sentence which is initially unintelligible to me only by coming to see what it is responsive to. Again, the requirement which presses itself upon the theorist is that a belief must be linked to something which we can experience.

We shall see that we can accept the idea that a belief is constitutively responsive to experience without committing ourselves to anything as strong as the verificationism of the logical positivists, for the kind of experiential consequences required of various beliefs will turn out to be very broad indeed. We do not need to say, with the positivists, that only scientific beliefs meet the standard. Nonetheless, certain hypotheses will be declared spurious.

The extreme form of the inverted spectrum hypothesis, for instance, would be declared spurious on our broad criterion. The thought that my colour spectrum might be inverted from yours, so that whenever you see black, I see white, etc., is such that, no matter how much evidence we gathered and argument we engaged in, we could never tell whether the hypothesis had anything going for it. The hypothesis is such that no evidence could be relevant to it. We shall see that this is not to say that we cannot understand it at all, but just that inquiry into it would be misplaced.

I suggested at the outset of this book that moral deliberation has many marks of objectivity – the distinction between thinking that one (or one's culture) is right and being right, the use of moral beliefs in inferences, the thought that we can discover that something is right or wrong and improve our views, and the thought that it is appropriate, or even required, that we give reasons and arguments for our beliefs, to name a few.

One additional mark of objectivity is that the practice of moral delibera-tion is responsive to experience, reason, argument, and thought experiments where we, for instance, place ourselves in another's shoes. Such responsive-ness is part of what it is to make a moral decision and part of what it is to try to live a moral life. It wouldn't be a moral life – it would not be engaged with the complexities of moral requirements – if we simply made our deci-sions about how to treat others by following an oracle, or an astrologer, or the toss of the dice. Such responsiveness meets the requirement set out above – an objective area of inquiry must be such that its beliefs are sensitive to something that can speak for or against them.

Our practice of justifying moral belief speaks against the non-cognitivist. It speaks against those who do not think there is good reason to see moral belief as being objective – those who think that the best explanation of a person's moral judgements is always a story about the person's cultural background or upbringing. A reason for trying to see morals as objective is that it is part of the phenomenology of inquiry that we are obliged to take seriously.

Here we are taken back to the thought articulated in the introduction to this book – to the idea that our philosophical theory must take seriously the picture various inquiries have of themselves. In this case, it must take account of the way in which our moral judgements are responsive to reasons. For that is a central feature of the phenomenon it wants to study – moral judgement.

Of course we must be prepared for the possibility that, as Bernard Williams thinks, 'ethical thought has no chance of being everything it seems' (1985: 135). But the commitment to keeping philosophy in touch with expe-rience and practice is such that we should not be too quick to jump to this conclusion. We shall see that we needn't reject the part of the phenomenology of moral inquiry which has us aiming at truth or at getting things right, where 'right' does not merely mean 'right by the lights of my group'.

One point I want to draw out from the requirement that theory be connected to practice is that, on the pragmatist view, a belief requires a justi-fication when, and only when, it has been thrown into doubt by actual inquiry. Those issues which perplex are the issues which call for justification – science's search for an effective anti-malarial drug or for a further sub-atomic particle, society's struggle with the question of euthanasia or abortion, etc.

Peirce argued that an inquiry begins with the irritation of doubt and ends with a stable, doubt-resistant belief. If we were to have a belief which would always be immune to doubt – which would forever fit with experience, argument, and the rest of our theories – then Peirce holds that the belief is true. But since we can never know that a belief is like that, he will tell the philosopher not to ask whether this or that belief is true, but to focus on inquiry and on getting the best answers we can to the questions that have arisen. We cannot follow Descartes and try to bring into doubt all beliefs for which error is conceivable. Such doubts would be, as Peirce argued, 'paper' or 'tin' – not the genuine article[9]:

> ... there is but one state of mind from which you can 'set out', namely, the very state of mind in which you actually find yourself at the time you do 'set out' – a state in which you are laden with an immense mass of cognition already formed, of which you cannot divest yourself if you would ... Do you call it doubting to write down on a piece of paper that you doubt? If so, doubt has nothing to do with any serious business ...
>
> (CP 5.416)

This leads to a second point. The key to avoiding an unthinking preservation of the status quo cannot be to begin again. Progress-jamming conservatism, in any area of inquiry, can be avoided only by recognising it as a possibility and then by trying to stay well away from it by listening to challenges to deeply held beliefs and practices. Those challenges can come from within, when my own judgements or principles conflict and I feel a pull towards revising them. And they can come from without, when I see that the judgements and principles of others, from within my circle or from afar, conflict with my own judgements and I feel a pull towards reconsidering them. I can then revise some of those beliefs and practices while holding enough unchanged against which the revision can take place.

So on the pragmatist epistemology, justification requires a fallible background of belief which is not in fact in doubt. Only against such a background can a belief be put into doubt and a new, better, belief be adopted. All our beliefs are fallible but they come into doubt in a piecemeal fashion. Those that inquiry has not thrown into doubt are stable and warrant our belief. What this means for epistemologists is that we have no choice but to begin our theory about truth and objectivity from where we find ourselves, laden with thoughts about what counts as evidence, about what truth and objectivity are, about where agreement is difficult to purchase, etc.

The Peircean model of inquiry, as Charles Larmore has pointed out, thus gives us the wherewithal to explain how our beliefs are rooted in our history and our practices, but nonetheless can be justified. This kind of epistemology, although it is entirely general, looks especially attractive with respect to our moral judgements. Moral theory should not be seen as 'a guide to eternity', whatever that might be, but as 'a code for problem-solving' (Larmore 1996: 60). We can carefully set out what we think are the principles of morality, and we can put these principles to use in our lives and in our policies, but they might well undergo revision as new experience and argument comes to light.

It is important to pause here to ensure that the thought that 'inquiry aims at truth' is not mischaracterised. We have in our various inquiries and deliberations a multiplicity of aims – empirical adequacy, coherence with other beliefs, simplicity, explanatory power, getting a reliable guide to action, fruitfulness for other research, greater understanding of others, increased maturity, and the like. What the pragmatist argues is that when we say that we aim at the truth, what we mean is that, if a belief really were to satisfy all of our aims in inquiry, then that belief would be true. There is nothing over and above the fulfilment of those aims, nothing metaphysical, to which we aspire. So when we say 'truth is our aim in inquiry', this is a way of expressing the thought that a belief is true if it is, and would continue to be, everything we want it to be. That is what we aim at in inquiry – getting the best beliefs we can. Truth is not some transcendental, mystical thing that we aim at for its own sake. It is not the be all and end all.

Science, some will want to interject here, aspires to truth and, whereas it makes sense to have that aspiration in science, it makes no sense at all in morals and politics. But I suggest that it would be a mistake, a begging of the question, to draw a hard distinction, at the outset, between science and morals. Similarly, it would be a mistake to draw an immediate analogy between science and morals so that the results of both are lumped into the undifferentiated domain of 'fact'. My suggestion is that we rather look to the aspirations of our inquiries in both morals and science, and see whether and how often those aspirations might be met. We shall see that the case for aiming at truth is indeed easier to make in science, but that matters are not quite so hopeless in morals. As Dewey says:

> To frame a theory of knowledge which makes it necessary to deny the validity of moral ideas, or else to refer them to some other and separate kind of universe from that of common sense and science, is both provincial and arbitrary. The pragmatist has at least tried to face, and not to dodge, the question of how it is that moral and scientific 'knowledge' can both hold of one and the same world.[10]

The final point that I want to make about the connection between philosophy and practice is that the very conception of truth which the pragmatist holds is a product of that connection. The pragmatist's view of truth keeps inquiry at the centre; it refuses to sever the link between truth and inquiry. A true belief is the best that inquiry could do; it is what we would find survives the test of experience at the end of a well-pursued inquiry.

Those views which would like to make truth something more absolute, something less concerned with the human business of inquiry, unlink the philosophical theory of truth from the practice of inquiry. They hold that truth transcends or goes beyond inquiry. Truth, says the correspondence theorist, is a relationship between a proposition[11] and the believer-independent world. And this is a relationship that holds or fails to hold whatever human beings find worthy to believe. No matter how good a belief might appear to us, no matter if it were to be as good as it could be by way of accounting for the evidence, fitting with our other beliefs, etc., it could still be false. It might fail to get right that independent reality and there might be no way we could ever have an inkling of the failure.

That, I suggest, is a spurious thought. Like the inverted spectrum hypothesis, the correspondence theory runs afoul of the requirement that theory be connected to experience. The possibility it envisions – that '*p* fails to correspond to reality, despite its being the best that a belief could be' – is such that nothing could speak for or against it.

A set of explanatory failures, related to its empirical emptiness, presses upon the correspondence theory as well. First, the correspondence theorist is at a loss to tell us just what it is that a true proposition is supposed to correspond to. For any attempt at articulating it involves our concepts, our sense of what is important, our background beliefs. Any attempt at articulating what the mind-independent world is like takes us away from that world.

Second, the correspondence theorist seems to lose her grip on why we should aim to get beliefs which are consistent, account for the data, have explanatory power, etc. For these desiderata are not linked – appear irrelevant – to our aim of getting beliefs which correspond to the mind-independent world. Indeed, the correspondence theorist has trouble saying that we aim at the truth. For on her view, we cannot have any access to it, cannot know when we might have it, and cannot even know when we are on the right track. In what sense, then, can we aim at it?

Peirce sums up the problems with the idea of correspondence to an unknowable 'thing-in-itself':

> You only puzzle yourself by talking of this metaphysical 'truth' and metaphysical 'falsity' that you know nothing about. All you have any dealings with are your doubts and beliefs … If your terms 'truth' and 'falsity' are taken in such senses as to be definable in terms of doubt and belief and the course of experience, well and good: in that case you are only talking about doubt and belief. But if by truth and falsity you mean something not definable in terms of doubt and belief in any way, then you are talking of entities of whose existence you can know nothing and which Ockham's razor would clean shave off. Your problems would be greatly simplified, if, instead of saying that you want to know the 'Truth', you were simply to say that you want to attain a state of belief unassailable by doubt.
>
> (CP 5.416, see also 5.572)

Here we have an early statement of the now-popular thought that we must deflate the notion of truth. The metaphysician has lost sight of the connection between truth and the less glamorous notions of experience, inquiry and assertion. Quine puts the point thus:

> What on the part of true sentences is meant to correspond to what on the part of reality? If we seek a correspondence word by word, we find ourselves eking reality out with a complement of abstract objects fabricated for the sake of the correspondence. Or perhaps we settle for a correspondence of whole sentences with *facts*: a sentence is true if it reports a fact. But here again we have fabricated substance for an empty doctrine. The world is full of things, variously related, but what, in addition to that, are facts?
>
> (1987: 213)

There are those who, in the face of the difficulties for the correspondence conception of truth, advise us to deflate truth so severely that we drop the notion altogether. We shall look in some detail at such a suggestion in the next section. We shall see that the trouble with this view is the trouble we encountered in Rorty's position. It deprives us of the substantial notion of truth we need in order to make some rather critical distinctions in inquiry. We will thus be taken back to the thought that inquiry requires truth, but not truth as the correspondence theorist sees it. And pragmatism, I shall argue, fits the bill.

Peirce insisted that we need a conception of truth which 'can and ought to be used as a guide for conduct' (MS 684: 11). We need a conception of truth which can guide inquiry and deliberation. With this in mind, he asked what we would expect of a true belief. We would expect a true belief to be consistent with other well-grounded beliefs, to fit with the data, to have explanatory power, etc. We would expect, that is, that the belief would survive the trials of inquiry; if inquiry relevant to the issue were pursued diligently, we would never want to revise that belief in light of further evidence, argument and other considerations.

The first way pragmatism delivers a notion of truth which can be used in inquiry is to give us a conception of rational belief. It closes the gap between truth and inquiry and explains why some of our current beliefs are considered rational, or more likely to be true, than other beliefs, even if we cannot know that they are true. If truth is the belief which would best fit with the evidence, were we to have so much by way of good evidence that no further evidence would overturn the belief, then a rational belief is the belief which best fits with the evidence that we currently have. If truth is what would be justified by the principles of inquiry, were inquiry to be pursued as far as it could fruitfully go, then a rational belief is one which is justified by the current principles of inquiry. There is no gap between what we take, after careful consideration, to be rational and what is rational. Although we are never in a position to judge whether a belief is true or not, we will often be in a position to judge whether it is the best belief given the current state of inquiry.

Second, unlike the correspondence theorist, the pragmatist can make sense of the fact that we aim at the truth or at the objectively correct answer. For such a belief would lie at the end of the process of inquiry of which the inquirer is a part. Truth is in principle not beyond investigation; it is in principle accessible.

It is also objective. For one thing, truth is what *would* be thought best to believe, and so it is independent, as Peirce said, of whatever 'you, I, or any number of men' think; it is independent of 'the vagaries of you and me'.[12] Truth is connected to human inquiry (it is the best that inquiry could do), but it goes beyond any particular inquiry (it is not simply the upshot of our current best attempts).

And finally, the pragmatic view of truth can justify a methodology, thereby guiding the inquirer in her deliberations. If truth were to be the belief which would best fit with experience and argument, then if we want true beliefs, we should expose them to experience and argument which might overturn them. Better to find out now that a belief is defeated by evidence against it, rather than down the line.

So the pragmatic conception of truth is a good one for the inquirer. It makes sense of and guides practice. We must think of truth in the down-to-earth terms of what it is to assert something properly – we must think of the relationship between truth and doubt, belief, experience, and perceptual disappointment. In the following sections we shall see just how this thought compares with some other kinds of deflationism about truth.

Pragmatism and disquotationalism

The objection that the correspondence theory rests on an unhappy metaphysics has seemed to many to be decisive against it. But even if we agree that grandiose metaphysics is to be spurned, even if we agree that our theory of truth should be a deflated one, the controversy does not die down. A variety of deflationist options present themselves. Some, such as Rorty, take the notion of truth to be so wedded to metaphysics that we are advised to abandon it. Others, such as Paul Horwich and Hartry Field, take the disquotational or equivalence schema – '*p*' is *T* if and only if *p* – to completely capture the content of the predicate 'is true'. And others, such as the best kind of pragmatist, argue that there is a conception of truth to be had which captures what is important about truth, is non-metaphysical, and goes beyond the triviality expressed by the disquotational schema (hereafter the *DS*).

I shall argue that the thought which lies behind the *DS* is a thought dear to the pragmatist: there is an unseverable connection between asserting a statement and claiming that it is true. But after this is accepted, we must look to the practice of assertion and to the commitments incurred in it, so that we can say something further – something about what truth *is*.

My aim in this section is to bring closer the pragmatist and those who place a premium on the *DS*. This will not be a surprising move to those who have noticed that Quine, who has provided one of the best statements of the disquotational view, has often flirted with pragmatism. I shall argue, against most expectations, that the pragmatist can come up to the anti-metaphysical standards of the disquotationalist. I shall also make a more familiar suggestion that the pure disquotationalist cannot adequately characterise perfectly good debates about whether a discourse such as moral discourse aims at truth or whether it is a radically subjective matter, not at all suited for truth-value.

Things are not, we shall see, made much better by Crispin Wright's attempt to show how a pluralism about truth, with disquotationalism at its heart, can reconfigure such debates. And of course, this book is an exercise in showing how the pragmatist can not only cope with, but flourish in, debates about whether the likes of moral judgements are candidates for truth-values.

We have seen that Peirce held that a true belief is one which would never lead to disappointment (CP 5.569). It would be 'indefeasible' (CP 6.485) or not defeated, were inquiry pursued as far as it could fruitfully go. I have argued that the pragmatist must refrain from putting this thought in terms of the end of inquiry, must refrain from suggesting that a true belief is one which would be believed in some cognitively ideal state or a state of perfect evidence. Rather, a true belief is one upon which inquiry could not improve, a belief which would fit with experience and argument and which would satisfy all of the aims of inquiry, no matter how much the issue was subject to experiment, evaluation, and debate.

We have also seen that Peirce was a resolute fallibilist and insisted that an inquirer could never know when inquiry had been pushed far enough for a genuinely stable opinion to have been reached. Far from suggesting with Rorty that a true belief is one which we find good to believe at the moment, he argued that since we cannot know when we have a belief that would never lead to disappointment, we cannot know when we have a true belief.

Nonetheless, when we offer a justification for '*p* is true', we offer a justification for the claim that *p* itself. This is the thought that lies behind the *DS*. The pragmatist holds it because she argues that what we do when we try to establish the truth of a claim is to show that, thus far, it fits with all the evidence and argument and that we have reason to think that it will continue to do so.

Peirce did not intend to specify the necessary and sufficient conditions for a belief being true. We must be sensitive here to the difference between an analytic definition and a pragmatic elucidation. What is on offer from the pragmatist is not the thought that agreement in the long run constitutes truth, objectivity, or legitimacy.

Peirce argued, generally, that a debate about a definition is likely to be a 'profitless discussion', unless the predicate to be defined is completely unfamiliar (CP 8.100). He would have railed against the contemporary focus on necessary and sufficient conditions and would have joined in Davidson's lament that '[w]e still fall for the freshman fallacy that demands that we *define* our terms as a prelude to saying anything further with or about them' (1996: 275).

More specifically, an analytic definition of truth tries to set out the necessary and sufficient conditions for 'p is true' such as 'p is true if and only if it corresponds to reality'. Peirce argued that such projects are unsatisfactory because they are often empty or trivial. The danger is that one word will be 'defined by other words, and they by still others, without any real conception ever being reached' (CP 5.423). These 'nominal' definitions are only useful to those who have not encountered the term being defined. Peirce was content to let something like the correspondence theory stand as a nominal definition of truth.

His theory of signs identifies three tasks for the theoretician. One part of what it is to know the meaning of a concept F – one aspect of understanding – is to be able to give a definition of it. Another is to be able to pick out what F refers to. A third – Peirce's own contribution to the debate – is to articulate the consequences which can be derived from 'x is F' or to give a pragmatic elucidation of F.

Peirce takes these three aspects of understanding to spell out completely what it is to grasp a concept and he takes the pragmatic aspect to be the most interesting and important. I do not, for instance, have a grasp of the concept of generosity unless I know that if a is generous then if she were to see a person in need, and if she had the resources, she would be inclined to help, rather than turn away with a dismissive scowl. I do not have a grasp of a concept unless I am able to see what further beliefs and inferences I am committed to if I believe that a is F.[13]

One reason for the pragmatic aspect's pride of place is that it serves as a criterion of meaning identity – a purported difference which makes no difference at all is spurious.[14] We thus ignore the third dimension of understanding at philosophy's peril.[15] We ignore it at the risk of getting theories which are empty, theories which are metaphysical in that they make a futile attempt to transcend practice and experience. A philosophical theory must be such that something turns on it – there must be some set of expectations we can draw from it. For those engaged in practice, in this case the practice of inquiry, something more enlightening than a definition of truth is required. We need to know how truth is relevant to inquiry. We need to know what to expect of a true belief; what the features of a true belief are. And of course, that is exactly what the pragmatic elucidation of truth tries to do.

We have seen that Peirce argues that what we can expect of 'p is true' is the following: if we were to diligently inquire into p, we would find that p

survived our inquiries – we would find nothing which would cause us to doubt it.[16] He spends much time elaborating this thought, for the pragmatic project does not lend itself nicely to snappy summaries. The thought at the heart of pragmatism is that a true belief is the best that inquiry could do. But this is just the beginning of a long discussion, not the end of it.

I have suggested elsewhere (1991: 127f) that in regard to the task of definition Peirce would, and should, be even happier with the *DS* than with correspondence. For we have seen that he expressed qualms about the idea of correspondence to an unknowable 'thing-in-itself'.

There are, however, two rather significant differences between the pragmatist and the classical or pure disquotationalist. First, we shall see when we turn to the issue of bivalence that the pragmatist must take the *DS* to hold of a statement only as a regulative assumption of inquiry and only when we are prepared to assert the statement or to think that it is a candidate for a truth-value. That is, the *DS* does not hold for all declarative sentences. It is a definition of truth only in Peirce's very loose sense of definition – it is a helpful introduction to the concept.

Second, the disquotationalist will be principled about not adding anything further to this equivalence. The infinite string of instances of the *DS* must stand alone as entirely capturing the content of 'is true'.[17] As far as truth goes, what we can say is that 'Snow is white' is true if and only if snow is white, 'Toronto is north of Buffalo' is true if and only if Toronto is north of Buffalo, and so on.

But the pragmatist thinks that something important comes on the heels of the thought that truth is bound up with assertion. What we know about a concept, our only access to it, is the role that it plays in our cognitive lives. It is these connections which give the concept body, as Davidson puts it (1996: 276).

The major role of the concept of truth, the pragmatist argues, is that we take truth to be our aim when we assert and when we inquire.[18] Even if I aim at misleading you with a 'false assertion', that is parasitic on aiming at truth. Only if you take my claim to be sincere – to aim at truth – will I succeed in my aim of deceit. The very business of assertion depends on taking assertions to be true. What we know about truth is that it is what we aim at when we assert, believe, or deliberate. So were we to forever achieve all of our local aims in assertion, belief and deliberation, were we to get a belief to be as good as it could be, that would be a true belief.

As Arthur Fine's (1986: 177) naturalism, California-style, puts it, we should not add anything philosophical to science, or to any other first order inquiry – 'no additives, please'. There is a point or an aim to any particular deliberation – to solve a problem, to build a better instrument, to decide what is just in the circumstances, or to confirm a hypothesis. Fine says that we mustn't move from this thought to the idea that there is one aim which all investigations have – truth. But, if we can wrench our gaze off of truth-as-correspondence, then, *contra* Fine, we can make this move. For on the pragmatist view of truth, 'truth' is just a catch-all for those particular local aims.

We have seen that when the pragmatist says that the aim of inquiry is truth, what is meant is that were a belief to satisfy all of our local aims in inquiry, (prediction, explanatory power, and so on), then that belief would be true. There is nothing over and above the fulfilment of those aims, nothing metaphysical, to which we aspire. But nonetheless, we can generalise and say that a true belief is one which would be the upshot of our inquiries. As we specify our cognitive ends, we specify our concept of truth.[19]

Let us turn to the disquotationalist and explore his thought that the philosopher should not make such generalisations. The disquotationalist agrees with the pragmatist about the metaphysics of the correspondence theory. Truth is not correspondence. But neither is it much else. The disquotationalist thinks that truth's role is so lightweight that precious little can be said about it. There is no underlying nature of truth or no general characteristic of true sentences, such as 'they get reality right' or 'they would be warranted were inquiry to be pursued as far as it could fruitfully go'. We do not need a theory of truth. All we need is an idea of how to justify this or that statement. The predicate 'is true' literally amounts to what is expressed by that infinitely long list of biconditionals expressed by the *DS*. In Horwich's words, 'in fact nothing could be more mundane and less puzzling than the concept of truth' (1990: xi). There is no 'essence' of truth; no 'special quality which all truths supposedly have in common' (1990: 6). So we should not inquire into its causal behaviour or its 'typical manifestations' (1990: 39). Believing that a theory is true is nothing but 'a trivial step beyond believing the theory' (1990: 60).

But Horwich in fact thinks that there is an important role for the predicate 'is true'. He does not claim that truth is not a property at all. It has one (and only one) use: a generalising function in logic.[20] It is a device for infinite conjunction and disjunction and for expressing propositions which we cannot identify. Consider: 'everything the Pope says is true', 'whatever Icabod said about her is not true', and 'not every belief of mine is true'. In the first case, I cannot identify the propositions because there are too many of them; in the second case, I don't know what Icabod said, but generally distrust his statements about the person in question; and in the third, I don't know of such a belief, but I'm willing to bet there is one. The predicate 'is true' is a simple way to express such propositions – propositions in opaque or indirect contexts, and whole classes of propositions. That is the '*raison d'être* of the concept of truth'; 'the truth predicate exists solely for the sake of a certain logical need' (Horwich 1990: 4, 2). It enables us to avoid cumbersome new forms of quantification (1990: 38).

This is what I call pure or classical disquotationalism. We are to hold on to the truth predicate for the sake of the logical need, but all the predicate amounts to is what is expressed in the *DS*. The role of truth in our conceptual scheme has, Horwich thinks, now been explained (1990: 42, 36).

Horwich says that his view differs from pragmatism because he is not offering an eliminative analysis or an analytic definition of the term 'true', but rather, an account of what a person understands when he understands claims about truth. He takes the pragmatist to offer an analytic definition of truth in terms of utility, presumably '*p* is true if and only if it is useful to believe *p*' (1990: 34, 47). Perhaps he has James in mind.

We have seen, however, that giving analytic equivalences is not in the spirit of Peircean pragmatism. As Sellars noted, the pragmatist[21] who helps herself to the *DS* will not then want to claim that truth is defined by or 'means' something like successful prediction in the long run. She will rather work out the relationship between truth on the one hand and coherence with our other beliefs, success, and the like, on the other. Sellars did not see that, on the pragmatist view of meaning, the working out of these connections *is* the working out of the full meaning of 'is true'. But his point stands: the pragmatist who helps herself to the disquotational definition of truth will then go on to do something else – to understand truth by looking at its links with our experiences and practices. And she will not take this to be the definition of truth.

If Horwich's objection to pragmatism should not be that pragmatism sets up an analytic definition of truth, perhaps he might then argue that the pragmatic elucidation which is offered, once the *DS* is accepted as a definition, is in some way spurious or metaphysical. We have seen that his own effort to get rid of spurious metaphysics in our talk of truth leads him to claim that there is no essence of truth, that truth is not a 'fundamental ingredient of reality' (1990: 81). But we must be careful not to slide with him from a perfectly good thought about the mysteriousness of essences to the thought that there can be no general characteristic of true sentences or no quality which all truths have in common, or even typically. A theory of *x* which identifies general characteristics of *x*s can be perfectly respectable for someone wary of metaphysics. Everything, of course, depends on what characteristics are identified and whether they are metaphysical.[22] And the offenders are states of affairs, facts, and the like, not anything the pragmatist puts out.

What I think Horwich really finds objectionable in a view which goes beyond the *DS* is that the extra step offends against his sense that 'truth has a certain purity'. Our understanding of truth, he thinks, should be kept independent of other ideas – such as the ideas of assertion, verification, reference, meaning, success, or logical entailment (1990: 12).

But it turns out that Horwich thinks that one should call the *DS* the theory of truth *and then*, if one likes, go on to explain the relationships between truth and those other concepts. We are to get ourselves the most simple, pure, elegant, separate, theory of truth and then we can 'conjoin that theory with assumptions from elsewhere' (1990: 26). In 'combination with theories of other phenomena', the *DS* will 'explain all the facts about truth' (1990: 26). There might be much that is right in other theories of truth, it is just that we are not to think of them as part of our *basic* theory of truth (1990: 115). A competing theory of truth might be a 'legitimate extension' of the minimalist disquotational theory, but it should not be seen as a 'tempting alternative' to it (1990: 115).

Here we encounter a fundamental difference in philosophical temperament between the pragmatist and the disquotationalist. The pragmatist thinks that the disquotationalist's quest for purity will result in something rather empty and useless, for the important work is in spelling out the relations between truth on the one hand and assertion, verification, success, etc. on the other. The way to deflate truth, the pragmatist argues, the way to make truth less metaphysical, is to link it with these other, more down-to-earth notions, not to claim an independence from them. Linkages with notions that we have workaday dealings with are the one and only way to get a grasp on the idea of truth.

Of course, the disquotationalist does argue that the truth predicate is connected to our practices in that it has a generalising function in formal logic. But once the truth predicate is retained in order to hold on to that use, the door is flung open to other uses. The pragmatist wants to jam a foot in that door and keep it open. How could we possibly think that the generalising function is the only function of 'is true' that we need to account for? If we stop with the disquotationalist here, we fail to give a full account of how truth is linked to our practices of deliberation and experimentation; we fail to live up to the demand of making sense of inquiry.[23]

In deciding which of these temperaments is most appropriate, we need to think about their motivations. Horwich's sense of purity, one guesses, is prompted by both the logician's concern for simplicity and by the fact that the *DS* seems to be the only uncontroversial thing that we can say about truth (1990: 126).

Here we ought straightaway to agree that claims about what arises from the *DS* — claims about the commitments involved in assertion and belief — are more controversial than the *DS* itself. The suggestions I shall offer below about these commitments are very much up for debate. But of course the fact that something is controversial says nothing at all about whether it is correct or important. So what Horwich leaves us with is an appeal to the desirability for the simple and sparse – to Quine's preference for desert landscapes.

On the pragmatist's side, we can focus on the fact that Horwich sees that the relationship between truth and those other notions is not unimportant or spurious. It thus appears to be merely a matter of emphasis whether one calls the theory of truth that infinite string of equivalences and then legitimately extends the theory or whether one calls the *DS*-plus-extension the theory of truth. If that is the case, then the pragmatist seems the more reasonable of the two. For he does not *deny* anything in the basic theory, but turns his attention to the elucidation of it.[24] The disquotationalist, on the other hand, says that the pragmatist, the coherence theorist, the correspondence theorist – any truth *theorist* – has made a mistake in thinking that there is anything more to say about truth than what is expressed in the *DS*. But this claim is in tension with the thought that the *DS* gets the basic theory of truth right and there is more to say then about the connection between truth and other concepts.

Pragmatism, superassertibility, and pluralism about truth

Crispin Wright is not such a purist. His own mimimalist[25] position intends to retain the disquotationalist's aversion to metaphysics or aversion to thinking of truth as identifying 'some especially profound form of engagement between language, or thought, and reality' (Wright 1992: 72, 37). But he wants to reinflate truth a bit. He thinks, with the disquotationalist (and, we have seen, with Peirce) that '*p* is true' amounts to the assertion that *p*. But Wright finds much more 'lurking behind the Disquotational Schema' than does the pure disquotationalist (1992: 72).

Wright takes the *DS* to suggest that to say that a sentence is true is to assert it and to assert a sentence is to say that it is true. The biconditional relation between assertion and truth is such that the norms governing assertion will also be the norms which govern the use of the predicate 'is true'. Reason to regard a sentence as warrantedly assertible is reason to regard it as true and vice versa (1992: 16–18).

One of the minimal conditions on a truth predicate, however, is that truth must come apart from warranted assertion – truth does not amount to mere warranted assertibility here and now.[26] Wright does not think, with Rorty, that truth is merely what passes for good belief. He thus turns his attention to a truth predicate which he calls 'superassertibility', a special kind of warranted assertion:

> A statement is superassertible ... if and only if it is, or can be, warranted and some warrant for it would survive arbitrarily close scrutiny of its pedigree and arbitrarily extensive increments to or other forms of improvement of our information.
>
> (1992: 48)

Here truth is a non-metaphysical property:

> superassertibility is ... an *internal* property of the statements of a discourse – a projection, merely, of the standards, whatever they are, which actually inform assertion within the discourse. It supplies no external norm – in a way that truth is classically supposed to do – against which the internal standards might *sub specie Dei* themselves be measured. ... In this way, it is metaphysically neutral, and betrays the metaphysical neutrality of the minimal conception of truth which ... it models.
>
> (1992: 61)

Wright's relationship with pragmatism is more complex than Horwich's. He thinks of Peirce[27] as holding the implausible view that there is an ideal limit to our efforts at getting warranted beliefs – a point when all relevant empirical information would be in. Moreover, he thinks that the Peircean view of truth requires that, were a person to be in such ideal conditions, she would know that she was; she would be in a position to acknowledge the fact (1992: 46). Since an inquirer could never have an intimation that she had somehow managed to get a state of comprehensive empirical information, the antecedent of the following conditional is 'conceptually impossible': were a subject to be in epistemically ideal conditions and were she able to acknowledge that fact, she would believe *p*. Wright thinks this is very 'bad news for Peircean views of truth' (1992: 46).

But we have seen that the pragmatist can and should stay away from the ideas of total evidence and epistemically ideal conditions. Inquiry, in the slogan 'truth is what would be believed were we to inquire as far as we could', is not to be thought of as global, complete inquiry, where every question is decided, including the question of whether inquiry is complete. We are to focus on inquiry into a particular issue and on whether our beliefs there are as good as they could be.[28]

And we have seen that Peirce the fallibilist will simply agree that a person could never know that inquiry had been pursued as far as it could fruitfully go. We might believe all sorts of truths, but we cannot know when we are in such a position, precisely because we cannot know whether we have a belief that would forever satisfy our aims. (We of course can have good reason to think that current beliefs satisfy our aims better than previous beliefs.) This is good news for the pragmatist, for she will not be tempted to pronounce prematurely on what would be the upshot of inquiry.

Once we see how Wright's criticism of pragmatism is misdirected, the difference between his superassertibility predicate and the pragmatist account of truth appears to evaporate. Peirce, we have seen, holds that what it is for a belief to be true is that it would not be improved upon. Both he and Wright are of the opinion that:

> Rather than ask whether a statement would be justified at the limit of ideal empirical investigation, or under ideal empirical circumstances, whatever they are, we can ask whether an ordinary carefully controlled investigation, in advance of attaining any mythical limit, justifies the statement, and whether, once justified, that statement continues to be so no matter how much further information is accumulated.
>
> (Wright 1992: 47, for Peirce's version, see Misak 1991: 150ff)

Peirce argues that there is nothing higher or better we can ask of a belief than that it would forever be assertible, by the standards which govern our practices of proper assertion. Truth just is that property of beliefs which are and which would continue to be warranted, no matter how far our inquiries were pursued.

It appears that Wright must be in full agreement here. But he is not. His proposal is that we take any predicate which satisfies the *DS* and which takes truth to be distinct from warranted assertibility to be a truth-predicate. There may be more than one perfectly good conception of truth.[29] Wright thinks that superassertibility is the truth-predicate of choice for certain discourses – discourses in which we think that if *p* is true, then *p* is knowable (1992: 58, 75, also 1996b). Other discourses have more robust truth-predicates.

We have seen with respect to Habermas' position that pluralism about truth-predicates comes at a heavy price. It comes at the price of some of the purported truth-predicates being downgraded – not grade A robust truth, but grade B sustained warranted assertibility. The problem is even more pressing for Wright than for Habermas. For we can multiply Wright's kind of impoverished predicates in the following way: 'warranted assertibility tomorrow', 'warranted assertibility tomorrow as well as the day after tomorrow', and so on until we reach some suitably durable warranted assertibility. None of these look like real truth, *if we have as a contrast something more robust*, something more like the truth-predicate the correspondence theorist has always sought.

Wright takes his project to be a rejigging of debates about realism and anti-realism in various areas of discourse, with moral discourse especially salient. Moral discourse meets Wright's minimal requirements for a truth-apt discourse – it is assertoric, imposes a discipline on itself, and, we suppose, truth does not amount to warranted assertibility here and now. Morality (as well as the likes of the comic, film studies and scientific cosmology) satisfies the minimal platitudes about truth and it does not need any 'metaphysical underpinnings' to show that it is up to the job.[30]

Wright worries that it will appear that his sympathies must lie with either of two unattractive options. One is a realism run rampant, where virtually every disciplined discourse is objective and thus morality is objective. The other is a 'bloodless' quietism, where we 'simply have to settle for the bland perspective of a variety of assertoric "language games", each governed by its own internal standards of acceptability, each sustaining a metaphysically emasculated notion of truth, each unqualified for anything of more interest or importance' (1992: 76).

He rejects both options. Yes, moral discourse is minimally truth-apt – we can help ourselves to talk of truth for it (1992: 16, 28, 36, 178). But a discourse meeting only the minimal requirements is one about which we must take an anti-realist stance.[31] The realist must show that the discourse in question does more than meet the minimum for truth-aptness. There *is* a basis for distinguishing claims about, say, the comic from claims about material objects, for a discourse can go beyond the minimum.

One such additional feature is that a discourse might display what Wright calls cognitive command. In such a discourse, it is *a priori* that intractable disagreements are due to one kind or another of cognitive shortcoming, such as insufficient or divergent evidence, faulty reasoning, inattention, oversight, or malfunction of equipment.[32] Wright does not think that this case can be made for moral discourse; it is not governed by cognitive command. But nonetheless, Wright feels that he has shown how the philosopher's debate about morals makes sense on his view and how its resolution leans in favour of the anti-realist or non-cognitivist.

What Wright wants to do here is to explain the difference between the realist and the non-realist without suggesting that the non-realist has to deny that the disputed statements aim at truth. We are all supposed to agree that minimal truth is had by all assertible sentences. And then we are supposed to go on to say how some discourses can be more objective than others. Those discourses will have a more robust truth-predicate – more robust than minimal truth.

But Wright himself verges on the admission that minimal truth is not really truth. He distinguishes, for instance, between truth *simpliciter* (minimal truth) and substantial truth (what one gets with cognitive command) 'merely for the ease of discussion' (1992: 89–90). And he thinks that it is just a terminological matter if we talk of the assertions in a discourse which meet the minimal requirements but fail to display cognitive command as aspiring to 'correctness', while those which also display cognitive command can aspire to 'truth' (1992: 232).

The problem is that it looks very much like Wright must say that the minimal requirements are *not enough* to get us the concept of truth. Just about every statement makes the minimalist grade and so that grade is indeed of little interest. It is not what we normally think of as truth – as what we aim at. Wright is a kind of anti-realist about ethics but that anti-realism begs to be stated in truth-theoretic terms. Moral judgements cannot be said to aspire to (robust) truth. This is bad news for a view of truth which insists that our theory of truth need not go beyond the minimal (non-robust) requirement.

Bivalence

One of the most pressing difficulties for those who take the very idea of truth to be linked to evidence, or to reasons we might have for a belief, concerns the status of bivalence and the corresponding law of excluded middle. Does the pragmatist not have to say that if inquiry would not decide upon a question, then it has no answer, that '*p* is true or *p* is false' fails to hold of the candidate answers? What about the statement that Churchill sneezed exactly 45 times in 1945, a statement for which the evidence has vanished? What about Goldbach's conjecture that any even number greater than four is the sum of two primes, a conjecture which cannot be confirmed and which may never be refuted?

Wright sees his pluralism as coming to the rescue here. The objection concerning bivalence will be put to the superassertibility theorist, who links truth with evidence. But there is something wrong 'with the shape of the objection' (1992: 51). It relies on a truth predicate which is out of place in a discourse, such as that about the comic, where we think that if *p* is true, then *p* must be knowable. It relies on a truth-predicate which is more robust than superassertibility and thus it begs the question. The objector says that there are *true* statements which are not superassertible. But the superassertibility theorist objects to that use of 'true' for the discourse in question. And all of the problematic examples concerning bivalence, such as the ones above, are imported from areas of discourse where Wright might think that truth is more than superassertibility.

I have argued that we are better off rejecting pluralism about truth. So how should the pragmatist, who plans to say something about truth *simpliciter*, think of bivalence? I have said elsewhere (1991, 1995) that she should not follow those who counterfactually spruce up inquirers so that they have superhuman abilities to, say, go back in time to answer questions about the remote past. (So the statement about Churchill's sneezes is bivalent – it is true if, were we to send someone back to 1945, he would count 45 sneezes, false if he would count some other number.) If the pragmatist does that, she loses the motivation for her view; she gives up on the idea that truth must be linked to *our* practices of inquiry, belief, and assertion, were they the best they could be.

It is also important to see that the pragmatist should not connect truth to inquiry with an indicative conditional, but rather, with a subjunctive conditional. It is not that a true belief is one which *will* fit the evidence and which *will* measure up to the standards of inquiry as we now know them. Rather, a true belief is one which *would* fit with the evidence and which *would* measure up to the standards of inquiry *were* inquiry to be pursued so far that no recalcitrant experience and no revisions in the standards of inquiry would be called for. Only then will pragmatism preserve the kind of objectivity that might suffice to attract those philosophers and inquirers who insist that truth is more than what we happen to think correct.

Peirce, who struggled long and hard with the issue of bivalence, ended up with the thought that bivalence is a regulative assumption of inquiry.[33] We must, for any given question, assume that there would be an upshot to our investigations, that it would emerge either that *p* is true or that it is false. Otherwise, we simply could not explain why we inquire into the issue. Such an assumption is one which we have to make in order to make sense of our practices of deliberation, investigation, and belief. The assumption of bivalence is our practice – it is part of inquiry.

Nothing, however, about the need to assume bivalence makes it true. Peirce argued that 'the only assumption upon which [we] can act rationally is the hope of success' (CE 2, 272). But he did not mean to imply that in fact there will be an upshot to our inquiries, for his point is a point about what inquirers must *hope* for if they are to make sense of their practice of inquiry. He is very clear that we are 'obliged to suppose' but we 'need not assert' that there are determinate answers to all our questions. The fact that an assumption is indispensable should not convince us of its truth. Unlike Habermas and Apel, Peirce sees that a necessary assumption is not a necessary truth. He compared the matter with the need to make the assumption that he has money in his account, if he is to write cheques on it. The indispensability never affected his balance in the least (CP 2.113).

He thus turned his back on the opportunity to elevate the principle of bivalence into a necessary truth:

> Logic requires us, with reference to each question we have in hand, to hope some definite answer to it may be true. That *hope* with reference to *each* case as it comes up is, by a *saltus*, stated by logicians as a law concerning *all cases*, namely the law of excluded middle.
>
> (NE iv: xiii [a saltus is a leap in argument])

We must make assumptions about inquiry 'for the same reason that a general who has to capture a position or see his country ruined, must go on the hypothesis that there is some way in which he can and shall capture it' (CP 7.219).

So refusing to assume the principle of bivalence is to impede the path of inquiry and that, Peirce argues, is something we should be loath to do (CP 1.135, 7.480). The principle is necessary only in the sense that it is required if we are to make sense of doing what we do by way of inquiry and deliberation.

In the light of this thought, the pragmatist will want to make a number of points about bivalence. First, she will not deny it of any statement which is the subject of a live deliberation. Any matter which we are seriously wondering about will be such that we think there is (or might be) a truth-value to be discovered there. As Hookway (forthcoming: ch.5) puts it, so long as we are aware of the dangers, we can use classical logic as a tool in our inquiries, for the propositions we make use of will generally be ones for which we believe bivalence holds.

Second, the pragmatist will not require the prospect of *proof* of a statement before sense can be made of its having a truth-value. We have reason to believe that Goldbach's conjecture is true, for, hard as we try, we have not been able to refute it. If a powerful computer program were to be run on Goldbach's conjecture and were it never to turn up an even number that was not the sum of two primes, then we would have a kind of inductive support for the conjecture. Just as the fact that we can never conclusively confirm a universal generalisation does not require the pragmatist to deny that it is bivalent, the fact that we do not have proof of Goldbach's conjecture need not have us deny that it is bivalent.

Third, even in the face of the strongest claim that we will have no evidence at all for or against a statement, we can still think that bivalence holds. For questions regarding the remote past, for instance, the fact that the evidence has dried up does not alter the truth-value of the following conditional: had we been able to pursue inquiry, were we to have the relevant evidence before us, we would believe *p* or we would believe -*p*.[34] As Blackburn (1989) has noted, we know what would count as having evidence for or against such statements; we know that they are the sort of statement for or against which evidence can speak. Or as Migotti (1998) puts it, we know that sentences about the remote past are instances of a general kind – and that kind of sentence is verifiable.

The pragmatist thus has a number of reasons for thinking that bivalence holds of those statements for which it seems that it must hold. But, nonetheless, bivalence must not be supposed to be a principle which governs every statement. There might well be underdetermination: some matters might not be governed by the principle of bivalence and the corresponding 'law' of logic, excluded middle: (*p* v -*p*).

Perhaps there are whole discourses for which our practice is not, or should not be, assumed to be bivalent.[35] A discourse such as that about the objective tastiness of recognisably edible foodstuffs might be a domain where we think that bivalence fails to hold, where it is reasonable to think that there is only underdetermination. For any statement '*x* tastes good', where *x* is something that some human beings are known to eat, and where the asserter refuses to qualify the statement with 'to me' or 'to so-and-so', we cannot say that the statement is either true or false.[36] The realist, not being able to avail himself of any hidden indexicality, will not want to say it, thinking that there is no fact that makes it true. The pragmatist will not want to say it, thinking that no amount of inquiry would settle on the right answer.

Perhaps there are also cases of genuine underdetermination in discourses where bivalence can be generally assumed to hold. Perhaps the question about whether light is a wave or a particle is such that there would be no univocal right answer.

Vagueness too interferes with the smooth holding of bivalence: 'Cheryl Misak is a junior faculty member' might seem neither true nor false, as 'junior' is a vague concept. So too may bivalence seem to fail of those statements which are such that by their very nature they are insulated from evidence. Statements such as 'being nothings nothing', 'the world and everything in it, including fossils and memories, was created five minutes ago', and 'my colour spectrum is an exact inversion of yours' are such that nothing *could* speak for or against them.

Finally, bivalence seems not to govern the liar paradox. For if 'this proposition is not true' is true, then bivalence fails: it is also not the case that 'this proposition is not true'.

The point of these examples is a slightly heretical one – it is to show that our intuitions about bivalence can pull against its unrestricted application and can thus pull against the *DS* holding everywhere. The disquotationalist, like the pragmatist, must try to cope with statements that seem not to be bivalent. The disquotationalist is committed to the view that any well-formed declarative sentence can be slotted in for '*p*' in the *DS*. But the sorts of sentences canvassed above seem not appropriately slotted in. Indeed, the liar paradox prompts a bald announcement from Horwich that the statement 'This proposition is not true' must not be substituted for *p* in the *DS*: 'permissible instantiations of the equivalence schema are restricted in some way so as to avoid paradoxical results' (1990: 41).

The disquotationalist, of course, has ways of trying to deal with what I have been suggesting are failures of bivalence. The principle of bivalence has it that every well-formed statement is either true or false and the disquotationalist might shift the burden to 'well-formed' in an attempt to understand as bivalent the examples I have marshalled. And Field (1994b) grapples with vagueness by adding a primitive 'definitely' operator, Horwich by distinguishing between 'ordinary truth' and 'determinate truth' (1990: 82).

My point is just that the disquotationalist also has some work to do here. The price of his coping strategies, I would argue, is added complexity, which is against the spirit of the *DS* and the proliferation of different grades of truth, which should be unwanted, I have suggested, by anyone.

Of course the pragmatist's view of bivalence also comes at a price. The *DS* can be accepted only conditionally – it will be said to hold only of those statements for which bivalence holds.[37] Pragmatism is in step with the thought which underlies disquotationalism – the idea that '*p* is true' amounts to the assertion that *p*, but it is very much out of step with the unrestricted application of this thought, for that entails the unrestricted application of bivalence.

The proof, I suggest, will be in the pudding – in whether the pragmatist view of truth and bivalence can make better sense of various areas of discourse and inquiry than the disquotationalist view. Of course, this standard of proof might well be weighted towards the pragmatist as it is a standard that requires theory to explain practice. But it is hard, I submit, to argue with it. We have seen that the importance of the phenomenology of our practices can be captured by the following entirely general and entirely plausible requirement: a theory of *x* must take seriously the practice of *x*. In this case, our account of truth must take seriously the thought that we aim at the truth. And it must take seriously the picture various inquiries have of themselves – whether, for instance, our practice in an inquiry is to take bivalence to govern or whether we take ourselves to be producing underdetermined judgements. It is not that our theory must try to ape these pictures. Rather, the requirement is that the theorist give principled reasons when her view is revisionist about the practice of inquiry.[38]

The disquotationalist has real difficulty in making sense of our inquiries. For one thing, it seems that he cannot fully engage the question of what kinds of statements the truth-predicate applies to, of what kinds of statements rightly aspire to truth. And these queries are not mere playthings of philosophers – it is often a critical matter whether statements about what is just or unjust, odious or acceptable, are such that they are either true or false, as opposed to up to the standards of some local discourse or other. We have seen in Chapter 1, for instance, that a pressing issue is whether liberal principles are merely some among many in the soup of culturally-bound principles or whether they are objectively right so that principles which are anti-liberal ought to be discouraged.

The pure disquotationalist is inclined to say, in Horwich's words, that 'every type of proposition – every possible object of belief, assertion, conjecture, and so on – will be a candidate for truth, for the device of generalization is no less useful when the propositions in question are normative than when they are naturalistic'.[39] There is no more to a statement's being the kind of statement which takes a truth-value than its being declarative and disciplined. Since all that one can, and need, say about truth is what the *DS* says, we are left without resources to deliberate about whether some statements are the sort that might be true or false. And that is an extremely heavy price to pay for keeping our account of truth 'pure'.

In response to this difficulty, Horwich argues that not only are such debates perfectly alright, but also that the non-cognitivist or subjectivist has the better view. He suggests that emotivism or non-cognitivism simply recharacterise itself so that it does not jar with his minimalism:

> the emotivist might attempt to characterize the unusual nature of certain ethical propositions by supposing ... that the meaning of '*X* is good' is sometimes given by the rule that a person is in a position to assert it when he is aware that he values *X* ...
>
> (1990: 88)

'Good' amounts to '*Y* believes that *x* is good', and so statements about the good will be true when what they are about is valued. Statements about the good can take their place in the *DS*, but what makes them assertible is just that someone believes them.

This tactic, however, seems to make truth something that it cannot be. Wiggins (1991b) argues, and one is hard pressed to disagree with him, that one minimal mark of truth is that *p*'s being true cannot be simply a matter of my thinking that *p* is true, or my willing it. One might bring in Wittgenstein's private language argument to support Wiggins here, but it is enough to note that truth just is like that – a statement is not true simply in virtue of someone's holding it to be true. That much seems clear enough even in the *DS*. So there is a tension in Horwich's suggestion that moral judgements can be slotted into the *DS* but that they are made true by someone's believing them to be true.[40]

Hartry Field is another disquotationalist who wants to make sense of what he calls factually defective discourse. His suggestion is that we think of evaluative statements as not being *straightforwardly* true or false – they are true or false only relative to normative beliefs (1994b: 436ff). This relative notion of truth might also fall foul of Wiggins' requirement. But it certainly encounters the difficulties associated with pluralism about truth. For it is hard to resist the thought that real truth is straightforward truth and that other kinds of truth are second-rate.

The pragmatist, I shall suggest, makes better sense of our inquiries, especially our inquiries regarding moral judgement. It can adequately characterise the long-standing debate about whether moral judgements should aspire to truth and can provide us with a notion of truth which can be used in all kinds of deliberation.

It is important to keep in mind, in what follows, that there is tremendous variety in the ways in which we think, explore, and deliberate in different domains. Inquiry is not a monolith – it is not, for instance, all about active testing of hypotheses or about arriving at definitive answers to well-formed questions. We shall see later in this chapter, for instance, that moral judgements often are a matter of direct perception – of seeing that some action is humane or that someone's behaviour falls into a pattern so that the person can be thought of as kind. But the bulk of this chapter is concerned with articulating some general and important thoughts about truth and inquiry. The reader will have to be patient and wait until Chapter 3, where the richness and the texture of our moral lives will be explored more fully.

The role of truth in inquiry

We have seen that there is considerable agreement that the concept of truth is internally related to the concept of assertion. For one thing, we cannot understand '*p* is true' without understanding that it is the assertion that *p*. In what follows, I shall suggest that truth is also internally related to inquiry, reasons, and evidence. For, reading the *DS* biconditional in the other direction, we get the thought that when I assert *p*, I assert that it is true. And I shall argue that when I assert *p*, I undertake commitments regarding inquiry, reasons, and evidence.

So let us look to the commitments we undertake when we assert or believe. Think of the difference between the phrases 'I suspect that *p*' or 'It seems to me that *p*', on the one hand, and 'I assert that *p*' or 'I believe that *p*', on the other. What I do when I use the first two is distance myself from the obligations which come with belief and assertion. (See Haack 1998.) Some of those obligations are as follows.

First, when I assert or believe that *p*, I commit myself to certain consequences – to having expectations about the consequences of *p*'s being true. Some of those consequences are practical. These will be specified in terms of actions and observations: 'if *p*, then if I do *A*, *B* will be the result'. And, as Peirce stressed, some of these consequences will be consequences for belief. When I assert or believe that *p*, I find myself bound up in a web of inferential connections. If, for instance, I believe that p and p entails q, then I am committed also to q.

Second, I commit myself to defending p; to arguing that I am, and others are, warranted in asserting and believing it. Of course, working out what it is to have warrant for a belief will be a difficult and controversial business and no one can always live up to the commitment. But that does not interfere with the thought that to assert commits one to engage, if called upon, in the enterprise of justification. Failing to incur the commitment, failing to see that one is required to offer reasons for one's belief, results in the degradation of belief into something like prejudice or tenacity.[41]

I also commit myself to giving up the belief in the face of sustained evidence and argument against it and to saying what *could* speak against the belief. We have looked at some arguments for thinking that genuine beliefs are such that they are responsive to evidence for and against them.[42] A 'belief' which thinks so well of itself that it claims to be immune from recalcitrant experience and reasoning is spurious; a 'belief' which is such that nothing could speak against it is empty.

Another way of putting the point is to say that part of what it is to be a belief, as opposed to some other mental state, such as entertaining an interesting but idle thought, a lie about what one believes, or a dogmatic opinion, is that there must be something that can speak for or against a belief and that belief must be responsive to what can speak for or against it. As Peirce insisted, there is a distinction between tenacity, or holding on to a 'belief' come what may, and genuine belief. Believing is a practice which is, by its very nature, linked to reason-giving or justification-giving.[43]

This idea certainly fits with a large part of the psychological reality of belief. A believer thinks that her belief fits best with the evidence and argument. I cannot get myself to believe that p by deciding that if the coin I am about to flip lands heads, I will believe it, and if it lands tails, I will not. In order to believe p I have to be convinced that I have good reason to believe it. If I were convinced that my coin had some special power to deliver true beliefs, then I could indeed get myself to believe p by its flip. But then I have made a prior (and most likely mistaken) judgement that my coin delivers beliefs which fit the evidence and argument. I still aim at getting beliefs which would fit with and respond to the evidence, I simply go about the business in a wrongheaded way.

If I decide to believe p if an expert believes it, I need not be making such a mistake. For I might have very good reason to think that the expert is the best judge of which beliefs are properly keyed to the evidence and argument. So if I take my physician's diagnoses as being probably correct, sometimes learning about the underlying causes and biology myself and sometimes not, what I acquire are indeed genuine beliefs.

Of course, sometimes it might seem better to *not* believe what is likely to be true or what has the weight of evidence in its favour – when the truth is too unpalatable or too uncomfortable. Here we must say that what we have is a case of wishful thinking, or 'denial', or self-deception, not genuine belief. Susan Haack makes a similar point and gives the following examples of what she calls 'pseudo-belief':

> think of those familiar psychological states of obstinate loyalty to a proposition you half-suspect is false, or of sentimental attachment to a proposition you have given little thought or none at all (when ... your verbal behavior is apt to be too vehement, and your nonverbal behavior unstable).
>
> (Haack 1998: 8)

Sometimes it might be rational enough to try to believe, against the evidence, the hypothesis which is most favourable to a desirable outcome, the hypothesis on which I can continue with what is important to me. If I believe that one physician is the better diagnostician, yet her diagnosis, if true, is disabling, whereas another's diagnosis is one on which I can continue to think of myself as healthy, then perhaps I am rational to try to believe the latter's verdict. Of course, there might come a point where the evidence speaks so loudly against the enabling view that I can no longer, or ought no longer, try to maintain it. The boundaries between, on the one hand, reasonably adopting an enabling assumption and, on the other, self-deception and denial are, of course, fuzzy.

In addition, there are assumptions which one *must* take for granted and this necessity might lead us to think that we do not have to offer reasons for what we assume. Certain beliefs are presupposed by all our inquiries and actions. We believe, for instance, that there is a world of enduring objects. But we would be *prepared* to offer reasons, however flawed or good they might be, for such presuppositions. Thus, our background of undoubted, stable, belief is rightly called belief – it is not held without reason. The reasons are just not things that we feel we constantly need to rehearse and examine.

Sometimes it will appear that someone has no reasons at all for something he claims – 'He believes, for no reason, that he is being followed' or 'She believes in God but says that reasons are inappropriate and that one must believe on faith'. On the view I offer here, these propositional attitudes, if they really are not keyed to reasons, must also not be genuine beliefs. The first is relatively easy to explain: the feeling that he is being followed is not responsive to evidence for or against it because it is caused by illness. If the paranoid person really 'believes', not for reasons, but because something has gone wrong, then he is not functioning properly and his state is a delusion, not properly speaking a belief.

The second, the case of religious belief, is especially interesting here. At first blush it might seem downright disrespectful to suggest that it too is better described as something other than belief. But if we take our cue from Wittgenstein, we can see that the view that holds that the religious do not believe, but rather, have faith, is actually more accommodating of the religious point of view.

Wittgenstein argues that it is a mistake to think of the religious life as being the sort of life which is led because the evidence points to the existence of God. To talk about evidence and reasons for belief, he says, destroys the whole business (1938: 56). If you tried to base religion on reason and evidence, your grounds for belief would be exceedingly weak and would not support the tremendous effect that your belief has in every corner of your life. Could you change your life, have your religious picture infuse your every action, if you merely believed, with some degree of probability, in the last judgement, in the existence of God, etc.? Wittgenstein thinks that it is obvious that you cannot and reserves his scorn for those who think that it is appropriate to search for grounds for their belief:

> I would say, if this is religious belief, then it's all superstition. But I would ridicule it, not by saying it is based on insufficient evidence. I would say: here is a man who is cheating himself. You can say: this man is ridiculous because he believes, and bases it on weak reasons.
>
> (1938: 59)

It is much better, much more friendly to religion, to see that reasons are not what count here. Religious 'belief' is a different sort of thing than scientific belief and belief in everyday matters. So Wittgenstein can say, of those who want to accuse a religious person of not evaluating the evidence correctly or of making a mistake in logic, 'for a blunder, that's too big' (1938: 62). A blunder is only a blunder in a particular kind of enterprise, a kind of enterprise which is not the province of religion. Thus with respect to religious matters, '[o]ne talks of believing and at the same time one doesn't use "believe" as one does ordinarily' (1938: 59). We have the words 'faith' and 'dogma' because religion isn't the sort of thing for which grounds are sought.

It strikes me, however, that we should not be quick to invoke this kind of explanation. The chances are good that there are reasons to which a purported belief would be sensitive. The paranoid might give what he takes to be evidence that someone is following him. And the theist might, contrary to Wittgenstein's advice, offer reasons for her belief – she has had a spiritual revelation, or takes some great revelatory book to be keyed to the evidence. Wittgenstein's scorn aside, plenty of people have reasons for their belief in God and these reasons can be such that if stronger reasons are presented, the belief will be shaken and perhaps revised or abandoned. Then we are presented with a case of genuine belief.

Thus the exacting notion of belief presented here is really very accommodating of what we usually call belief. The believer must simply take her belief to be responsive to reasons, for that is what is required of a propositional attitude that is aimed at truth. We might have other attitudes toward propositions – for instance, we might, against the evidence, hope or wish that p is true. But whenever a mental state is sensitive to reasons, it is a belief.

In this quick account of what we are committed to when we assert or believe something, we have gone far beyond the *DS*. Truth is bound up with the practice of assertion, which then binds it further to expectations for experience, reasons, and inference.

A question arises about moral judgements. Can they meet the standards for genuine belief? Can they aspire to truth? I suggest that here is the ground upon which the pragmatist should conduct the debate (and it will be a substantial one) about the status of moral judgement. My bet is that the debate will point to a kind of cognitivism, one which is not a mere by-product of a quietism which holds that *every* disciplined discourse admits of truth. For the various discourses, including moral discourse, will have to struggle to meet the pragmatist's requirements. A discourse might to some extent fail or even fail outright.

Indeed, even within a discourse like morality, we might, with Wiggins (1991b: 161ff), find that certain kinds of judgements are more viable candidates for truth than others. Practical judgements of the sort 'I must *x*', 'she should *y*' might be less suited for the truth-predicate than judgements about the application of concepts such as 'good', 'odious', or 'cruel'. For instance, it might not be such that someone who judges 'Eva should give blood' is committed to thinking that the reasons for Eva giving blood require anyone to give blood.

That is, there is an important distinction between a judgement being a mere candidate for a truth-value and its being a good or likely candidate. A judgement which appears to aim at truth and which is subject to some discipline is a candidate for truth. But we have yet to satisfy ourselves that we are reasonable in thinking that it has a truth-value, that it has a good shot at fulfilling its aspirations. When we have done that, then we can say that the judgement and the discourse of which it is a part, is, for want of a better word, objective.

Moral discourse has the requisite basic discipline; it is full of candidates for truth. We aim at getting things right, we distinguish between thinking that one is right and being right, we criticise the beliefs, actions and cognitive skills of others, we think that we can make discoveries and that we can improve our judgements, etc. These marks of objectivity indicate that moral judgement aims at or aspires to truth.

But we must ask whether or how often such aspirations might be met. I have suggested above that one feature a viable candidate for truth requires is that there be consequences of the belief which could in principle support or speak against it. A second feature is that there really be some discipline – some shared standards of deliberation – not just an appearance of it. What causes us to ask whether moral discourse is objective is that it is far from obvious that morality is like that. There is much disagreement about what standards of deliberation ought to be adopted; we often find issues to be contestable, thorny, and underdetermined. And much work must be done to make plausible the idea that moral judgements are responsive to evidence and argument which might overturn them. There is no guarantee in advance that these challenges can be met by the cognitivist.

The rest of this book is an attempt at showing how they might be met. Thus far, I will be content if I have managed to establish that if we are to understand what truth is, we must link the notion to our practices. The disquotationalist, insofar as he holds that there is no distinction between '*p* is true' and the assertion that *p*, joins the pragmatist in this project. But once one has accepted the point which underlies the *DS*, there is no good reason to stop oneself from going on to trace the implications of the relationship between truth and assertion, and plenty of reason to go ahead.

Experience: taking it seriously

Lest the impression be given that pragmatism faces few difficulties, let us turn now to some problems which immediately arise for it. What, we might well ask, constitutes a well-pursued inquiry, who is counted in the 'us' in the slogan 'the truth is what is best for us to believe', and what counts as experience? These questions, I shall argue, rather than setting up insurmountable obstacles for pragmatism, can be answered in such a way as to make pragmatism especially attractive. For the answers infuse pragmatism with a radical egalitarianism and provide a justification of tolerance and a reason for resisting the Schmittian view.

The pragmatist must be extremely careful to avoid stipulating what constitutes a well-pursued inquiry. We cannot say that the kind of inquiry that would arrive at the truth is the kind with our favourite features (an inquiry which turns on experimentation, open deliberation, crystal balls, or whatever). Peirce was so conscious of this requirement that he sometimes said that *any* kind of inquiry which was in fact successful at settling belief is the right kind. But eventually he saw his way out of the difficulty. Let us follow that route first for sensory judgements and then for moral and political judgements.

Peirce insists on a minimal characterisation of good inquiry, as that which takes experience seriously. This characterisation is partly due to the thought that the methods of inquiry may well improve and thus the philosopher would do well to hesitate before identifying the current methods as the objectively best methods. But we shall see that his motivation for the minimal characterisation is also that it alone can be justified.

Peirce recognises that 'going back to the first impressions of sense' 'would be the most chimerical of undertakings' (CP 2.141). We do not have access to anything raw, unconceptualised, or 'given' in experience. Some philosophers have thought that sensory judgements have an exalted status because they are infallible. Even had this idea not pretty much died with logical positivism, it has no place in the fallibilist epistemology articulated here. Nonetheless, sensory judgements do seem to be paradigmatic cases of judgements which have a chance at truth and objectivity. So we need to search for some other feature of these judgements which enables them to aspire to truth and which provides something for beliefs to respond to.

We must, however, be careful in this search not to beg the question in favour of the moral sceptic by beginning with beliefs which arise from our senses and asking what features they have. We must not set up science as the standard bearer and then notice that nothing else measures up. Beliefs, I have suggested, must respond to experience, but experience characterised minimally and prior to the discussion of various sorts of inquiry.

The fact that our senses do not provide us with information about how the unconceptualised world is provides Peirce with a starting point for a non-question-begging account of experience. Once we give up on what Sellars called the Myth of the Given, it seems that what we have are 'perceptual judgements'. These are descriptions or interpretations (of whatever hold a person had on what actually impinged on her) which can be true or false and subject to error. Peirce says:

> Practically, the knowledge with which I have to content myself, and have to call 'the evidence of my senses' instead of being in truth the evidence of the senses, is only a sort of stenographic report of that evidence, possibly erroneous.
>
> (CP 2.141)

Experience does not give us an accurate picture of the external world. Sensory perceptions only 'provide positive assurance of reality and of the nearness of their objects' (CP 4.530). Perception is cognitive – it is a matter of seeing that *p* – but it is also direct in that no inference is involved. What we do when we perceive is make a judgement.

Once we stop thinking of the authority of sensory perceptions as arising because they accurately report on how the cognition-independent world is, their authority needs to be accounted for. After all, we do (and we think we should) take them very seriously. Peirce argues that we have no choice but to take seriously the force of experience. Indeed, that is what an experientially-grounded belief is – any belief that is forced upon one. A perceptual judgement is what we are compelled to accept; we have no control over the matter. Since 'it is idle to discuss the "legitimacy" of that which cannot be controlled', observations have 'to be accepted as they occur' (CP 6.522). Sensory judgements are authoritative in that they force themselves upon us. The 'hardness of fact' lies in 'its entirely irrational insistency' (CP 7.659).

This does not return us to the thought that something is 'given' to us in experience. There is a difference between a fact being brute and stubborn and its being bare and naked.[44] Not only do perceptual judgements involve our concepts, but we have seen that Peirce is an unflagging fallibilist and thinks that all of our judgements, including the most simple perceptual ones, are revisable in light of further experience.

On this view of perception, the senses need not figure in an essential way.

The key feature of perception, observation, or experience is its insistence. And that is fully general. Experience is not tied to what our ears, eyes, nose, and skin report. Peirce says:

> ... anything is ... to be classed under the species of perception wherein a positive qualitative content is forced upon one's acknowledgement without any reason or pretension to reason. There will be a wider genus of things *partaking* of the character of perception, if there be any matter of cognition which exerts a force upon us....
>
> (CP 7.623)

Any judgement that is compelling, surprising, brute, unchosen, or impinging is an experience, regardless of what causes us to feel compelled and regardless of whether we can identify the source of the compulsion. All 'compulsions of thought' count as experience (CP 8.101).

Peirce argues that there are two kinds of compulsions – sensory experience and experience in which

> ... operations upon diagrams, whether external or imaginary, take the place of the experiments upon real things that one performs in chemical and physical research.
>
> (CP 4.530)

These diagrammatic experiments or thought experiments figure in mathematical and deductive inquiry.[45] They involve

> experimenting upon [an] image in the imagination, and of observing the result so as to discover unnoticed and hidden relations among the parts.
>
> (CP 3.363)

The mathematician, for instance, draws subsidiary lines in geometry or makes transformations in algebraic formulae and then observes the results:

> his hypotheses are creatures of his own imagination; but he discovers in them relations which surprise him sometimes.
>
> (CP 5.567)

Since surprise is the force of experience, the upshot of such reasoning counts as experience.

Peirce insists that the distinction between kinds of experience cannot be firmly drawn. External facts are simply those which are 'ordinarily regarded as external while others are regarded as internal' (CE2, 205). The distinction arises, he says, because the inner world exerts a comparatively slight compulsion upon us, whereas the outer world is full of irresistible compulsions. But nonetheless, internal experience also can be 'unreasonably compulsory' (CP 7.659): 'the inner world has its surprises for us, sometimes' (CP 7.438). He intends to leave the difference between the two sorts of experience vague:

> We naturally make all our distinctions too absolute. We are accustomed to speak of an external universe and an inner world of thought. But they are merely vicinities with no real boundary between them.
>
> (CP 7.438)

Peirce's characterisation of good inquiry is just this – good inquiry takes the force of experience seriously. It exposes beliefs to experience which could overturn them. And we are justified in identifying this feature as good, we are justified in adopting such a method, because, for one thing, we have no choice.

This is not a kind of justification that will make all philosophers happy. It does not, for instance, show that the method is bound to lead to beliefs which correspond to reality. That would be a high profile justification and Peirce, setting the tone for the pragmatists who will follow him, thinks that sort of justification impossible and not what philosophy should be after. We happen to be compelled to face experience and our method of inquiry should acknowledge this compulsion:

> As for this *experience*, under the influence of which beliefs are formed, what is that? It is nothing but the forceful element in the course of life. Whatever it is … in our history that wears out our attempts to resist it, that is *experience*… The maxim that we ought to be 'guided' by experience means that we had better submit at once to that which we must submit at last. 'Guided' is not the word; 'governed' should be said.
>
> (MS 408, p. 147)

So on Peirce's view, experiencing something as *x* is not an infallible judgement, but it is a judgement that we cannot swiftly brush aside.

We can make this point with respect to perceptions of what is valuable as well. All we have to go on in our deliberations about what is valuable is our experience – what we see as valuable and our refinements of those thoughts, in light of the arguments of others and in light of reflection. Of course, as Elizabeth Anderson notes, to judge that something is valuable is to judge that it is properly valued, not that I happened to find it valuable on some occasion or other. Finding something noble, for instance, does not make it noble (1993: 2). Our experiences are fallible. But there is no other route to the concept of nobility other than relying on what impinges upon us, immediately and after discussion and reflection, as being noble.

The same holds for perceptions of injustice. The experience of injustice does not prove that there has been injustice. Most of us know how easy it is to whinge about how we are hard done by. Nonetheless, we cannot answer questions about injustice without taking what is experienced as unjust into account.

It is not, however, only that we have no choice but to adopt it that the method which has experience at its centre is justified. Peirce also argues that the aim of inquiry is to get true beliefs, which, on his view, are beliefs which would forever fit with experience and argument. The best means to this aim is clearly a method by which we test our beliefs against experience. A physicist who refused to take into account any of the experimental results of, say, the British, would be adopting a very bad method for getting beliefs that would stand up to experience.

Similarly, those engaged in moral deliberation who denigrate or ignore the experiences of those who are of a certain skin colour, gender, class, or religion are also adopting a method unlikely to reach the truth. And, of course, in moral and political deliberation, we are often discussing how best to live our lives together. When the assumption made by so many of those discussed in Chapter 1 really operates – the assumption that we want to get on with others in peace and harmony – then the experiences of others take on special importance.

To anticipate the discussion in Chapter 3, let us notice here that some predicates might be such that an outsider lacks the requisite qualification to contribute profitably to a discussion about them. A twentieth century, single, urban stockbroker might not be able to get a grip on the idea of nobility, as it was understood by medieval knights, or on the idea of familial responsibility, as it is understood by the Amish only a few hundred miles away. His experiences might not connect with, might not be relevant to, such ideas, just as my experiences are irrelevant to discussions of quantum mechanics. One can lack the requisite background knowledge and thus one can be, for good reason, disqualified from being a serious participant in certain inquiries.

The Schmittian thinks that everyone who is defined as an 'other', everyone outside of the defined homogeneous culture, is disqualified from participation. The Schmittian denies that truth is what is best for all to believe. The boundaries of the truth-seeking communities will fall along political lines or racial lines. There is no such thing as the general community of knowers. I might, for instance, have to consider a tax on me in order to help others in my community, but I have no duties to those outside of that community – no international duties, as it were. If this is right, then the truth-seeker does not have to take the experience of all others seriously.

But much speaks against the general Schmittian claim. Not all predicates, not even all predicates about what is valuable, require specialised cultural knowledge and countless predicates cross political and racial boundaries. Think of 'x is round', 'x is unkind', and 'x is generous'. Each of these predicates, although they admit of plenty of controversy, both within and across cultures, are such that they can be translated into other languages, understood by those in other cultures, and used in communication and debate.

That there is controversy about their application suggests that we understand what is at issue, even if we disagree about the details. That we might
disagree about the application of such concepts suggests that we share
enough against which the disagreements can manifest themselves. That we
might disagree suggests that we can make sense of a deliberation with others
about how to apply the concepts and, in turn, that suggests we should take
the experience of those others into account.

This kind of justification of taking the views of others seriously will also
not make all philosophers happy, for it is merely a conditional justification. I
argued in Chapter 1 that certain conditional justifications are too weak in
that they cannot engage those who do not see anything worthwhile in the
antecedent of the conditional. Here, the conditional is as follows: *If* we want
to arrive at true beliefs, we ought to expose our beliefs to the tests of experience. There is a whiff of circularity here: we test beliefs because we want
beliefs which are true – beliefs which will stand up to testing.

The circularity, however, evaporates once the pragmatist is explicit that
we in fact value the truth. We can see that this is the case when we see that
the assertion that *p* is the assertion that *p* is true. Belief and assertion aim at
truth. And it is very difficult for a sceptical opponent to suggest that he does
not have beliefs or make assertions. Those who we want to criticise (for
instance, flat-earthers, National Socialists, and the upholders of apartheid)
also have beliefs and make assertions, even if they claim (wrongly) not to be
seeking the truth.[46] So the argument against racists and nationalists is that
their interest in truth speaks against their racism and nationalism.

This argument gets us farther than Rawls' move or Habermas' move, for
not everyone is interested in maintaining mutually cooperative relations with
others. If we have established that we want to get on with others in a mutually cooperative way or if we have established that we aim at the truth, then
we can say that someone misses something if she only wants to get it right
for herself or for her group. But it is much easier to establish that belief aims
at truth and that all functioning humans are believers than that all functioning humans aim at peace and harmony.

It might be objected that, with respect to beliefs about tables and chairs
and science, it is fine to suggest that everyone wants beliefs which will stand
up to experience, but the suggestion is less plausible in the moral domain.
Again, what about those who assert that what they want is for their preferences to be satisfied or for their group to dominate – those who say that they
do not aim at getting beliefs which best account for *all* experience?

One possibility here would be to side with the non-cognitivist and hold
that in morals and politics we do not have genuine beliefs with truth as their
aim. It will be clear that I am committed to exploring the other, cognitivist,
possibility. What I require is an argument for a kind of epistemological
holism – an argument for including the moral and political domain within
the scope of truth and knowledge. This argument will require a whirlwind
detour through empiricism.

Holism and radical holism

The guiding thought of the holism I shall advocate is a thought about inquiry. Rather than begin by driving a wedge between various sorts of inquiry, we ought to try first to identify, in an entirely general way, those features of hypotheses which make them candidates for serious investigation. I have suggested that one such feature is that a hypothesis must be sensitive to evidence and argument against it, a suggestion with an empiricist bent. But in what follows we shall see that this empiricism is one with a number of twists.

Empiricists have always shown respect for mathematical and logical statements, despite the difficulties they pose. Traditional empiricists (think here of Hume or the logical positivists) maintain that all meaningful beliefs originate in experience and, if they are justified, are justified by experience.[47] But it seems that this does not hold for mathematical and logical beliefs. These empiricists avoid the conclusion that such beliefs are not meaningful, objective, or candidates for truth-value by withdrawing the requirement that they be connected to experience. They do this via the distinction between, in Hume's terms, 'relations of ideas' and 'matters of fact' or, in more contemporary terms, 'analytic' and 'synthetic' statements. Analytic statements, such as 'all brothers are male', are supposed to have a special status because when they are true, they are true in virtue of meaning and are therefore unrevisable. Synthetic statements, such as 'there is a peach on the table', are not true in virtue of meaning and they must prove their legitimacy by passing a rather strict empiricist criterion. Hume argued that they must correspond to sensory impressions and the logical positivists argued that they must entail observation statements or be verifiable.

Quine (1953) rejects the distinction between the analytic and the synthetic, but nonetheless retains respect for the statements of mathematics and logic. With Duhem, he argues that no scientific statement is confirmed or disconfirmed on its own. For the statement being tested does not by itself entail an observation statement. Only when taken in conjunction with countless auxiliary hypotheses does a statement entail that 'if we do x, we shall observe y'. Thus, rather than the statement in question, any of those auxiliary hypotheses could be taken to be confirmed if we do x and observe y, or disconfirmed if we do x and do not observe y. It is a whole theory, or a substantial part of one, that faces the tribunal of experience.

One corollary of the Quine/Duhem Thesis is that 'synthetic' statements cannot show themselves to be legitimate by passing an empiricist test. For no statement by itself entails observation statements.

Another corollary is that mathematical and logical statements are on a par with sensory ones. They are part of any scientific theory and so they also face the test of experience – they are not unrevisable. Because of their central place in our fallible, evolving, and interconnected web of belief, they will not be easily overturned. But logically, they are as susceptible to discon-

firmation as any other judgement and, practically, inquirers may find themselves in a position where it seems best to revise a mathematical/logical
belief. (Such a fate has sometimes been suggested for the law of the excluded
middle in light of quantum mechanics.)

So the Quinean empiricist joins the traditional empiricist in taking logic
and mathematics to be genuine branches of knowledge. They are a part (the
very core) of our system of belief and knowledge and all that legitimacy or
objectivity amounts to, in Quine's view, is having a place in that effort to
make sense of experience.

But Quine puts the brakes on holism here. The analytic/synthetic distinction has been a dogma of empiricism and needs debunking. But the
distinction which encourages the thought that moral judgements are not
candidates for truth-values, the fact/value distinction, is fine as it stands.
Moral judgements have no role to play in the Quinean web of belief. They
are not a part of science; they do not face the tribunal of experience. Aside
from a 'salient marker' or two, there are only 'uncharted moral wastes'
(1987: 5, 1981a: 63).

The traditional empiricist will agree with Quine here. Whatever moral
judgements are, they do not enjoy either of the kinds of content that have
the traditional empiricist's respect. Thus Hume, on one reading, argued that
it is we who spread moral properties onto the world; they aren't there to be
found. And the logical positivists argued that moral judgements fail the verificationist test of significance; they merely express feelings of approval or
disapproval.

Since Quine rejects the traditional empiricist dichotomy, he ought to be
hard pressed to say why the exclusion of moral judgements from the web of
belief is more than mere prejudice. If there was anything good about the
correspondence theory of truth, which argues that a statement is true if and
only if it corresponds to the mind-independent (one might as well read
'physical') world of objects, that theory could be invoked to exclude moral
judgements. For the correspondence theory virtually guarantees that only
statements which assert something about the properties of physical objects
will be candidates for truth-values. But, as we saw in our discussion of deflationism, Quine rejects this account of truth.[48]

The empiricism that I wish to explore is one which sheds the Quinean
prejudice against morals. If, as I will suggest (and as Quine sometimes
appears to suggest), we should view truth simply as the best that our
inquiries could produce, the best that we could do by way of accounting for
and explaining our experiences, there is no *prima facie* reason for denying
moral inquiry a place in our search for truth. Scientific theories (with a
mathematical/logical core) certainly are a part of our attempt to understand
experience. But given a broad enough account of experience, so are moral
theories.

Indeed, we have seen that there is an important consideration against
expelling moral judgements from the scope of truth and knowledge: the

phenomenology of morality is that it aspires to truth. We argue, debate, and agonise over our moral judgements and choices as if there really is a truth of the matter at stake, something that we are trying to discover. On the pragmatism offered here, this thought is preserved. Moral inquiry is aimed at finding the right answer and at improving our beliefs through considering more evidence, argument, and perspective. I shall return to the issue of truth below, but first, we need to see how moral judgements could be seen to be objective by the empiricist who embraces holism.

The radical holism that I suggest the pragmatist adopt takes from Quinean holism both the rejection of the analytic/synthetic distinction[49] and the thought that we must view knowledge, truth, and objectivity in terms of Neurath's metaphor. We have developed a body of beliefs for making sense of our experience and we modify these beliefs in light of recalcitrant experience. We are to imagine ourselves as mariners adrift on a ship, making piecemeal repairs as they become necessary. There is no land in sight – no destination that we are bound to reach or are even trying to reach. We are rather trying to stay afloat the best we can, trying to construct the most seaworthy vessel we can.

But radical holism is more thoroughgoing than Quine's because it does not privilege or prejudice any domain of inquiry at the outset. It does not pronounce that there are separate orders of fact and value or of the causal and the normative and then go on to glorify the factual/causal and denigrate the evaluative/normative.

Rather, it takes from traditional empiricism the thought that, in order for a subject matter to qualify for a place in our system of knowledge, or in order for it to qualify as an objective area of inquiry, it must pass an empiricist test. It must meet the criterion discussed above – one which demands of a belief that it *answer to something*. The empiricism that I want to argue for undercuts the distinctions between analytic and synthetic and between fact and value by setting up an unbiased account of experience and then seeing what sorts of beliefs respond to it.

Russell's hypothesis 'the world and everything in it, including fossils and memories, was created five minutes ago' will be defective on this account just because nothing could serve as evidence for its truth or falsity.[50] If moral judgements are in some way like that, then Mackie (1977) is right that the common belief that they legitimately aspire to truth is mistaken. But if moral judgements can be shown to be responsive to experience in the way that the radical holist demands, then they are good candidates for truth-values; we are right to think that they aspire to truth.

How, it might be asked, can a holist embrace any kind of verificationism? Verificationism seems to rest on the claim that some statements carry with them their own bundle of empirical content which can be verified or falsified, a claim which is the target of the Quine/Duhem Thesis.

But notice that Quine himself can be described as a verificationist who thinks that the unit which must have empirical consequences is a whole theory. This is why he takes it for granted that physics but not morality is a part of our web of belief. Moral theories do not answer to sensory experience. Despite his arguments against verificationism, Quine seems to hold that a judgement must be a part of a theory which entails observation statements.[51]

An alternative kind of verificationism for the holist might be as follows. We have seen that the pragmatist and Quine embrace fallibilism: no belief is immune from revision. A direct consequence of this view is that a judgement must be such that it is *not insensitive* to evidence for or against it. Any judgement, that is, can be toppled by evidence. A judgement which pretends to be above experience is in fact not so lofty. It pretends to be something which it cannot be. That is the kind of verificationism which is perfectly compatible with holism.

The thought that no judgement must be taken to be immune from evidence seems to be in tension with the Quine/Duhem thesis, which has it that any judgement can be held true come what may if we are willing to make radical revisions elsewhere. But the fact that someone might tenaciously hold on to a belief does not mean that the holist must applaud such an attitude. The holist can criticise someone who is prepared to say in advance that she will not revise a certain judgement, no matter what evidence may come to light against it. Such a person, I have argued, is not engaging in genuine inquiry, is not aiming at truth, and does not have a genuine belief. We ought not take any judgement to be true come what may, although people certainly do sometimes adopt this attitude.

The significant point of departure from Quine's position is the radical holist's denial of Quine's claim that the only acceptable kind of evidence is sensory.[52] We are in debt to Quine for the thought that sensory evidence can topple both beliefs which arise from the senses and mathematical/logical beliefs. But the pragmatist wants to extend this idea. Presumably, Quine also thinks that beliefs which arise from the senses justify many of our beliefs. But, unless one takes the unattractive Millian path of holding that sensory evidence justifies mathematics, we require an account of what does justify our beliefs about mathematics. Whatever that is might as well be called a kind of evidence.

We take ourselves to be justified in holding a mathematical or logical belief if either there is a proof for the statement in question or if the statement strikes us as obviously right. We are then pressed to ask whether these sorts of considerations can topple beliefs which arise from the senses. Given his holism, Quine must respond 'yes'.

We have already seen that mathematical/logical beliefs are susceptible to revision if such a drastic change is needed to save beliefs about sensory phenomena. So we can have what we might call mathematical evidence against a belief which arises from the senses and sensory evidence against a mathematical belief. Once we have made this move, there are two kinds of evidence in the field of inquiry. We need no longer pejoratively label what strikes us as right in mathematics as 'intuition', as if to distinguish it from *real* evidence.

This sort of talk may seem to threaten holism, insofar as it may seem to reinstate the analytic/synthetic distinction by distinguishing between mathematical and sensory evidence. But no holist wants to deny that there is any difference between mathematics and science. Rather, the holist's claim is only that the distinctions are not hard and fast and that, as far as susceptibility to evidence goes, both sorts of statements are logically on a par. I want to add that recalcitrant experience can be had in the context of a proof, in a clash with a mathematical/logical belief, in a clash with a belief which arises from the senses, or, as we shall see, in a clash with yet other kinds of belief. These are all *reasons* we might set against (or for) a belief.

We have seen that traditional empiricists argue that mathematical and logical statements are empirically empty but exempt from the rigours of the test for significance. Peirce is not pressed to adopt such an *ad hoc* procedure. In his own debunking of the analytic/synthetic distinction, he suggests that we ought to expose mathematical and logical statements to the empiricist criterion. Experiments performed on diagrams will provide the relevant observable data for such statements. It is not that these observations verify or falsify the statements and thus grant them meaningfulness. Rather, the fact that the statements have consequences in such experiments makes them candidates for truth-values. This is what the empiricism of radical holism amounts to: every non-spurious belief must have experiential consequences. It must answer to experience of one kind or another. Let us rest with this sketch of the Peircean notion of experience and see how far it takes us in the domains in which we are interested.

Seeing that a piece of litmus paper is blue clearly qualifies as a perception on this account. A certain view – that the paper is blue – is compelling. There is, to borrow a phrase from Wiggins, simply nothing else to think. Such beliefs are quite fallible (the light, for instance, may be bad) but nonetheless, there is nothing else for me to believe. Moreover, such a belief is not independent of human perceptual and conceptual capacities. It is in virtue of having the capacities that we do that we call a certain phenomenon blue.

Similarly, when a scientist observes the tracks of an electron, the observation is not a theory-free observation. For one will only identify those black marks as electron tracks if one's background beliefs include a complex theory, if one knows what the cloud chamber apparatus is, etc. But once one has that set of beliefs, there is nothing else to think but that those are the tracks of an electron. Again, this is not to say that the belief is *true*, merely, that it is forced upon those with certain capacities, training and background beliefs.

The Peircean idea thus fits well with sensory judgements, both colour judgements and judgements in more theoretical contexts. The idea that experience is what we cannot help but take seriously captures what goes on in science and yet does not invest sensory observation with the fairy-tale features of being infallible and free from any subjective influence.

Peirce clearly thought that his idea lent itself nicely to mathematical and logical judgements. Proofs and valid deductive arguments are such that we cannot see how we could believe otherwise than what they conclude (CP 2.96, 6.568). If we understand a proof, we have no choice but to accept the result. Indeed, we often do not require a proof in order for a mathematical or logical statement to impose itself upon us. '2 + 3 = 5' and '$-(P \& -P)$' do so without further ado. But again, understanding here requires much in the way of background belief and again, as both Quine and Peirce insist, such statements are fallible. Although we cannot easily imagine circumstances under which we would revise them, they are in principle subject to overthrow. With respect to mathematical and logical statements, we are taken as far as we need to go by the Peircean idea.

One does not want to rely too heavily on an analogy between the moral and the mathematical or the moral and the perceptual here. The analogy I am prepared to draw between a scientific theory and moral theory is not that we perceive that certain acts are right or wrong and thus confirm or disconfirm general principles which constitute the theory. If we try to squeeze moral inquiry into the scientific mould like this, the dissimilarities or lack of fit is what ought to strike us. For one thing, the important local goals of science will include better prediction, whereas in morals they may be something more like getting a conception of ourselves that will facilitate our becoming the best we can be. And in, for instance, colour perception, there are physical objects in the world which have properties which interact with our physical sense organs and cause us to have the response we do, whereas there are no such objects and no such organs involved in our moral responses. So the analogy and the attempt to elevate the status of moral judgements would be dubious. In the mathematical case, there is a different disanalogy, for the moral and the mathematical are surely similar in that neither is primarily about physical objects. The disanalogy, rather, is the striking absence of agreement in moral matters and the striking presence of agreement in mathematical matters. Again, the attempt to elevate moral judgements, if it rests entirely on a comparison with a 'respectable' sort of hypothesis, founders because it will seem that there is more dissimilarity than similarity between the two cases.

Rather than try to show how moral judgements are like other sorts of judgements, we would do better, I think, to develop the minimal Peircean notion of experience and see whether it extends to the moral realm. By beginning with the minimal idea rather than with an analogy between fully-specified areas of inquiry, we shall not be tempted to think that all inquiry is more or less the same. We shall be encouraged, rather, to think of all inquiry as aspiring to truth and then to explore the different aims and methods of the various kinds of inquiry.[53]

Moral inquiry

However problematic it can seem to be, a case can be made for perception or experience in the moral domain. We often find ourselves compelled in moral matters and, as in mathematics, this compulsion can take two forms. The first is something like what gets called 'intuition' or 'felt response' – upon observing a group of teenagers bully and torment a younger child, we simply 'see' that it is cruel and wrong. The second is that we find some reasons, arguments, imagined situations, and thought experiments compelling and may, in light of them, revise our moral judgements. We can learn from debate and discussion, 'morals' we find in novels, morality plays, *Aesop's Fables*, the parables of the *New Testament*, and from the philosopher's hypothetical situations and counterexamples. The force of experience can be felt in the course of this kind of argument and experiment.

Again, my use of the term 'moral inquiry' is not intended to privilege the second kind of moral experience – the kind where we test our intuitions. The first kind of experience, where we perceive something, is just as important and perhaps more prevalent. And here too, experience is not uniform. Moral perception is sometimes akin to direct perception, where we see that an act is generous without much reflection. And sometimes it is more complex, where we see a behaviour as following a pattern or where we see how a set of character traits hang together.

'Force' and 'compulsion' have pernicious connotations from which I, of course, want to dissociate myself. Often the powerless are compelled to do much that is not in their interests and a totalitarian regime can force ideology on its subjects. But the notion of force and compulsion used by the pragmatist is just the notion of finding ourselves unable to believe otherwise, just as a single mother on welfare is unable to believe that she has enough funds to cover her basic costs, a feminist is unable to believe that patriarchy is good, and you are unable to believe that you are a brain in a vat, manipulated by some mad scientist. It is just the notion that is used by many when they talk, for instance, of a narrative being compelling.

We need not, and must not, suppose here that we have a special faculty for perceiving right and wrong or that our intuitions are self-evident or indefeasible. We need only suppose that we find things compelling about moral issues as well as about issues regarding the properties of ordinary objects, colours, and mathematics. As with other kinds of observation, observation in the moral domain is fallible. What is intuitively obvious in any kind of inquiry can be discredited – think of initially plausible stereotypes in the social sciences and the fact that Einstein's relativity theory was taken at the outset by many to be intuitively false.

Indeed, our very ability to recognise mistakes like these turns on the idea that what strikes us as obvious is subject to further interpretation and experience. As Michelle Moody-Adams (1997: 146ff) has put it, understanding our own moral experience requires sophisticated interpretation and self-scrutiny. One often finds oneself *mistaken* about what one experienced – self-deluded, perhaps, or unaware of what was really going on. In order to get a more accurate idea of what one experienced, conversation with friends or a therapist and some self-reflection can be helpful. We can do things to improve our interpretations.

We can, that is, be critical of our 'intuitions'. As Anderson has so nicely argued, we in fact adopt many strategies here (1993: 105ff). We can try to create a reflective equilibrium between our intuitions and our other considered judgements; we can ask whether they fall short of our ideals; science can show us that a purported fact which underlies a moral intuition is false; and we can be challenged by someone who does not share our intuitions. The situation in the last case is similar to the situation in which I alter my aesthetic intuitions by having someone invite me to appreciate a work of art in unfamiliar terms. A stranger, that is, can make me rethink a moral matter. This can be done by argument and persuasion, or by showing me new possibilities by manifesting new-to-me qualities of courage, mercy, etc.

Here is a way of understanding one of those 'objective' phenomena in our moral lives – the phenomenon that an individual can get external help in improving her beliefs about what is good, even a belief about what is good for her, about how she should lead her life. Here is a way of understanding how such beliefs are truth-apt. My beliefs about how I should lead my life are sensitive to experience, both my own experience and the experience of others. I try out the life of the aesthete and find that it is not for me. Or perhaps I read an account of how self-indulgent a particular aesthete is and I see that such a life is not for me. Or perhaps a friend argues that, given my dislike of pretence, such a life is not for me. 'Personal' conceptions of the good are not so personal and immutable after all – they are responsive to experience, argument, thought experiment, and reasons.

But, despite the fact that they are up for revision, our initial intuitions must be given weight. We have no choice but to take our background beliefs seriously in inquiry; if we did not, inquiry would grind to a halt. Without background belief, one is not empowered to see things, to make distinctions, to reason.

Furthermore, we need a body of stable belief against which to judge new evidence and hypotheses. One of the most fundamental pragmatist premises is that some beliefs must be held constant if revision of other beliefs is to take place.[54] Plausibility, obviousness, or coherence with our other beliefs must speak, at least in the first instance, in favour of hypotheses. If I judge that Serbian acts of genocide are wrong, I must do this against a set of background beliefs – perhaps my belief in the moral equality of human lives and my belief that disagreements caused by the identification with race and culture are best worked out non-violently.

Of course, those engaging in genocide may not have these background beliefs and so they will not judge that it is wrong to try to eliminate the other in one's midst. It will thus seem to some that the sort of experience relevant to morality is so liable to vary from person to person or from culture to culture, that it cannot count as evidence for or against a judgement. We are again brought up hard against the problem set out in the first chapter.

The pragmatist ought to admit straight away that morality is such that there will be much disagreement about what is compelling, for there will be differences in people's capacities, education, and belief systems. It may be that, as Wiggins has stressed, while moral judgements aspire to truth, not all will attain it. But this thought should simply be taken on board; it should not lead us to abandon talk of correctness in moral matters. For no judgement stands apart from theory or background belief. We might say merely that the baggage which accompanies the sort of experiential judgements relevant to science and mathematics is more uniform than that which accompanies the sort of experiential judgements in morals. That is, the background beliefs, education, and capacities of scientists and mathematicians are usually to a greater extent shared.

We might also say that moral judgements require more collateral information. The judgement that the bullies are cruel requires, for instance, that we know that they intend to cause distress.[55] We might also say that science has a more precise theory of error and that disagreement can often be explained by citing error or shortcomings – malfunctioning or misuse of equipment, abuse of statistical methods, etc.[56] Perhaps moral inquiry exhibits what Ian Hacking has called a looping effect, where reflection changes the nature of the thing studied. Reflection on the nature of generosity, for instance, can eventually change what we mean when we say that a person is generous.[57] Perhaps the scarcity of goods and resources explains some kinds of conflict in the moral and political domain. And, of course, morals and politics often require immediate decision-making – decision-making in advance of having anything like enough to go on.

All these things said, we must be careful also to notice the tremendous amount of underlying agreement in moral matters as well as the diversity of background theory and belief in science and mathematics. And science has also to act on partial evidence, hunches, and vague theories. Just think of clinical medicine here. And, as Putnam (1987) and others have argued, nothing very uniform can be said of the sciences over and above a few thin methodological points – points similar to the one I have articulated above about taking experience seriously.

That thin methodological point, however, is a workhorse. With respect to morals, it gives us something to say to and about someone who is, for instance, keen on ignoring, denigrating, or eliminating the other.

For those beliefs which the methodological point does not address, the pragmatist advises that we acknowledge and applaud diversity in our moral lives. Rather than damaging pragmatism, this thought indirectly supports it. For it, in tandem with the rest of pragmatist epistemology, leads to explanations of some troubling phenomena.

Take, for instance, the phenomenon of moral blindness – of the inability to see that some atrocious act is atrocious. On the view offered here, if someone does not have certain background moral views or capacities, or if they find themselves unable to take the perspective of others, then we ought to expect that they will not be able to see that a certain act is wrong.

We also have the makings of an explanation of the disagreement so prevalent in morals. Without similar background theories and capacities, one will not be able to see what others can.[58] Hence the importance of trying to expand, educate and refine our moral responses.

And we can explain how it is possible to reasonably change one's mind or discover something about a moral matter, a phenomenon the non-cognitivist struggles with. (If there is nothing to respond to, why do we sometimes revise and improve our beliefs in light of evidence and argument?) I might come to see an act in a different light or from a different perspective. Or someone might point to certain features of the act that have been missed or thought to be unimportant. That is, because experience is bound up with interpretation, not only can (and should) we expose ourselves and others to new experiences, but we can also arrive at better interpretations. We can revise our intuitions.

It will seem to some that moral inquiry is not aimed at truth because moral judgements are self-confirming in a way that scientific judgements are not. Our background beliefs might be such that we only manage to confirm our prejudices. But again, this does not distinguish morality from science – the history of science is full of examples that show that those in the sway of a particular theory will find that their observations tend to confirm that theory.

Again, we can see our way to an explanation of the troubling phenomenon on the view offered here. As in science, there is a constant dialectic between perception and the background theory. The theory facilitates certain observations and then those observations have to be squared with the rest of the theory. Through critical reflection, exposing oneself to more experience and perspectives, one's background beliefs can be improved and one's judgements revised, despite being able to see only what one's theory allows.

We can also see our way to an explanation of why it is that we can sometimes get out of the rut of confirming our prejudices. We can have an experience which makes us revise our judgements. That is, we can be *challenged* by new experience. Coming face to face with 'the other' might force us to modify our understanding of them and behaviour towards them.[59] A racist, for instance, might get to know a member of the despised group and see, at least, that his generalisation is wrong. South African prison wardens on Robben Island, white men with little education and virulently racist views, quite often were radically transformed by the experience of contact with Nelson Mandela and his fellow political prisoners. Some ANC prisoners saw such transformation as part of their work.

Indeed, it is not only that we might revise our principles in light of experience. Our principles will often only be completed or become determinate when we see how practical conflicts, when they arise, are to be resolved. Moral and political situations, with all of their complexities, must actually be *faced* in order for our principles to be worked out.[60]

Thus, while it may seem at first glance that the force of experience in moral inquiry is intolerably variable, moral judgements can be seen to be responsive to experience in the required way. Their responsiveness differs, to a certain extent, from that of mathematical and scientific beliefs, but those differences are only to be expected and receive explanation at the hands of the pragmatist. None of the differences need be immediately destructive of the general case for morals.

If we pay attention to that distinction between genuine belief and tenacity, we will want to retain, against the obstacles, the thought that moral judgements are responsive to experience. We have seen that what it is to assert, to make a claim, to believe, to judge is also to be engaged in a process of justification. It is to commit oneself to giving reasons – to be prepared, in the appropriate circumstances, to justify the claim to others, *and to oneself*. Those claiming to hold a belief, something which has a truth-value, commit themselves to being open to evidence and argument. If we are to retain the distinction in moral philosophy between mere tenacity and belief, then moral beliefs must be in principle responsive to evidence and argument.

Another way of putting this point is that if we engage in moral deliberation or inquiry, as opposed to holding on to our moral beliefs come what may, we must take those beliefs to be responsive to new reasons, arguments and experiences about what is cruel, kind, odious, just, etc. If one is committed to never revising an opinion, no matter what evidence against it is brought to light, then that is something like blind dogmatism and not a genuine judgement about what is true. Moral discussion, for those who engage in it, is experience-driven, example-driven, and argument-driven. And we do sometimes, if not always, engage or try to engage in real moral deliberation rather than in mere tenacity.

The pragmatist thus supports a kind of radical democracy in inquiry. Belief involves being prepared to try to justify one's views to others and being prepared to test one's belief against the experience of others. Thus, the differences of inquirers – their different perspectives, sensibilities and experiences – *must* be taken seriously. If they are not, reaching the best or the true belief is not on the cards. As Putnam says, democracy is 'a cognitive value in every area. Democracy is a requirement for experimental inquiry in any area. To reject democracy is to reject the idea of being experimental' (Borradori 1994: 64).

In the next section, I address some pressing questions about true beliefs being those upon which we would agree – about the idea of the end of inquiry.

Convergence and the end of inquiry

It is supposed to be a pillar of the pragmatist position that our beliefs would converge in some kind of ideal limit of inquiry. We have seen that we can quiet some worries about that ideal limit by reformulating the pragmatic maxim in terms of beliefs that could not be improved, rather than beliefs we would converge upon under certain conditions. But even when that is cleared up, the idea of convergence can be responsible for much misunderstanding and subsequent dismissal of pragmatism. Quine has suggested, for instance, that Peircean pragmatism takes the notion of successive approximation, which is defined for numbers, and hopelessly tries to apply it to theories (1960: 23, 1981b: 31). I want to make it clear, by running interference on some confusions, just what ought to be meant by the claim that a true belief is one which we would agree upon.

The pragmatist takes correct judgement not to be a matter for the individual, even though it is the individual who does the judging, but as a matter for the community of inquirers. Peirce was adamant that the 'Cartesian Criterion' – 'Whatever I am clearly convinced of is true' – makes individuals judges of truth, which is 'most pernicious' (CE 2, 212). But this is not supposed to be the thought that the community is the epistemic agent – that it is the community which does the knowing or which has the beliefs, so to speak. Individuals are the possessors of belief, but whether or not a person's belief is correct is a matter of what the community would determine. What fits with *my* experience is not of paramount importance as far as truth is concerned. What is important is what fits with all the experience that would be available, what the community of inquirers would converge upon. A hallucination, Peirce says, is a compulsion which does 'not fit into the general mass of experience' (CP 7.647).

One misconception about this community-based view of truth arises with respect to how the force of experience is supposed to encourage convergence. It might be right to say the following kinds of things. If we find that a person feels nothing for the plight of battered women, then taking him to a shelter for women where he can see for himself, as it were, how women experience battering, is something which we think ought to compel him to think differently. And we think that someone who is unmoved by the suffering of those under her employ in, say, apartheid South Africa is missing a moral cog – her failure to be compelled by the experience of others speaks against her.

But we should not leap from these thoughts to the idea that we will in fact be compelled so frequently by the experience of others that we will converge in our opinions. That is not what is meant by experience being compelling. We will often improve our views by taking into account what other people find compelling. But this does not entail that there is one set of beliefs to which we will all gravitate.

There is also a clutch of misconceptions which begin with a failure to notice that it is *only* the methodology that we ought to take seriously the experience of others (the democratic methodology, if you like), which is justified at the level of theory. The pragmatist should not be interested in setting out a list of standards for inquiry, standards which will make convergence likely. The pragmatist, at this level of abstraction, must remain agnostic about the details as to how inquiry (of any kind) should go. She will say that inquirers must expose themselves to new evidence, argument, and perspectives. For if truth is that which would best fit with the evidence and argument, were inquiry to have proceeded as far as it could fruitfully go, then the best way to inquire about the truth is to take in as much and as varied evidence and argument as one can.

Beyond that general principle, the methodological principles and standards of rationality which are best are those standards which would evolve, were inquiry to be diligently pursued. Those standards might turn out to be very different from what now gets counted as rational.[61] In science the standards will be set by scientists and those few historians and philosophers of science who have an impact on actual inquiry. In morals, the standards will be set by those engaged in moral inquiry. This does not mean only, or even mainly, philosophers, 'experts' who sit on ethics boards in hospitals, and those novelists and essayists who engage particular issues. As feminists have stressed, we must not underestimate the value of listening to ordinary people's own *stories* – their accounts of how injustice, for instance, has played a part in their lives.

Perhaps this is the flip side of the fact that there is so much underdetermination in ethics. Moral deliberation displays a kind of epistemological democracy. We are all involved in moral discussion and in experiments in living, to borrow a phrase from Mill. Moral judgement is inextricably bound up with our relations to others and anyone who stands in such relationships has plenty of engagement in moral deliberation. Truth requires us to listen to others, and anyone might be an expert.

This, of course, does not mean that everyone is equally good at seeing when something is kind, unjust, or phoney. It just means that anyone, whatever their formal training, might be very good at it. One suspects that good novelists[62] are amongst the best, but so might the man on the Clapham omnibus.

Indeed, there is some reason to be suspicious of experts in morals and politics. As Dewey said, experts may well become 'so removed from common interests as to become a class with private interests' themselves and not at all good at arriving at the best judgements in social matters (1976: 245). Ian Shapiro adds to this that purported knowledge about politics is regularly undermined by events and usually the experts turn out to be on somebody's side after all (1996: 128–9).

The point that only the general democratic methodological principle can be justified by a philosophical argument is important. Failure to attend to it can put the radical democratic core of pragmatism at risk. This is what is wrong, I think, with a certain interpretation of Hilary Putnam's pragmatism. Putnam, in *Reason, Truth and History*, argued that truth is what would be believed by an ideally rational inquirer. Brian Ellis, taking this ball and running with it, argues that we need the concept of an ideally rational being not only in order to 'define how people would think if they were ideally rational', but also to serve as a 'regulative ideal ... to tell us how we ought rationally to think'. We may never realise the ideal, but nonetheless, we are somehow to construct the ideal out of what we currently take to be rational. For in arriving at a model of rationality, the 'ideal of rationality ... should appeal to the normal intellect as a rational ideal' (1990: 235).

But there is too much emphasis here on what seems natural, or normal. If we earmark certain (fallible) claims about what is good by way of belief and glorify them by making them part of the ideal, the danger is that we will confirm our prejudices and block the path of inquiry. We must not take for granted the system of epistemic value which is now taken to be the best. The open-endedness of inquiry and the commitment to taking other perspectives seriously must be preserved if we are to have any hope of reaching beliefs which really do account for all experiences and argument. For surely what strikes the 'normal' intellect, or the scientific intellect, or even the best intellect around, as epistemically valuable is not guaranteed to be valuable.

So the pragmatist must be careful not to suggest that the way in which we are converging on the truth is that we are getting closer and closer to some specified ideal. In suggesting that, he seems sure to get the ideal wrong. Pragmatism is not a view about the standards of our present human practices. We must not identify an ideally rational person with what we now take to be a good inquirer. Nor must we identify an ideally rational person with the scientist. Not only has science often failed to live up to its own ideals, but we do not know that those ideals will remain the same. Our standards even there evolve and we can never reach a point where we can say that they are fully evolved.

Indeed after the moral horrors of this century, surely no one will even want to say that we are marching forward in this domain – that we are getting closer to the truth. This should not prevent us from thinking that here and there we have made improvements, corrections, and progress, as opposed to changes in whim or fashion.

Of course, in making judgements about what is rational to believe, we cannot help but use the standards we presently think best. But again, we must be prepared for the possibility of a revision of those standards. The pragmatist, being a fallibilist, will leave room for radical revision of our methodological principles and this room will be made by paying attention to the views of those outside the mainstream. If there are standards and values that are characteristic of some group or other, they must be a part of this dialectic. It is not just the participants of a practice who must be heard. Those who would like to participate, but are barred, those affected directly or indirectly by the practice, and those who simply react to what they perceive in a distant practice also have something to say. We must be open to learning from them.

We also should not think that one set of standards will certainly emerge as best. As Ian Hacking (1982) has gone so far to show, there are different styles of reasoning and it might be agreed that various styles are suitable for various inquiries. We might even be prepared for the possibility that some styles of inquiry are most prominent in a certain kind of inquirer. It has been suggested, for instance, by some feminists, that women and men have different ways of approaching a problem.

So on the pragmatist view, we will not turn to the notion of an ideally rational inquirer to settle our debates. The view of truth offered here is not a version of the ideal spectator position, on which the truth is what a certain kind of ideal spectator, in ideal circumstances, would take to be true. For we have seen that we cannot fill in the details about what an ideal spectator would be like (impartial, sympathetic, utilitarian, interested in simplicity, or whatever) and then settle our debates by asking how such a spectator would settle them.

We must be careful with the Peircean notion of the end of inquiry. It is not some God's-eye view, where, if we could only guess what God (or whoever else occupies the view) would see, we would have the truth and a foundation for knowledge. Rather it is the down-to-earth view which involves the outcome of our actual human practices, if they were to be informed the best they could by evidence and argument. Sensitivity to context and situations will be a primary feature of moral inquiry. We must settle our debates the best we know how, paying careful attention to the particulars of situations, with the assumption that, were inquiry to be pursued as far as it could fruitfully go, there would be a best answer which would make itself apparent.

That 'would' is of crucial importance. We have to pay special attention to Peirce's insistence that the expectations of a true belief be expressed with a subjunctive, not an indicative, conditional. We expect that a true belief is one which *would be* right to believe, were inquiry to have progressed (by way of evidence, argument, and standards) as far as it could fruitfully go. A true belief is not one that *is* now agreed to be best. If this point is missed, pragmatism turns into something that no one should want to hold.[63]

Despite the emphasis on this subjunctive, the end of inquiry is not to be pictured as some point in the future, where we would find ourselves with perfect and complete evidence. Neither is it to be pictured as a body of statements that constitutes the complete truth, a body where every statement is assigned a determinate truth-value. Truth is a regulative ideal of inquiry, and as Dorothy Emmet puts it, a regulative ideal differs significantly from an utopian blueprint (1994: 47ff). A blueprint, such as Marxism, is thought to be in principle realisable, but in fact unrealised. A regulative ideal, on the other hand, is not thought to be realisable. Its role is to set a direction and provide a focus of criticism for actual arrangements.

This brings me to the last thing that I want to say about convergence and the end of inquiry. Although all moral judgements may aspire to truth, not all will attain it. This does not entail that truth and falsity fail to apply to moral discourse; it does not entail that moral discourse is not truth-apt. Our deliberations in morals and politics are, I want to argue, regulated or governed by standards of correct and incorrect assertion – standards of when we have got something right and when we have made a mistake. It is important to see, however, that our discourse can measure itself by such standards, can be disciplined, without every case admitting of a right answer.

Again, the pragmatist must keep a cool head about convergence. A statement's being true is not a matter of its being such that every person would come to believe it under the right circumstances. And a discourse or an area of inquiry admits of truth not when we can expect convergence about every statement in that discourse. Rather, convergence enters into the pragmatist's account of truth as a way to mark the thought that a belief is true if it would be found to be the belief which would forever best account for all the experience and argument. The pragmatist says, loosely, that we would agree upon, or converge upon, the best belief. But the pragmatic account of truth is very tolerant of disagreement. It does not suggest that the reasons offered in the deliberative process must be ultimately acceptable or convincing to all.[64]

We can turn much of the current talk of convergence on its head. The expectation of convergence is a regulative assumption of inquiry – it, like its more formal partner, the principle of bivalence, has, in Simon Blackburn's phrase, imperative force (1993: 25). It tells us what to look for, what to hope for, of our practice. It requires us to keep looking for reasons, despite the fact that we might expect, in a discourse such as that of morals and politics, that there would be countless underdetermined beliefs.

As Joe Heath (1998) argues, we should not think of ourselves as examining a given discourse to see whether it is objective; to see whether it is about the world; to see whether the world here produces convergence of belief. Rather, the expectation of convergence is a normative presupposition of inquiry, differing in strength as our needs for convergence differ. The assumption, that is, presses itself on our practice more in some cases and less in others.

Heath suggests that one discourse which imposes a strong convergence constraint on participants is discourse about physical or natural events. We need to expect convergence here, we work hard in order to align our beliefs, because that is required if we are to interact or coordinate our actions with others. If we are going to have reasonable beliefs about how others will behave, we need to expect that we all assign pretty much the same probability to events.

In legal argument, too, the belief in an objective physical reality is maintained in the face of evidence to the contrary – contradictory accounts of what happened, for instance.[65] The assumption made by a traffic court that there is a single correct story about what caused a traffic accident is an assumption which here exerts a firm regulative grip on practice. It is taken to be unfalsifiable and the failure to maintain it is subject to various forms of social control. We wonder about the sanity of someone who thinks that contradictory descriptions of an accident are both in fact correct. That is just not how we think of 'what happened'.

We are not talking here of a case where two narratives can be correct in a 'duck-rabbit' kind of way, where if you look at the picture one way you see it as a duck and if you look at it another way, you see it as a rabbit. When two narratives conflict about whether or not the car jumped the curb, we assume that only one can be correct. Because of the expectation that we can converge on a correct answer to our question, we pursue the inquiry. The expectation comes first and is in part responsible for the degree of convergence that follows.

Beliefs about moral requirements also command a high expectation of convergence. Heath points out that with migration and increased communication and transport, we find pressure for standardisation or convergence of our practices. In order for social interaction to go smoothly, it will often be important to share values (such as respect for persons).

With respect to desire, there is less call for agreement. We must share a vocabulary of what it is to have a motive, intention, and the like, but our actual motives and intentions can diverge without presenting too many difficulties. And where agreement is less important, where the norm of convergence is less a presupposition, we can happily agree to disagree.

We have seen, in our discussion of Habermas and Apel, that this kind of point must be kept in its place. The expectation of convergence – the expectation that there is a truth of the matter – might be necessary to maintain a particular practice of inquiry, but it is not for that reason necessarily right. A practice might be entirely wrongheaded. Or we might find that we have an *unreasonable* expectation of convergence – we might find that our hopes are dashed with respect to a domain of inquiry and we have to revise our expectations and our practice. Preserving our regulative assumptions, preserving those thoughts without which we could not go on, does not entail that they are true. That we cannot imagine circumstances under which the need for them might disappear is not decisive. Even our methodological assumptions can be up for grabs, as can the best belief at any stage in inquiry.

The pragmatist, however, is set on exploring the other option – on making the best case for our expectation that moral inquiry is disciplined and properly aimed at truth. My attempt at an epistemology that respects the aspirations of morals has been as follows. We engage in the practice of scientific, mathematical, and moral inquiry. Each has its evolving standards of criticism and evaluation and each has a kind of experience most relevant to it. This experience, and the possibility of clashes with other sorts of judgements, constitutes a domain of evidence that could be for or against a hypothesis. The fact that the branch of inquiry in question is responsive to experience in part justifies our belief that it aims at the truth.

There are differences, to be sure, between the three inquiries and the prospect of judgements in some inquiries commanding consensus differ from those of others. But this should not lead us to think that science, say, is the sort of thing that might achieve a correspondence with an independent reality, for no thing is that sort of thing. Scientific hypotheses are laden with our concepts and theories – they are part of our attempt to make sense of what impinges upon us. The same holds for moral beliefs. We are in both cases adrift on Neurath's boat. We have our practices and their standards of success. To borrow an apt phrase from Wiggins, in prosecuting those practices, 'we shall reach wherever we reach, for such reasons as seem good and appropriate' (1987: 207). And if we were to reach a stage where we could no longer improve upon a belief, there is no point in withholding the title 'true' from it.

In addition, and against Rorty, there is a point in thinking that we aim at true beliefs. For, as Peirce argues, an assumption of inquiry into any matter is that there is a hope of reaching the truth. Without the hope that there is an answer to the question at hand, there would be no point in debate or investigation. If we are to leave the path of inquiry unobstructed, we must assume that there is a truth of the matter with respect to the issue we are investigating. Those contemporary pragmatists who would replace the notion of truth with that of warranted assertion betray their commitment to taking seriously the practices of inquirers, who take their business to be that of trying to reach true beliefs.

In the next chapter, I try to show how moral and political deliberation might be characterised on this pragmatist epistemology. One thing is clear: ensuring that the multiplicity of voices is heard is a political matter. So a part of the pragmatist package must be the claim that such politics must be allowed to be fairly played out. There will have to be redistribution of cultural resources like access to opportunities to speak in public forums. And often considerable effort will have to be expended to hear those who have more immediately pressing things to do – the poor, for instance. Otherwise, what results from inquiry will not be truth and knowledge. It is to this kind of issue that we now turn.

3   Moral deliberation

Truth-seekers and reason-givers

I have presented an entirely general pragmatist epistemology, with remarks along the way about how the view might be friendly to moral and political judgements, about how moral and political judgements might be truth-apt. One of my central points has been a conceptual point about how moral belief and assertion, like any other, must be responsive to experience and to reasons. Part of what it is to hold a belief about what is good, even about what is good for me, is to be committed in principle to giving reasons for that belief, to defending it. Here I want to draw out the implications of this idea.

Let us begin with a question posed by David Wiggins in 'Truth, and Truth as Predicated of Moral Judgements' (1991b). He asks what is significant about the discovery that I can offer no persuasive reasons on behalf of a proposal or claim of mine. For I tend to be disturbed if what has impinged upon me does not impinge upon others. If something can be said about the origins of and reasons for this disturbance, something will have been said at least about how we think of objectivity.

Another way of putting this query is as follows. Assertion, belief, truth, and objectivity, I have suggested, are not private matters.[1] What it is to have a belief is to be committed to giving reasons for that belief. And if there is a truth of the matter, I expect my reasons to be persuasive to others. Of course, my reasons can fail to impress others and the belief can nonetheless be true, but what is needed then is an *explanation* of this unhappy situation.

Wiggins points out that I might explain *away* the failure to have my reasons impinge on others. If the explaining away is that the others are not in the appropriate position to feel the force of the evidence or arguments or that the others are defective in some way, my disturbance will disappear. But in absence of such explaining away, one must feel uneasy, for:

> If … there were no prospect at all that arguments founded in what made me think it true should have non-random efficacy in securing agreement

about whether *p*, I should be without protection from the idea that (unless I was simply wrong) there was just nothing at issue.

(1991b: 149)

One thing that might be going on when I cannot explain away the fact that no one else sees anything in my arguments is that my arguments are wrong. We have seen that Cohen, Nino, and Bohman suggest that when my reasons fall flat on others, I might be moved to arrive at better reasons. I might think that objectivity requires that I rethink my position.

But, if I cannot bring myself to do that – if my arguments continue to seem correct to me and if I cannot get anyone else to see their force – then perhaps there is no truth of the matter to be had about the issue. That is, another thing that might be going on when my reasons fail to persuade others is that there is no right answer to be had. If an issue is to be thought of as an objective issue, with a right answer or set of answers, then I have to say something, by way of explanation, about why others do not agree with me.

Nuance about the kind of question at issue is required here. If the issue is about how it is best for me to live, then we have recourse to a psychological explanation. If, for instance, I fail to persuade others that it is best for me to go off and be a hermit in the hills, the explanation of this failure might be that I have an unusual set of preferences or psychological makeup – a makeup which makes it best for me to do something which others find incomprehensible. Or the explanation might be that I have made a mistake, even about what is best for me. Sometimes the information obtained from others can enlighten me about my own desires. Since self-deception, denial, and lack of self-insight are common enough phenomena, sometimes an outsider's view can be the most accurate.

If the issue is about what justice requires in a particular case, my failure to persuade others is likely not to be explained away by an appeal to my idiosyncratic set of preferences or psychological makeup. But it might be explained by my having made a mistake. I might think this if I see that others, who are generally epistemically competent, and who have been in similar circumstances and have thought about the matter, see no point at all to my claims. Or it might be explained by there being no objectivity – no right answer – to be had in the matter.

Non-cognitivists will latch on to this last kind of explanation. They will say that there is nothing in the moral and political domain to get right or wrong and that is why reasons and experiences which pull on me can fail to pull on others. But we have seen that if that explanation is accepted as all-embracing – as holding everywhere in the moral and political domain – then the advocate of tolerance has nothing to say to the Schmittian. And she has nothing to say *to herself* about why she is right in thinking as she does rather than as the Schmittian does. If my reasons are parochial and latch on to nothing which is common to all, then they might as well have as little persuasive power with me as they do with others. It is hard to resist the thought that I have *no reason* for advocating tolerance other than that it is what strikes me as right. And I have no reason to criticise the Schmittian, no reason to be passionate about my belief in tolerance, and no reason to think that coercion is ever necessary. As Wiggins suggests, we need protection against this idea – the idea that there is nothing at issue in morals and politics.

Pragmatism, I have suggested, can offer such protection. Unlike non-cognitivism, it does provide the theoretical wherewithal to think that one's reasons are more than just what one happens to think. For a judgement aims at being true, where being true amounts to being the belief which would best fit with reasons and experience. And pragmatism provides the theoretical wherewithal to criticise others. For a methodological principle has been justified: engaging in genuine moral inquiry – searching for principles and for particular judgements which will not be susceptible to recalcitrant experience and argument – requires that we take our beliefs to be responsive to new arguments and sensibilities about what is good, cruel, kind, oppressive, worthwhile, or just. Those who neglect or denigrate the experiences of others because of their gender, skin colour, or sexual orientation are adopting a very bad means for arriving at true and rational beliefs. They can be criticised as failing to aim at truth properly.

This methodological criticism will come into play in relatively few cases. The project is not to derive the whole of morals and politics from a general and proven principle. The methodological point is not a fountain from which all policy must flow, although it supports a certain direction for policy, rich and possibly radical. For the most part, moral debate will be conducted in the usual way, with reasons offered of the sort: that someone fails to see how much pain she is causing; that lying to a person in order to get what you want is treating him as a means to an end and that this is an inappropriate way to treat a person; that keeping a class oppressed in order to maintain a luxurious lifestyle indicates a perverse ordering of the importance of various needs, and so on.

That is, once the pragmatist/cognitivist ethics is up and running, there will be countless familiar principles which will provide grounds of justification and criticism. But these principles will not have the general justification that the methodological principle enjoys. Their justifications will be even more low profile and fallible. Agreement on this or that issue must always be taken to be possibly wrong, for we do not know that inquiry or debate has been pursued as far as it could go. We have seen that not even the methodological principle should pretend that it is necessarily true and this holds even more sharply for the first-order principles.

But the fact that our judgements are fallible does not mean that the arguments for them are weak. We can have good reasons to think that a way of life, a conception of the good, a comprehensive doctrine, a religious commitment, a norm of behaviour, an ideal of virtue, a kind of character, a cultural value, or a recommendation for action in a particular context is right or wrong.

It is clearly crucial for the pragmatist theory that wanting to get the truth is something which cuts across whatever divides us from others. Luckily for that theory, we are indeed hard pressed to find opponents in our moral and political lives who do not assert or believe or claim that their position is true, or best, or that which ought to be enforced. This is all we need in order to see them as participating in inquiry and all we need in order to see them as bound to the minimal requirement of taking experience seriously. Once our Schmittian and other illiberal opponents are brought into the epistemic fold, they can be criticised as failing to really hold beliefs – things which are responsive to reasons. For they refuse to take the reasons of all seriously.

So despite the fact that the pragmatist's methodology is sparse and is something that is relatively easy to accept, it gives us what Habermas wants and what everyone should want – critical bite. And despite the fact that the pragmatist says that we must start our theory with ongoing practice, that theory can provide us with a guide for future practice. We can debate substantive moral issues and, over and above the first-order criticisms which we will level, we are guided by a methodological normative principle. An inquirer can fail to aim at truth, can fail to hold genuine beliefs or genuine assertions, or he can follow a method that is unlikely to get him true beliefs.

The first-order reasons we may invoke for or against some proposal are not reducible to the second-order reasons – to the epistemological arguments about truth and inquiry. The epistemological arguments tell us what it is to have a belief which aims at truth, moral belief being a special case of that general type (a case where arguments about the rightness of respecting others happen to take primacy of place). The first-order reasons will be about moral properties, such as the fair distribution of resources and how we ought to treat others when we interact personally with them. It is the first-order reasons which will constantly come into play in our ethical and political lives, unlike the epistemological reasons. And there will be plenty of first-order reasoning which bears on the question of whether we ought to treat the experience of others with respect. But that does not damage the point that the epistemological arguments give us something additional to the first-order reasons to say to ourselves about why and how we can criticise those who denigrate the experiences of others. It does not damage the point that the epistemological arguments give additional weight or justification to the idea that we must take the experiences of others seriously.

David Estlund (1997) and Henry Richardson (1997) can be seen as offering the following justification for deliberative democracy, which has affinities with the justification offered here. Assume that impartiality and fairness are a part of our aim in morals and politics. We have a preference for deliberative over random ways of achieving these aims. We think that flipping a coin would be a bizarre method of making political decisions, even though it exemplifies a kind of impartiality. This preference reflects something – it reflects that there are standards which require our respect. A legitimate procedure must be answerable to reasons – it must be capable of paying attention to the reasons that matter. If, for instance, a vote – which exemplifies another kind of impartiality – failed to provide minimal resources to the most needy, we would reject it. For it would fail to meet standards of charity or generosity which demand respect. Since reasons come out in debate and deliberation, a legitimate procedure must be one that proceeds by debate and deliberation. Flipping a coin or simple voting cannot guarantee that standards and reasons will be respected and so we *need* to deliberate. That is the only methodology which is justified for those who hold that random methods of impartiality are not preferable over methods which pay attention to reasons.

My argument, along similar but more all-embracing lines, is that any method for arriving at genuine beliefs (beliefs which aim at truth) must be a method which is driven by reasons and experience. The argument embraces more because having a belief that is aimed at truth, or at getting things right, is something that every believer is committed to, whereas impartiality is not. So the point I have been urging is stronger than Estlund's and Richardson's. The shared point is that if you want to have your beliefs governed by reasons, then you will have to expose yourself to different reasons, different perspectives, different arguments. You will have to engage in debate and deliberation. The stronger point is that a case can be made that any opponent is committed to having her beliefs governed by reasons, so any opponent is committed, whether he acknowledges it or not, to debate and deliberation.

It will be asked here whether I am not trying to give a sort of transcendental argument for the principle that we must take the experience of others seriously – a kind of argument for which I criticised Habermas and Apel. Do I not also try to have democratic principles fall out of the very ideas of belief, assertion, and truth?

Indeed, my argument is that the requirements of genuine belief show that we must, broadly speaking, be democratic inquirers. But the argument avoids the difficulties which accompany Habermas' and Apel's view. First, many problems for Habermas and Apel arise because their account of the necessary preconditions of communication seems to rest on an unintuitive definition of communication as an attempt at mutual understanding. Communication often, it seems, flies in the face of the democratic principles. I have argued that certain things are required for genuine belief and my argument, I hope, is based on a plausible and thin understanding of what is involved in the concept. A belief is something that one gives, or would give, or could give, reasons for, something that one takes to be responsive to the way things are. And that seems right.

Second, I have offered an independent argument for the thought that truth is what would be agreed upon. I do not take for granted an identification of truth with the results of inquiry when I try to justify the democratic method. And one of my arguments for that method – that adopting a method which ignores the experience of others is a bad means for getting beliefs which best account for all experience and argument – has no transcendental ring at all to it. It does not suggest that the possibility of language or communication depends on a certain conception of how to live (i.e. freely and equally). Rather, it is a hypothetical imperative of the sort: if you want beliefs which will withstand the force of experience, then do such-and-such. The additional empirical or sociological claim is then added – virtually everybody claims to be after such beliefs.

So my argument rests on a conception of deliberation or inquiry which tries to be relatively uncontentious. All it takes for someone to be a participant in these practices is a commitment to wanting beliefs which will not be overturned by subsequent experience and reason. Again, it is extremely easy for a state to qualify itself as a belief on this view. All it takes is that acknowledgement, explicit or implicit, that the belief *answers* to something. This is not Popper's claim that a belief must be straightforwardly falsifiable. A belief merely must be sensitive to something. And in those cases in which I fail in my commitment to have my belief sensitive to reasons, all that can be said is that I fail to have a genuine belief aimed at truth, not, contra Habermas in some moods, that my humanity is compromised. I merely do not aim at the state I say I aim at, or I adopt a method which is not appropriate to my stated aim.

One reason for the thin conception of inquiry here is to avoid the kind of difficulties that face Habermas and Apel. But another is to avoid an objection often put to liberalism. The charge is that the liberal tries to elevate a particular conception of the good – something like 'rational' debate – to the status of an obvious and universal good. Rawls, for instance, has been accused of having a conception of the self as a rational chooser who wants to maximise her own advantage. The charge is that it is far from obvious that such a conception of the rational self ought to be written in stone for all.

I try to defend a view which has it that all conceptions of good be on the table for discussion. There appears to be no built-in bias here, no bias which will ensure that certain conceptions will be declared best. But is the pragmatist not sectarian in that she thinks that the life of active citizenship, or the life of deliberation, or some other variation on a liberal ideal is the life we must live?[2] Some will see in pragmatism an unpleasant privileging of the inquirer, the debater, or the investigator. Perhaps pragmatism merely enshrines the culturally specific values of argumentation, impartiality, and experimentation.

We shall see in the following sections that, for a number of reasons, this is not right. The pragmatist does not think that deliberation is always appropriate. And the nature of deliberation is left entirely open. For hand in hand with the idea that truth would be the product of human inquiry is the idea that what is true, what is rational, and what the standards of good deliberation are is a matter of what human inquiry would take to be true, rational, and good by way of standards of inquiry. There is no truth beyond our human inquiries, which always take place in a particular context. So even the kind of deliberation that is appropriate is something that will come out only through thought and deliberation. Indeed, the self will only be formed through thinking and decision-making. It is only in the midst of inquiry that we discover who and what we are, what we want, and what fits best with the evidence and argument. But we shall see that this kind of process can take all kind of forms, not all of them resembling self-conscious, organised, and systematic investigation.

Again, the point is that it is much more plausible to think that all inquirers aim at getting beliefs which will not disappoint them than to think that all inquirers aim at being rational, in the fairly narrow sense meant by some Western academics. The pragmatist rejects the idea that the nature of reason (that it is neutral, that it abides by first-order logic, or whatever) is identifiable in advance of inquiry. Rather than require all to conform to such purportedly objective standards, the pragmatist makes the thinner and more plausible requirement that all inquirers aim at getting beliefs which will stand up to the test of experience. It is very easy to qualify oneself as an inquirer on this conception of inquiry.

Neutrality: three senses

Although the pragmatist puts forward a methodology for moral and political deliberation which is thin and low-profile, it would be a mistake to suggest that it is thereby neutral, in the sense most often meant by liberal political theorists. 'Neutral' is one of those words that is so overused that confusion about just what is meant often accompanies it. The sense of neutrality which I am concerned to distance myself from is what I shall call the neutrality principle and it is the pillar of many a liberal theory.

The neutrality principle holds that government should not encourage or discourage conceptions of what it is to lead a good life. On this kind of neutrality, as long as the pursuit of a conception of the good does not directly harm others, the state should take a principled position of non-interference. The view is often summarised by saying that conceptions of the good are off the public agenda – the state cannot explicitly encourage them and citizens, in their public roles, cannot appeal to them in debate and argument. I shall argue, on the contrary, that often an appeal to reasons which refer to one's conception of what is valuable can and should be made in public deliberation. If the relevant distinction is between the neutral and the public/political willingness to judge ways of life, then we shall see that the pragmatist wants to allow for such judgement and declare this kind of neutrality unwise.

There are other distinctions, which issue in other senses of neutrality, which we would do well to keep in mind. One is between the neutral and the committed and another is between the neutral and the biased.

We have seen that central to the pragmatist's argument is that it is impossible to be neutral in the first sense – to be uncommitted.[3] There is no way of thinking of neutrality as a kind of perspectivelessness. One must have some perspective, some commitments. If being impartial involves the thought that an individual can rise above a particular context and somehow make a judgement which stands apart from her background beliefs, then impartiality is indeed not to be had.[4] Our policies and beliefs arise from deliberation between individuals with particular, partial, views, views laden with the reasoner's background beliefs, education, and cultural expectations.

It is, however, possible and desirable in politics to be neutral in the second sense, to try to eradicate bias. A person is biased if he holds to his commitments in such a way as to close his mind to other beliefs. So being unbiased requires, amongst other things, that one try to put oneself in the other's shoes, so to speak – that one try to imagine what it would be like to see the issue from the perspective of others.

If we pull together the thoughts regarding these two distinctions, we can see that having commitments, being steeped in a fallible point of view, having a perspective, need not be a form of illusion, bias, or distortion. As with one's location in perceiving an object, one must perceive from a particular perspective. But a range of perspectives will be consistent with each other and consistent with a particular description of the object or situation. If we are careful to try to shift perspectives, we can get a more complete take on matters.[5] An individual occupies a perspective, and can occupy any one of a number of perspectives. Attention to these possibilities can produce a judgement that is not biased.

There are of course difficulties in drawing the line between having a perspective and having a bias. For instance, in 1994 the Ontario Court of Appeal dealt with a charge of bias against a member of a Police Services Board of Inquiry into the conduct of officers who strip-searched a black woman in public. The board member in question was the president of a Chapter of the Congress of Black Women of Canada and the majority in the court agreed that the statements about the prevalence of racism, which the Congress had made in the past, created a reasonable apprehension of bias. The dissenting judge, however, noted that affiliation with an organisation which by its very nature might be said to favour one side in a dispute could not be enough to show bias. The other board members, after all, were recommended by the Ontario Police Association and the Ontario Association of Municipalities.[6]

The difficulty is that a board member on a tribunal always has some view, fallible and defeasible, about what constitutes discrimination and what should be done about it. Did this woman's having the view she had constitute a bias that made her unsuitable to make judgements of improper searches by police officers? Should a candidate be disqualified from being a Constitutional Court judge who has to decide on same-sex gender legislation because he believes that homosexuals should have the same rights as heterosexuals? Should he be disqualified if he is a gay rights activist? What makes it more likely that someone who is a believer in 'family-values' can be fair in thinking about such legislation? They also have a view or a perspective.

The fact that it is difficult to draw these lines does not mean that we can or should avoid thinking about them. We must make judgements about when someone is biased. One way I have suggested making them is to ask whether that person is taking the experience of all seriously. And there will be a host of other kinds of searching questions to be asked.

There are of course limitations on the exercise of viewing matters from different perspectives. (Can I really get a sense of what it is to be a black unemployed male with no prospects at all?) But again, we must not draw a too-pessimistic conclusion from the difficulties. They do not entail that one should not do one's best. Indeed, as Kymlicka argues, without the attempt to get into the shoes of another, elected representatives cannot even begin to do what they are supposed to do (1995: 140f). If understanding the needs and interests of those who differ from oneself is impossible, then those who are supposed to represent citizens cannot do so, for they are sure to differ in some respects from all whom they are supposed to represent. We assume that empathy with others can produce some understanding.

Indeed, the assumption behind our attempts to understand others must be right, if we accept the point which is stressed by Onora O'Neil and Donald Davidson. If we can translate and interpret the utterances of others, if we can communicate at all, this reveals a great deal of shared belief. (Davidson argues that in order to have an idea or a concept at all, we have to communicate and thus share a picture of the world.) If we succeed in talking together and thinking together, if we succeed in disagreeing with others, rather than simply failing to comprehend others, then we share a great deal. Agreement and disagreement are parasitic on mutual understanding. And thus the idea that we have different conceptual schemes, that we live in different worlds, so to speak, is scuttled.

Let us now turn to the neutrality principle, the principle on which a central dispute between the pragmatist and the mainstream liberal lies. The advocate of this kind of neutrality holds that politics is not the place for debate about what is good. He thinks it always undesirable or impossible to judge, in a public forum, the way of life or the practices of another. The pragmatist argues, on the other hand, that we sometimes can and ought to make these judgements.

In what follows, I shall show how the pragmatist can shut out the neutrality principle without shutting out the things that it is designed to promote – autonomy, equality, and tolerance. The upshot will be that multi-culturalism must be promoted by the institutions of a pragmatist democracy. The liberal who thinks the neutrality principle important will be attracted to a policy of benign neglect of minority groups. We shall see that the pragmatist, on the other hand, will think that a policy upon which minority groups are encouraged and perhaps even granted special group rights and powers might be warranted.

We might, that is, find ourselves heeding Kymlicka's advice to treat different kinds of group claims differently (1995: 58–60). For instance, what is in the interests of justice for African-Americans, with their history of slavery, segregation and exclusion from the majority culture, may not be in the interests of Native Americans with their history of forced inclusion into the majority culture. 'Colour-blind' laws may be what is required in the first case, but not in the second.

The 'may' here is important. The negative side of colour-blind laws is that they can rule out affirmative action and encourage laws which are merely 'facially neutral' – for instance, heavy mandatory sentences for crack cocaine in the US, which tend to impact severely on blacks. So one has to go carefully before making such a recommendation. As I shall argue below, it is not the philosopher's place to say that such-and-such a policy is what is required. It is the philosopher's place to make theoretical room for the controversies to come to the surface and for the right public policy to be made.

The principle of neutrality

The liberal neutrality principle is prompted by a worry. History shows us that if the state takes it upon itself to evaluate conceptions of the good, then the likes of homosexual acts, possession of soft drugs, and divorce can get prohibited. For such things can be thought by those in power to be worse than worthless. So Ronald Dworkin expresses his reasons for the importance of the neutrality principle thus:

> Government must... leave people free to live as they think best so long as they do not harm others. But the Reverend Jerry Falwell, and other politicians who claim to speak for some 'moral majority,' want to enforce their own morality with the steel of the criminal law. They know what kind of sex is bad, which books are fit for public libraries, what place religion should have in education and family life, when human life begins, that contraception is sin, and that abortion is capital sin.
>
> (1983: 1)

If we want to keep at bay the likes of the moral majority, we must prohibit appeals to any particular parochial morality (in this case, the fundamentalist Christian morality) in politics.

That some moral majority will enforce their beliefs upon all is indeed a worry. But it is just a worry. It is not a necessary result of allowing conceptions of the good a voice on the public agenda. And the worry might be quieted by any one of a number of different policies, the neutrality principle being one of the many. We ought to be concerned about the possibility that certain ways of life will be wrongly denigrated, but neutrality may not be the only, or the best, way to prevent that from happening.

One argument for the neutrality principle begins from a scepticism about morality. If it is impossible to make objective judgements about what is valuable, then a government cannot do it. And citizens, when they are arguing about policy and about justice, cannot do it either.

We saw in Chapter 1 that Schmitt turns this argument on its head so that it is an argument not for, but against the idea of liberal neutrality. If it is not possible to aim at making rational and true judgements about the good, then all that one can do is plumb for one's own conception. Some of these conceptions will undermine the liberal framework, and thus that framework only *thinks* itself neutral, when in fact it really cannot help but be an upholding of the liberal view of the good under the bogus name of neutrality.

So a consideration against the argument from scepticism is that it crumbles internally and that it just as easily leads to intolerance within a society, not tolerance. Another consideration against the argument is the bundle of reasons given in Chapter 2 about how we are better advised to think of moral judgements as genuine beliefs and assertions which aim at truth. There is a perspective – a human, not a God's eye perspective – from which values and conceptions of the good can be judged.

Not every advocate of the neutrality principle, however, is a sceptic about moral judgement. Some argue that even if it is possible to adjudicate between conceptions of the good, governments ought to avoid it and leave such deliberation to individuals in private forums. These arguments start from the thought that something like autonomy, or equality, or respect for persons, is basic.[7]

Dworkin, for instance, argues that equality and respect require neutrality: a government which forces or encourages its citizens to live what it takes to be the good life puts constraints on citizens which 'they could not accept without abandoning [their] sense of [their] equal worth' (1983: 3). If a government is going to treat its citizens as equals, it must be neutral with respect to the nature of the good life.

Or one could claim that if individuals are to retain their autonomy – their capacity to stand apart from their current interests and aims in order to revise, question, discover, and choose their ends – their ends cannot be chosen by an authority. They must be free to choose what kind of life plan they will adopt, free to change that plan, and free to make mistakes. Governments ought not to decide what the best lifestyle is and use their coercive power to then interfere with individuals who fail to adopt it or happen to fall outside of it.

I shall suggest that the pragmatist can have autonomy, equality and respect for persons, without adopting the neutrality principle. This is a good thing, for I shall also set some arguments against the non-sceptical version of the neutrality principle.

One argument is Andrew Kernohan's recent claim that the liberal's commitment to the moral equality of persons requires the liberal to think that governments must act, in a non-neutral way, to discourage a polluted cultural climate (Kernohan 1998). An oppressive culture, such as one in which women are treated as inferior, and encouraged to see themselves as inferior, can cause real accumulative harm. It can undermine self-respect, it can cause stereotypes to be internalised by those who are oppressed,[8] and it can harm our interest in knowing the good. Thus a government which is committed to liberal principles of equality and respect for persons should not be neutral about such oppression – it ought to use its persuasive power to try to reform a polluted climate.

I think that this argument is a very good one. But the point against the neutrality principle that I want to concentrate on is perhaps best made by concurring with an observation made by Will Kymlicka.[9] It is a kind of Schmittian point without the horrible Schmittian conclusion.

Governments in pluralistic societies, Kymlicka argues, cannot in fact be neutral towards ethnic and national groups within their boundaries, since just about every policy or law promotes some conception of the good. A crucial requirement for the survival of a culture, for example, is that its language is the language of the government and its institutions:

> When the government decides the language of public schooling, it is providing what is probably the most important form of support needed by societal cultures, since it guarantees the passing on of the language and its associated traditions and conventions to the next generation. Refusing to provide public schooling in a minority language, by contrast, is almost inevitably condemning that language to ever-increasing marginalization.
>
> (Kymlicka 1995: 111)

A state has no choice but to make choices and it thus promotes a particular culture in countless ways. The law often takes a controversial position on what is good. In our regime it recognises monogamous marriages and punishes bigamous ones, allows spousal benefits for heterosexual cohabitants, but not for homosexual cohabitants (perhaps not for much longer), prohibits digging up corpses, defecating in public, and so on. Statutory holiday schedules, national anthems, oaths, and the like also reflect certain values. In my society these are Christian values, despite the fact that not all citizens are Christian. My state advertises on television and on the subway against the drug culture; encourages 'high' culture by subsidising the arts, but not tag-team wrestling; offers tax credits for contributions to 'recognized charities', but doesn't recognise white supremacist groups who want to set up a charitable foundation for 'victims' of affirmative action; regulates against pornography and against using the F-word, as my seven-year-old says, during prime time television, and so on.

Neutrality, that is, is a myth. As Patrick Neal (1997: 20f) puts it, governments do not passively respond to autonomous demands, interests, and preferences. They play an important role in shaping those demands, interests, and preferences. Governments shape the social fabric and that fabric is what maintains the range of lives which we take to be good. Governments have to support something and their support always involves some kind of coercive power. They might as well encourage what they think is good, rather than what they think is worthless. Otherwise the cultural climate might well become such that the worthless or the polluted reigns supreme.[10]

It might be thought that the point that every policy supports some value speaks against only a very strong version of the neutrality principle. In an earlier paper, Kymlicka distinguished between consequential and justificatory neutrality and pointed out that the latter is what most liberal theorists want to uphold.[11] Consequential neutrality has it that a government should not adopt policies which have the effect of promoting a particular conception of the good. This is the impossible requirement. Justificatory neutrality suggests that the justification of a policy should not be that it promotes a particular conception of the good. This, one would think, is an easier requirement to meet.

But the distinction is difficult to maintain.[12] Let us assume that a government does not explicitly reason that legislation against Sunday shopping promotes the Christian way of life over others. They just reason that one day a week should be kept relatively clear so that shop workers can have an identifiable, predictable day off. But it is pointed out to them that the initial rationale against Sunday shopping was that people should be in church. This gives the Sunday shopping laws a residual whiff of Christian justification, a whiff which can offend those who must work on the day of rest specified by their own, non-Christian, religion. Keeping Sunday the day of rest makes things easy for Christians and difficult for others. The lack of will to change the policy supports the thought that the implicit rationale of the policy is indeed to promote Christianity; that it is indeed a way of implying that Christian values are the primary values of the society. And of course, one can always find (just think here of the United States) plenty of politicians and citizens who betray these intentions by explicitly asserting that it is important to maintain Christian values and not others.

I have said that the pragmatist can preserve the freedoms that the neutrality principle seeks to uphold without the neutrality principle – without the commitment to the thought that government must take an attitude of benign neglect towards the value of a way of life. The society that the pragmatist envisions, and goes some way to justifying, will leave space for individuals to decide how to live. It is not a society with a government that takes it upon itself to see to it that people live what it takes to be a high-quality life. It is not a society in which those with power repress the ways of life of those without power. The pragmatist does not fail to see that lives tend to go better when governed from the inside – from the values and beliefs of the individual who is living that life. And the pragmatist does not fail to see that the good cannot be *imposed* on people, that discovering the good for oneself is vital to a good life.

The pragmatist's route to the preservation of autonomy, equal moral worth, and respect for persons is that preserving these things is a vital part of deliberation aimed at the truth. Respect for persons is required, as we must take account of how others report their experiences if we are to have any hope of arriving at the best answers to our questions about justice and fairness. Autonomy is required, as, at least in the first instance, I am able to articulate my own experiences in a more accurate way than someone else. What is good for me will thus largely be an internal matter, be a matter for me, not for experts or politicians. We have seen in Chapter 2 that these initial judgements are defeasible and revisable in the light of further experience, reflection, and input from others. But the fact remains that the concern for autonomous choice will play a central role in debates about the good.

So the pragmatist argues that if we are to take seriously the experiences of all, we must let ways of life flourish so that they can be articulated and we must let people articulate them for themselves. And until we can be reasonably sure that we really comprehend what is going on with a group very different from ourselves, we cannot even begin to make judgements about what is good for them. It is hard to see how anything but a principle of tolerance could be the upshot of the methodological principle to take the views of others seriously. We must listen to those with whom we disagree, as long as their views take the views of others seriously.

We can thus argue that laws against homosexuality, for instance, are bad on better grounds than that they are not neutral. They are bad laws not primarily because they enshrine one parochial conception of morality over other parochial conceptions. They are bad laws for the first-order reasons that they are oppressive and that they claim a harm to individuals and to society where there is no harm. And they are bad laws for the second-order reason that they try to make the public ear deaf to the experiences of those engaged in what the moral majority takes to be a sordid way of life.

The fact that perhaps relatively few judgements will be made on methodological grounds by our pragmatist (perhaps relatively few positions will turn on denigrating the experiences of others) does not damage the argument against the neutrality principle. That principle just is not a part of the pragmatist picture. We do not have to be silent on matters of greatest importance. We can see that some conceptions of the good – those which turn on denying the experience of some group – are wrongheaded.[13]

The point against neutrality, however, is not entirely negative – it is not only that we should deny the thought that we cannot speak, in our public voices, about unacceptable kinds of lives. The view sketched in this book is a cognitivist moral theory, a theory on which it makes sense to say that we aim at truth in our moral deliberations. We hold out hope of getting answers to questions about what is in fact good. We try to improve upon that battery of beliefs, reasons, and principles which form our moral outlook.[14]

When it comes to imposing those beliefs on others, the pragmatist will tread very cautiously. We have seen that there is no pretence here that a neutral framework for society has been provided. Governments have a hand in shaping their citizens' conceptions of the good life and we should concentrate on the debate about where to draw the myriad of lines, which will be somewhat arbitrary, while not being entirely unprincipled, as to when a government is being reasonable in doing so and when it is being oppressive. One clear enough line is that governments should not use the likes of force and torture to try to ensure that citizens prefer poetry to pushpin.

It must also be kept in mind here that it is very difficult for a government to promote a conception of the good, even if it has no choice but to encourage what it takes to be valuable. People are usually resistant to such pressures. It is also very difficult to promote waning cultures so that a conception of the good can enjoy continued articulation. Some cultural options are simply closed off by the march of human history. As Bernard Williams points out, it is no longer possible to live out the life of an Athenian democrat or of a Roman emperor, for the cultures in which such lives were possible no longer exist (1981: 140).

This is not a moot point or a point that might apply only to small bands of enthusiasts. For many yearn for a return to a way of life that the industrial and the information revolutions have virtually made impossible. It might be that Native North Americans are in such a situation. Their culture was shattered by invaders and now that there is at least in principle an acknowledgement that those wrongs should be righted, it seems that there is no practical way to do it. The option does not exist, for instance, for the Plains Bands to return to a life that centres around the buffalo hunt – there is a lack of sufficient animals and a lack of sufficient space.

The same sort of situation, although far less dramatic and insidious, might be true of French-speaking Canadians, whose birth-rate is declining and whose language is being chipped away by the national and international dominance of English. It is not at all clear that the language laws in place in Quebec, laws regulating, for instance, the use of English in shopkeepers' windows, will have any long-term effect. The call to separate from the rest of Canada is no doubt in large part based on the thought that a separate Quebec will be better able to preserve language and culture. But it may be that even in that event, Quebecois culture will be swallowed up by the Americanisation of North America.

The upshot of these points is that the pragmatist position will not advocate quick and easy intervention into people's lives, in an effort to cultivate in them the right conception of the good. The idea is not that we can identify the good, or rank conceptions of the good, and then try to force the good upon citizens. There will be countless conceptions of the good which will not violate the pragmatist's principle that we must respect the experiences of others. So gross intervention will hardly ever be justified. And even when it is justified, it might be impossible or too difficult to do. These points do not, however, alter the fact that governments, in making policy and law, are not neutral – they intervene in a value-laden way all the time. What we have in the rejection of the principle of neutrality is a parallel of the epistemological quandary of having no choice but to start where we find ourselves, immersed in a set of beliefs and practices. We must now make further value-laden judgements about where to go from here, modifying our beliefs and practices bit by bit, trying to make them the best they can be. We have no reason to think that we are on our way to objectively true, impartial, and neutral principles. That is not possible. But we can aim at getting judgements which are as respectful of others, respectful of the autonomy of others, and as unoppressive as they can be, given the circumstances. We do not need a principle of neutrality in order to invoke these values in our reasons.

There is, then, a great gap between the mythical situation of government neutralism, where a government does not encourage a conception of the good, except when it is protecting citizens from direct harm, and the totalitarian nightmare, where a government forces its conception of the good on an unwilling citizenry.

There is even a great gap between neutralism and the less nightmarish government which takes it upon itself to provide the sole forums for debate about the good, a government which fails to see that debate about the good is often best conducted in free associations between individuals – in non-governmental settings such as families, friendships, churches, bars, and the like. We will thus get nothing like 'state perfectionism', on the pragmatist view, where the state takes it upon itself to rank values.[15] While the state cannot get out of the value-adjudication business, it is not the sole practitioner.

The theoretical work is in finding principles to guide us in drawing our lines on this continuum, in deciding when it is appropriate for a government to encourage or discourage a lifestyle and when it is inappropriate. The dangers of having the coercive power of the state involved in deliberations of the good must be squarely confronted. But the best way to avoid such dangers is not to pretend that the state can stay out of people's lives. The best way to avoid the dangers is to see that the state must be involved in encouraging and discouraging conceptions of the good and then deliberating about when enough is enough.

Public/private

A part of the difficulty with the neutrality principle is the distinction between the public and the private. We have seen that those liberals who place a premium on neutrality would like substantive judgements about the good to be kept out of public debate and confined to one's private morality. Ackerman makes this dichotomy most stark when he suggests that deliberation is the stuff of public life, not of private morality: dialogue is 'fundamental' to our lives as citizens, but it is of not much importance when it comes to our personal moral integrity.[16]

The view I have put forward is a kind of holism, by which I simply mean that it treats all of our beliefs as an interconnected whole. There is in this view no room for any hard and fast distinction between what kinds of reasons can play a role in our private and in our public decision-making. But there are other considerations for rejecting the public/private distinction, considerations independent of the attractions of holism. We have seen in Chapter 1, for instance, that two questions loom large for it. What makes anyone think that we can pull off the trick of isolating our public, citizen selves from our substantial moral beliefs? And why might this be thought to be desirable?

The distinguisher will respond to the second question by arguing that keeping our moral thoughts to ourselves will allow us to live together in harmony. If questions of the good are at issue in politics, then we shall find ourselves in a battle of traditions, each fighting for supremacy. Ackerman, for instance, thinks that:

> If we cannot find a way to talk to one another neutrally, we do not seem to have much choice but to ... return to the age-old effort to base political life on the truth, the whole truth, and nothing but the truth about moral life.
>
> (1989: 13)

If politics engages with its citizens' private conceptions of the good and if citizens think the political arena is a suitable place to make arguments about what is good, then politics will become a battle between such conceptions – between those centring around this or that religion or this or that nationalist ideal. Such a battle would presumably involve disregard of the choices of others, since one's commitment to the truth of a way of living would require the belief that others simply had got it wrong. Is this Schmittian scenario the fate of pragmatist politics?

I have argued not. Fight-to-the-death certainty is not the only option to neutrality. One can think of conceptions of the good life as being on the table for discussion, without thinking that one conception will win, that there is one best answer. Indeed, someone might even think, with respect to a particular issue, that there is one right answer to the question of how best to live, but object to coercing others to go that way. Making judgements about what is good, I have suggested, does not entail that we should interfere with people in order that they have the good. Raising the standard of living so that people can *choose* the good is much more effective, one would think, and much more respecting of that important value of autonomy.

But even that scenario – where one thinks that there is one right answer, but is loath to enforce it – is unlikely. The view sketched here, we shall see, is one on which we *expect* underdetermination about the question 'which way is best here?' So the desire to live together in peaceful toleration of one another is not enough to justify keeping matters of substantive morality off the political table. We can aim at living together and still discuss the good in public. And it is better to have such a discussion, for reasons best stressed in the last two decades by the feminist thought that the personal is political. No aspects of life or of our practices should be in principle excluded from public debate or required to remain hidden and private. The women's movement has succeeded in getting some important issues out of the private closet – wife battering, unequal division of housework, and date rape, to name a few. As Seyla Benhabib has put it, the struggle over what gets included in the public, what gets put on the public agenda, is itself a struggle for justice and freedom (1992: 94). To prejudge the question is to beg it.

Gay activists too have made a public issue out of what has often been taken to be a private matter. Attempts, for instance, have been made by various educational authorities, always vehemently protested, to publicly display the gay lifestyle in a positive manner. As noted in our discussion of Rawls, this kind of attempt to publically portray a conception of the good as being worthwhile seems unavailable to the neutralist.

Neutrality theorists sometimes offer another reason why substantive moral judgements should be kept out of public life. They suggest that politicians are not very likely to get the best results from their debates about what is right and wrong. Better forums for moral inquiry are to be found in private life – in discussion with family and friends, in solitary reflection, and in the church.

We have seen that the state cannot be prohibited from enforcing morality, for it cannot help but enforce what is thought good. Neutralists might well be right in suggesting that politicians and government agencies are ill-suited to the business of guiding individual lives. But since they are, and must be, in that business, it is best that they acknowledge their limitations and try to be more sensitive to those who are perhaps better-suited to the matter. The way to try to make good policy is for the state to see that politicians should not go it alone with respect to morals. The thoughts of the clergy, the family, novelists, etc., can and should be fodder for political deliberation.

That is, we must be careful not to agree to too meagre a characterisation of public deliberation. One must not think that because we have institutionally enshrined modes of specialised public reasoning, such as parliament and courts, that other, less formal, kinds are less important or that courts and parliament must be the model for deliberation. For, in the absence of a serious program for state funding of court challenges, and in the presence of the need to have a tremendous amount of money in order to mount a campaign for public office, this kind of dialogue is limited to a very small number.

Indeed, the dialogue of a parliament, where elected members are supposed to represent the views of their constituents is problematic on a number of fronts. Representation is at best partial, as a member of parliament obviously cannot represent the various views of all of her constituents and minority views are far less likely to be heard in parliament.[17]

As Bohman (1996: 23) points out, modern constitutional democracies already enshrine certain rights which open up space for many forms of public deliberation – freedom of speech and freedom of association, for instance. Debate which takes place in school boards, parent-teacher associations, trade unions, city councils, neighbourhood associations, academic journals, talk shows, newspapers, the Internet, the streets, shopping malls, and bars is a crucial kind of public debate. These are kinds of public space, the space of ordinary politics, as opposed to the space of formal constitutional politics.

We must, therefore, take care that such spaces remain public. With the disappearance of public squares in many cities, policy might well have to be made regarding some of these private commercial spaces, such as shopping malls, where 'loiterers' and union pickets can be thrown out. Obviously, not all of the forums mentioned are such that anybody can participate. Academic journals and newspapers have limits on who can participate – those with the requisite skills and training. And bars have age restrictions. But malls threaten to take over the role of the unrestricted public square and it would be unfortunate, to say the least, if a conglomeration of shop owners dictate who is allowed and not allowed to participate.

We must, however, be prepared for many to choose to stay out of formal or informal public debate. There is nothing in pragmatism which *requires* a person to participate. Some might not enjoy it, some might think that too much participation in political deliberation takes time and energy away from other important things, and some might genuinely prefer to leave it to others.

But for those who want or feel the need to engage, the arenas will include (for the select few) well-established institutions such as the debate one finds in parliament in a parliamentary democracy and argument before a Supreme Court. For the bulk of the citizenry, other forums will be required.

Here, Benhabib's distinction between models of political public space is helpful. She identifies a number of ways of thinking about public space: for instance, the 'civic virtue' or 'agonistic' model, the 'liberal' or 'legalistic' model, and the democratic-socialist discursive model which she takes to be implicit in Habermas' work.

Benhabib associates the agonistic view with Hannah Arendt and ancient Greece and Rome, but it is also Schmitt's concept of the public. Here, public space is where 'moral and political greatness, heroism and preeminence are revealed, displayed, shared with others' (1992: 93). It is a space where agents compete for recognition and acclaim – a space where they try to achieve a kind of immortality. Arendt, with Schmitt, thought that modernity brought the loss of this kind of public space, and mourned it.[18] Benhabib points out that such a conception of the public is only available where there is a great class of servants, slaves, subordinate women, and the like to make possible the leisure in which a few can pursue such a romantic political life – in which the elite can vie for excellence with their peers (1992: 91, 93).

On the second, liberal, model public space is a public dialogue about legitimacy or the justification of power. It is a discussion about how different groups, with different values, can decide to coexist. There are constraints on this dialogue: a person cannot assert that his conception of the good is better than someone else's or that he is intrinsically superior to others. When we disagree with others, we should say nothing at all about the matter and talk only about what we do agree upon. We have seen that Rawls and Ackerman conceive of public space in this way. Benhabib takes such a minimal conception as unable to make sense of social movements and revolutions as reconfigurations of what counts as public.

On the Habermasian discourse model of public space, things are better. Habermas takes participation to be not exclusively political, but all-pervasive. Discourse, we have noted, is for him at the heart of self-identity. It is not something engaged in by an elite, as the agonistic model has it, but is everybody's game. As Benhabib puts it, '[t]he public sphere comes into existence whenever and wherever all affected by general social and political norms of action engage in a practical discourse, evaluating their validity' (1992: 105).

We might add to this thought something from what Benhabib calls the 'associational' model of the public, which is close in spirit, I think, to the Habermasian model. Here, any space where people act together and where freedom can appear is public space. Such space needn't be institutionalised. Any demonstration, secret meeting of dissidents, etc., counts as public on this account.

Benhabib thinks, however, that there is an important limitation in Habermas' discourse theory of public space. Any theory of public space, she says, will have to assume that there is a distinction between the public and the private. Habermas has been criticised for upholding a model of the private, where maintaining the household, reproducing and caring for offspring, and the like are intimate matters, not matters of public discourse.[19] But this kind of distinction has traditionally served to keep women confined to the space of the private and it cannot account for the fact that the lines between private and public get renegotiated in struggles such as the women's movement.

Benhabib decides that the discourse model can take this point in its stride. Indeed, she argues that there is an affinity between the discourse model and movements such as feminism. If the agenda in discourse is radically open, as it must be, then there can be no preclusion of a discussion of whether the sphere of the private is constructed as it should be. There is no way to preclude feminists, for instance, from arguing that housework should be paid work. The distinction between public and private will itself be reinterpreted in a radically open discourse.

So on Benhabib's model of public space, a model which she upholds as an appropriate ideal for the deliberative democrat, debate is radically unconstrained. The only constraints are those which are articulated in the core principles of discourse ethics, and even they are not immutable. I have argued in Chapter 1 that the principles of discourse ethics which Habermas and Apel think are essential cannot be adequately justified. But the principle that we must take the experiences of all seriously can be justified. And then the other democratic ideas (that different perspectives which might be brought to debate must be encouraged, that everyone has an equal right to participate, etc.) follow on the principle's heels.

Modesty and the philosopher

We can summarise much of the argument of Chapter 2 with the thought that the pragmatist stands somewhere between the radical particularist[20] and the system-building philosopher. The radical particularist thinks that moral judgement is a matter of perceiving the relevant special features of a situation, with no recourse to general principles. Judgements will always be heavily contextualised: it is correct or right for me, at this time, and in this very context, to do x. The system-builder thinks that the job of philosophical theory is to articulate those principles or rules under which we can make correct moral judgements; to give us a way of determining what judgements are categorically binding on everyone or on anyone who might find herself in a certain situation.

The pragmatist cannot see how either of these views could be right. Both generalisations and contextualised judgements might be true or false. With respect to the first, it is hard to see how we could make particular judgements without having some general rule in mind. So some general principles must be right in order to even see the moral issues which are relevant in particular contexts. We must be prepared for those principles to at times be in conflict with other principles, in the way that 'lying is wrong' sometimes conflicts with 'being kind is right'. That is, we shall see that our generalisations will not often be universal – they will not often take the form: 'Everyone must do x, in every circumstance in which the question of doing x arises'. Our ethical norms will be, as Richardson puts it, 'explicitly open and flexible, ... qualified with a "generally speaking" rather than with a logically universal "in all cases"' (1995: 130). But they nonetheless will be norms which can be articulated in a way that makes them not about specific situations, but about what is right in a kind of situation.

With respect to the second, it is also hard to see how we can avoid contextualisation. Circumstances will quite literally shape the available options, especially in politics. For instance, when a new nation is trying to decide what to do about the human rights abuses committed by the previous government, security forces, legal system, and bureaucracy, the principles it should invoke will depend on such things as the role the armed forces played during the oppression and how widespread complicity with the regime was. If virtually every family had someone who was entangled in the complicity, retributive justice is likely to hurt everyone and have only a destructive effect. If an armed elite was pretty much responsible for the oppression, perhaps symbolic trials where justice is seen to be served is a better vehicle of getting over the past. Volumes have been written about such complexities[21] and the point is that such complexity – such dependence on historical circumstance – is what we should expect. We should not want our moral and political philosophy to make it go away.

On the picture of inquiry outlined here, we will give what we think are good reasons for our judgements. Those reasons will be drawn from a great store of ideas that come into play in our moral deliberations. In this store are insights from various schools of thought about morality – utilitarian calculations about maximising happiness; Kantian principles about treating people as ends in themselves; Aristotelian thoughts about virtue; feminist suggestions about the importance of our relationships with others; thoughts about what serves our interests and desires, etc. Each of these schools or moral frameworks, I suggest, latches on to something important about morality, but none provides us with the one thought from which we can derive our moral principles. None provides us on its own with a complete model of deliberation,[22] such as 'decide what to do by determining what will produce the greatest happiness for the greatest number'.

The suggestion that our values do not all promote one supreme good, or that there is no principle which is foundational, distances the view offered here from some other sorts of cognitivism. The pragmatist will not think that we can have moral knowledge because we know we must always act to maximise utility or because we know that there is a contradiction in acting on principles which we could not will as universal laws. Rather, our values call on the diverse concerns and interests which make up our malleable and complex nature – which make up, as Isaiah Berlin (1991) has said, 'the crooked timber of humanity'.

For one thing, the pragmatist will insist that our principles arise and can be articulated only within a practice, not from abstract considerations about rationality, human nature, or whatever. Reflecting upon and examining our practice can make us see those principles and the point of those principles more clearly. Donald Ainslie (forthcoming) makes this point nicely regarding bioethicists' focus on general principles about harm and confidentiality when debating what should be disclosed to the sexual partners of HIV-positive gay men. In North American urban gay communities, a practice of taking responsibility for safer sex has arisen in order to deal with the question of how to live ethically within the constraints of the disease. This moral response to the epidemic is to engage in sexual activity as if one knows that one's partner is infected. Thus gay men can continue to express their value of affirming gay sexual life, the value of refusing the closet, while not endangering others. Bioethicists have largely continued to support the principle of the duty to warn, even when many of those most affected by the AIDS epidemic have rejected it and rejected it for reasons.

The way to get at the right principle here, says the pragmatist, is both from above and below – from a consideration of general principles and insights and from a consideration of the principles which have grown up in the practice in question. Bioethicists should not gloss over how people affected by a disease try to make moral sense of its impact on their lives.

So the pragmatist thinks that issues will be resolved on a case by case basis, with the particular context and history of the conflict taking its place on centre stage alongside general principles. Issues will be resolved politically and philosophically.

The highlighting of the normative work involved in theorising from practice as opposed to from the lofty heights of abstract principle has ramifications for how the philosopher sees her business. Obviously, she will not search for an overarching principle which will make sense of all of practice. That kind of systematising theory will no longer be the business of philosophy.

Hand-in-hand with this thought goes the following. In the face of evil, the pragmatist will not absurdly launch into a treatise about truth and inquiry. The pragmatist's point about having to take seriously the experience of others is not supposed to be the starting point from which all deliberation and inquiry flows. To the neo-Nazi who is about to commit some real atrocity, we shall observe the evil of the proposed actions and do what we can to intervene. If we are in a position to talk to him about it, we shall offer what we think just might get him to see things right – concerns about equality, impartiality, cruelty, autonomy, suffering, and so on. It is only when, or if, those reasons fail to get a grip on him, that we invoke the thought (and given our failure to persuade him, we will be invoking it mostly to and for ourselves) that he has adopted a method of deliberation which betrays the commitment he incurs by claiming to hold a belief which is oriented at the truth. It is only then that we discount him as a moral inquirer, always pending his enlightenment. Our first-order reasons for objecting to the neo-Nazi are merely fortified by the philosophical argument about truth and inquiry.

In other words, I do not want to maintain that the argument about genuine believers and genuine truth-seekers is that to which we will want always to appeal in our moral deliberations. It is not the only, nor indeed the primary, route to criticism. When we condemn or praise beliefs and actions, we will appeal to a range of considerations and maxims which we hold dear – maxims which we might well order in importance and which might seem immutable. Perhaps the most important consideration here will be the thought that we owe something to others because of their equal moral worth. This sort of reason is the stuff of moral deliberation and it will still be what is most visible in our moral lives. But it is not something foundational, not something that must be presupposed to get morality off the ground. Justification is something at which we arrive through open deliberation, but deliberation does not have to be open because we are all committed to the idea of the equal moral worth of persons. Justification is something we arrive at through open deliberation, because justification is a matter of paying attention to the tug of reasons and if we are to really justify our beliefs, we must hear the reasons of all.

Perhaps it is best to portray the argument for listening to others as occurring on three levels. The first is a general epistemological argument, one which applies to any domain of inquiry. I can learn from others and enhance my truth-seeking capacities. I listen to the opinions of others because I hope that things will come more into focus for me.

A second kind of argument is less about knowledge and more about morality. I ought to listen to others because that is how one ought to treat people – with consideration and respect. I think that self-reflection, self-direction and autonomy are values and so I should respect these characteristics in others. One way of doing that is to take what they say about how they experience moral and political life seriously. This argument arises from substantive principles of morality that I am willing to assert. I expect that it is a moral truth – it would be the upshot of considered moral deliberation – that it is right to listen to others. When I think that a person is deluded, in the grip of an incoherent or false ideology, or just not very wise, I shall only have the moral reason, not the epistemic reason, for paying attention.

The final argument is the argument which finds its expression in deliberative democracy. If we listen to others and if we offer others reasons which they can in principle accept, then political decisions are more likely to be taken to be legitimate. Here, too, the argument can be in play even when we do not stand to learn from others. With respect to political questions, even more so than with questions about whether we have a complete list of sub-atomic particles and even more so than with questions about how to go about living a life, we have an additional reason to listen. For listening to others increases the likelihood that law and policy will be accepted.

We can see, then, that philosophy will play a minor role in our moral and political deliberation. As Hume saw, it has its limits:

> ... where one is born of so perverse a frame of mind, of so callous and insensible a disposition, as to have no relish for virtue and humanity, no sympathy with his fellow creatures, no desire of esteem and applause ... my philosophy affords no remedy in such a case, nor could I do any thing but lament this person's unhappy condition. But then I ask, if any other philosophy can afford a remedy. [23]

Some people, and Rorty is one, are over-impressed by the fact that philosophy is powerless in the face of evil. But why hold up such ambitions for philosophy?

I have suggested that views about matters such as truth and objectivity can provide me with a reason for being critical of the likes of the neo-Nazi, a reason I can offer to myself, above the hurly-burly of first order reasons, so that I can take my reasons to triumph decisively over his. That is what philosophy is good for in the face of evil. Of course, there are other good things that might come from engaging in philosophy. Perhaps the more important benefits have to do simply with how much one gains from just going through the exercise of thinking hard, for instance, about issues such as truth and objectivity. We can, for instance, hope for increased self-under-standing, enhanced awareness of the local issues and of their complexity, and a reduction in our tendency to simplify. But when it comes to offering knock-down arguments against those who are doing wrong, philosophy can only go so far.

A further thought follows on the heels of the observation that the prag-matist will not talk abstract philosophy in the face of evil. The pragmatist does not mean to suggest that what is *wrong* with humiliating someone, or with being cruel, or with treating someone as an inferior, is that it gets in the way of inquiry and truth. The pragmatist does not make the mistake, with Benhabib (1992: 32–8), of suggesting that the reason we ought not inflict unnecessary suffering on others is that doing so would undermine the possi-bility of an ongoing conversation with them. What is wrong with such things has most to do with the effects on the mistreated and the effects on the moral integrity of the mistreater. Such things are wrong, that is, for substantive moral reasons, not for epistemological reasons.

So discovering the texture and the ins and outs of a moral claim is not the sole province of the moral epistemologist. It is something for all those who take an interest – the novelist, the cultural commentator, the rabbi, the priest, and the ordinary person caught up in moral tangles. Philosophy, I have argued, must be reluctant to pronounce in any detail on how that deliberation should be conducted. It cannot, apart from giving us some rough guidelines, tell us which moral judgements are correct. But it can tell us how to make sense of moral judgements. It can tell us how to think of moral belief and assertion because it can tell us how to think of belief and assertion.

But, it might be asked, does this view not promote quietism – does it not require the philosopher to be quiet and let the status quo march along in its plodding and oppressive way? Well, the philosopher, on the pragmatist view, will have to be quieter than she sometimes has been. She cannot, for instance, claim to have uncovered a decision procedure, based on the 'science' of rational choice theory or on the categorical requirements set out by this or that philosophy, for the worthiness of action. But, although the philosopher cannot justify a system of rules from which we can derive our answers about the right and the good, although the philosopher will not be able to deliver anything like a perfectionist ranking of conceptions of the good, or anything like a decision procedure, there will be plenty of things to say. Moral reasoning or justification is not a closed book to the pragmatist, for she is one of those interested parties, both in virtue of her humanity and in virtue of her readiness to think carefully about such matters.[24]

That is, it is not only in pressing the inclusion requirement, the requirement that we must take the experiences of all seriously, that the philosopher can engage in moral debate. She can advance first-order reasons for why an action is odious or laudable. Perhaps the philosopher, in virtue of having thought in a sustained way about morality, will have especially important contributions to make. But they will not come in the form of universal generalisations, or universal rules for behaviour.

There is thus much that the pragmatist can say about a moral matter, but it will not fall directly out of considerations about epistemology. And that is the way it should be – epistemology will not give someone the requisite skills to be a good person. We see a further reason here for the thin conception of inquiry. The philosopher should not try to second-guess or, worse, legislate for, inquiry. Nothing about being a philosopher grants that kind of ability. Dewey was on the right track when he argued for a philosophy which 'humbles its pretensions'.[25]

The pragmatist moral cognitivism which I have outlined has remained on a fairly lofty theoretical plane (it has been an account of how it might be that moral and political judgements can fall within the scope of truth and knowledge). But it trains its gaze on moral practice. And indeed, there are practical implications which fall from the theory. Deliberation must be encouraged and political institutions and mechanisms for decision-making must be as inclusive as is reasonably possible. The pragmatist voices the requirement that we try, at least until such attempts fail, to include rather than exclude others. This entails listening carefully to the marginalised in society.

Nelson Mandela's treatment of the right wing, as he took his place in post-apartheid South Africa, is an instance of the kind of decision the pragmatist commends. Mandela took great pains to include the Freedom Front – the right wing Afrikaner nationalist group – in his negotiations for the new structure of the country. Their joining in had the happy effect of splitting the Afrikaner right into those who would talk and those who refused. The latter group quickly became regarded, by just about everyone, as mad. They lost legitimacy and ceased to be major players on the political landscape. The group that would engage in deliberation, on the other hand, had its claims taken seriously. And some of those claims had bite – the Afrikaners, after all, became nationalists to escape real oppression by the British. Those on the right who accepted the invitation to negotiate found that they had to participate seriously in working out a generally acceptable solution to the political problems. And, by talking to those with very different views, those on all sides of the political spectrum started to talk a different language.

Conflict, difference, and community

A set of tensions seems to arise for the cognitivist who wants to focus on particular situations. How can it be that we aim at getting the correct judgement – for all – but also that we will take the features of particular situations seriously? Is there really any ground intermediate between the system-builder and the radical particularist? How can it be that we aim at getting a judgement which is best for the community of inquirers, but also that we want to preserve and commend diversity? What we encounter in our moral lives is that there often seems to be no one right answer or answer which is best for all. In the next section I shall show how these tensions can be resolved or at least coped with so that they are less destructive of the cognitivist project. In this section, I shall address some preliminary issues about conflict, difference, and community.

I have suggested that there is no reason to think that debate will tidily resolve all issues. We must be prepared for underdetermination and even for questions with no decent answer at all. What our theory does is provide justification and encouragement for debate and for taking others seriously and tell us that, were we to reach a belief which could no longer be improved, that belief would be true. It does not tell us that we are bound to reach the one right conclusion. And it does not tell us whether any particular debate has been pursued as far as it might fruitfully go. These are important points and they are again corollaries of the fallibilism which is at the heart of pragmatism. Fortunately, justification for action does not require that we be certain that our judgement would always withstand doubt or that it is a judgement which would be best for everyone. We will justifiably act on the most reasonable belief, given all of the available evidence, experience and argument.

Some have suggested that the multiplicity of values which are carried to moral deliberation is a modern phenomenon, perhaps the defining feature of modernity. Whatever the accuracy of this kind of story of how our values and insights came to be so numerous, the diversity of values is certainly a prominent feature of our moral lives. And it is a feature which presents a great challenge for the moral theorist, especially for the cognitivist who is drawn to looking at the particulars of moral situations. Christine Korsgaard has said that views which hold that we 'happen to be subject to an unsystematic plurality of duties that can of course conflict' offer 'pat' explanations. They 'make sense of the complexity of morality at the expense of depriving morality itself of sense' (1997: 320).

But putting the multiplicity of value at the centre of one's moral theory need not cause such distress. Such a view might deprive morality of its systematicity, but it does not for that reason deprive morality of its sense. The thought that duties cannot be derived from one foundational set of principles does not entail that there can be no such things as duties. I shall argue in the pages that follow that the pragmatist can hold on to the thought that we aim at true and reasonable beliefs, despite the fact that we encounter a plurality of conflicting values. And the pragmatist can also hold on to the thought that morality can furnish us with reasons for action that are categorical in that they are not conditional upon any desires we might happen to have.[26] If I see that it is my moral duty to, say, give blood, I cannot cease to care about that duty and the reasons for it if the duty conflicts with my squeamish desire to not be punctured.

I suggested in the previous section that the reasons which we give for our judgements will come from a great variety of sources. Any plausible list of such sources will at the least include the various schools of thought about morality which together make up what we might think of as the moral tradition of Western philosophy – utilitarianism with its idea that the good is a matter of maximising happiness, Kantianism with its idea that people must be treated as ends, not as means, Aristotelianism with its idea that we must ask what it is to lead a virtuous life. But it will also include newer ideas and imports, such as thoughts garnered from Buddhism and from feminism with its focus on what is said to be the way that women approach morality – with an eye on maintaining relationships, bonds, etc. The point is that there is no one thing that we try to maximise in our moral deliberation. Our values do not all promote one supreme good – they call on diverse concerns and interests.[27]

My suggestion has been that the philosopher or theorist should not take any system or any one set of rules to be such as to give us a procedure for making correct moral and political judgements – things are more complicated than that. The pragmatist thus builds the full complexity or the full richness of our moral lives into the position at the outset. The reply to Korsgaard is that a systematic theory makes sense of morality only at the expense of losing its grip on how morality *is*.

One thing we should notice about the complexity of moral life is that it is not only general principles of competing moral frameworks which can clash. Ideals within a framework, such as the liberal ideals of freedom and equality, can also be in tension.[28] Feminists have argued, for instance, that the pornographer who exercises his right to freedom of expression by depicting women as sex slaves interferes with the right of women to be portrayed and treated as equals. Here either freedom or equality must give way. We cannot respect both values. And there might be agreement that liberty and equality are valuable, but those who place liberty before equality favour a laissez-faire economy with few constraints and those who place equality before liberty favour a regulated market in a strong welfare state.[29]

Obligations can conflict as well, as when we must either break a promise or help someone in great need. And, of course, acceptable comprehensive conceptions of the good life can conflict and an individual might find such conflicts within her own idea of the good.

We have seen that, for the most part, the pragmatist will think of moral and political debate as being conducted in the usual way, with all of our values vying for our attention. Some will press harder than others in certain contexts. And some will press harder than others when the consequences of failing to do one thing are particularly severe. Someone might well think, for instance, that treating someone as less than an equal might be justified when great loss of life is the consequence of treating them as an equal.

This is just another way of suggesting that no one value is foundational – not equality, maximising happiness, pleasing God, etc. Many of these values will be bound up with each other but untangling them, if it were possible, would not, I surmise, show one to be the source of all others. And it would not show one, or one set, to always trump others. The pragmatist can (and ought to) be open-minded about the possibility of one system showing itself to be correct, but the thought here is that, given how untrue that scenario is to the texture of moral deliberation, it is unlikely.

It is unlikely, that is, that the best way of understanding a moral dilemma is to find the set of principles with which we ought to govern our moral lives and then apply those principles to the dilemma. Here is a thought experiment given by Richard Brook:

> You are at the zoo with two children who are making a scene. Becoming angry, you toss them into the lion's den. Horrified, you come to your senses and notice that they can only be saved if you toss a third child (who just toddled along) into the back of the den. The beast would be distracted and you could quickly leap in and save the first two.
>
> (1991: 197)

The thought behind such philosophers' examples has often been that they will help us see which principles really are most important. Ought we to refrain from doing an evil thing (then let the two in the den be eaten) or ought we to maximise utility (then do the evil thing – throw an innocent passing child into the den – so that only one child, not two dies)? The thought experiments are supposed to make it clear to us which of two conflicting principles *really* carries the most weight.

But perhaps we should not be appealing to such thought experiments in an effort to work out which principles are most important. Apart from the fact that there is no reason to think we are any good at taking a morality which has evolved for real cases and applying it to artificial ones (see Blackburn 1998: 233), we should not care so much whether we can order our principles in a hierarchy.

We need to ask how the pragmatist can think that there is a multiplicity of unrankable and sometimes conflicting values while holding on to the thought that a belief is true if it were always to best meet our expectations. For this thought seems to hold out hope for an agreement which will level all difference. It seems to be the view Blackburn characterises as being not quite right:

> The first near miss would take its stand on the actual convergence of attitude and sentiment 'in the long run'. The idea here is that, at least under some kinds of circumstances, the divergences of moral opinion we find would disappear.
>
> (1998: 301)

But actual convergence seems not to be on the cards. And it can also seem undesirable. Disagreement in the form of an opposition is, after all, a sign of the health and vitality of a democracy[30] and a world of agreement on what is good and worth pursuing seems a bland world indeed. The diversity of conceptions of the good adds to the richness of our lives by providing a range of possibilities and options for the people who we are to become. Indeed, when we deliberate, we often *generate* disagreement by forcing ourselves and others to confront and engage with diverse views,[31] a confrontation which, on the view presented here, is something required if we are to have any hope of reaching true and rational beliefs.

So the question is this: How can the pragmatist cope with the many guises of value pluralism without smugly insisting that there is a belief to which everyone would eventually come? The answer will require us to see that pragmatism does not have just one, general, thing to say about how it is that moral judgement is truth-apt. It is happy with the thought that some judgements may command agreement more easily than others and with the thought that some judgements may not take truth-values. It does not try to idealise inquiry by requiring it to aim at getting the one answer for all. Moral judgement can be seen as being truth-apt without denying that disagreement might well persist and without denying the fact of pluralism or watering down what is good about pluralism. The idea that we search for right answers does not, I want to suggest, obliterate differences, even irreconcilable ones. Unlike some of the views canvassed in Chapter 1, the pragmatist does not focus on the idea of a contract or on the idea that everyone might be able, in principle, to agree, or on the idea of some reasons being convincing to everyone. The complex and problematic character of our moral and political lives requires a corresponding complexity of responses.[32]

Such a view might seem to lead us towards communitarianism, which argues that we ought not to aim at the pipe dream of universal agreement, but rather, for agreement within a tradition or community.[33] Only within a community can the good be identified. Does the pragmatist agree with this thought and then argue that there is an answer to the question of which communities get it right enough and which arrive at unacceptable results?

The pragmatist might indeed say, in the spirit of communitarianism, that many questions about what is right and wrong will be able to be answered only by participants in a way of life. The reasons for it being good for a Christian Southern Albertan to organise his life around the nuclear family and the church may not bear on the question of what is good for a Southern African Xhosa.

But the pragmatist can go on to say, against the communitarian, that the Xhosa and all of those who are affected by Xhosa decisions do not have a monopoly on experiences relevant to Xhosa morality. Perhaps the native Southern Albertan dispossessed of his land by colonial settlers, or a Japanese Southern Albertan forcibly removed from his farm during the Second World War, or a rural Southern Albertan whose life can be devastated by the vagaries of weather can speak knowledgeably about what the Xhosa may face. It is not that these Southern Albertans belong to the same community as the Xhosa, but they share some things. We must be careful, as Michelle Moody-Adams (1997: 64ff) puts it, not to fetishise difference as being exotic.

The pragmatist will also pull away from communitarianism by noting that it is extremely difficult, if not downright impossible, to define or individuate a culture, community, way of life, or a conception of the good. The boundaries of communities constantly shift and with every shift people will be left on the margins. Indeed, even leaving to one side the problem of the margins, there is nothing like complete agreement between members of a 'core' community. Communities will overlap and there will be plenty of internal tensions in any given conception of the good.[34] For instance, in Turkey a traditional moral code has it that family honour requires an unmarried girl be a virgin. Impending forced virginity examinations, backed by the government's Women's Affairs minister, recently resulted in the attempted suicide of five girls from state-run foster homes. The attempted suicides sparked a public outcry within Turkey, with women's rights activists and the Human Rights Minister leading the campaign.[35] How could one even ask which values constitute *the* values of this community?

Even adherents to a worldview as well-set out as Catholicism will interpret and specify it differently. Pope John XXIII of Vatican II and the current Pope John Paul II surely share a conception of the good, but disagree strenuously about what to do and believe.[36] And most conceptions of the good will be less rigorously characterised than those of formal religious or well-worked-out philosophical systems.

Indeed, the fact that someone might not *think* much about his conception of the good – the fact that he might not point to any principles which govern it – does not entail that no conception is in play. Someone's life might seem to me to drift along, without much regard for what is valuable. But perhaps that drifting and that disregard for talking about the valuable is what is taken, implicitly, to be a good way of living.

So while the communitarian may be on to something when she says that what is right is only identifiable from within a community, the notion of community and of what demarcates a group is so difficult to pin down that nothing much follows from the communitarian's thought.

We should note that where difference flourishes, there might well be claims that the experiences of one group are so different from that of others that they must separate. Some nationalists, separatist feminists, Afrikaner traditionalists, etc., want to set up their own 'homeland' and exclude others from it. Such a move might well be unobjectionable, on the view outlined here. As long as what such a group is after is the discovery of what is possible within one way of life and as long as they do not displace others or suggest that there is something inferior with those who are excluded, then the plan seems innocuous.

But of course, often there is a dark underside to such moves – an underside which denigrates those not in the separate group. Canadians got a glimpse of this when some Quebec separatists, defeated in the 1995 referendum on secession by the narrowest of margins, blamed 'money and ethnic votes' for the defeat.[37] And of course, we have seen the dark underside in all its horror many times this century.

Issues about communities and about when it is acceptable to speak and act against them are extremely difficult. The pragmatist must walk many tightropes here and the fact that she teeters so does not speak against the position. For any epistemology which did not find these issues hard would be, I suggest, simplifying matters so much as to be in danger of being simple-minded.

I have indicated that pragmatism is friendly to difference and to the multitude of competing values. But I have also been sympathetic to the idea that we all share a tremendous amount, that there is only one community of inquirers, that we must think of inquiry as embracing all peoples and cultures.[38] It takes a lot of work to keep these two thoughts simultaneously afloat. It takes a lot of work to think of the 'us' in the slogan 'truth is what is best for us to believe' as embracing everyone, while acknowledging that there is inevitably, and healthily, lots of conflict and difference in the world.

One thing we shall want to say here is that those positions which stress difference at the expense of similarity, those positions which would have us living in different worlds, are wrongheaded. The pragmatist, that is, does set herself against the kind of view which thinks that irreconcilable differences are more important or more significant than similarities.

Pragmatism, we have seen, is committed to the thought that our philosophical views must have a good effect on practice and a focus on irreconcilable differences would, it seems, have disastrous consequences. Take, for instance, the view put forward by a few feminists that there are two ways of looking at the world and two realities. On the one hand, there is the experience of men leading to a male understanding of the world and on the other hand, there is the experience of women leading to the female way of understanding the world. But if these theories are really incommensurable and latch on to different realities, then inquiry is paralysed. If there is no experience and reality accessible to all, then discussion about what is right and wrong, both in the way of belief and action, is impossible. In that case, one must wonder whether a world composed of both men and women can survive.

If we want our philosophy to have a salutary effect, we should commit ourselves, if we can, to the thought that we all belong to one community and bring to it our differences. This, I have suggested, might be compatible with some groups exploring their way of life apart from others. But that practice can only be taken so far.

The moral experiences of women might of course be different from that of men.[39] No one thinks that men and women experience jokes about rape in the same way. There would be no point to the pragmatist epistemology I outline here, if there were not divergence in experience. But that epistemology does not suggest that women's experience is so different that it is simply incomprehensible or not understandable by others.

It of course remains true that I cannot get under your skin and feel what you feel from the inside, as it were. So, in some sense I cannot fully comprehend your experiences. But I comprehend enough, something which is shown by the fact that I can speak to you about them, interpret what you say or write about them, and learn something about what it is that you feel. This is just that point again that language and communication are public. The fact that we communicate, interpret and translate shows that we share a tremendous amount.

We have seen that the inquirer must be committed to taking the beliefs and viewpoints of others seriously. If what we are after are the beliefs which would best stand up to all experience and argument, then we had better not ignore a part of that experience and argument. The plurality of competing perspectives and beliefs must not merely be allowed, but encouraged. And of course, giving difference a chance to manifest itself will require that the conditions for such views to be articulated and to mature will have to be put in place. Difference must flourish if we are to fully explore what it is to lead a good and full human life.

Thus one kind of institution we might applaud is the commitment the Canadian federal government made in the 1980s to providing public funds for groups to make Charter challenges. They saw that fostering deliberation required the financial wherewithal to let those without money mount expensive court cases. In the same spirit, public funding of cultural practices of minority groups, relaxing dress codes in the Royal Canadian Mounted Police so that Sikhs can wear turbans, and the like, might be required in order to prevent minority cultures from being swamped by the majority culture.

Indeed, rights of self-government might also be required. Any institution which tries to expand the range and the confidence of voices is a good institution in the eyes of the pragmatist. For one thing is clear: if we are to have any chance at getting at truth or the right thing to do, we must provide arenas for people to put matters on the agenda and participate in debate.

But also required are measures to reduce material inequality, for one obstacle in the way of participation in debate will often be that one's energies are focused on more physically and economically pressing matters. Of course in a straightforward sense, having things arranged so that people have adequate health care, education, and jobs is more important than having things arranged so that people have a voice. But the formulation of those policies regarding health, education and employment require voice and participation. This is the lesson that the international aid community has learnt the hard way.

Also required is extra effort to listen to those whose communication skills are underdeveloped, those whose lives are such that they have more demanding concerns than engaging in public debate, those who cannot muster the energy or the inclination to participate. And the pragmatist must not underestimate the influence of power, which will manifest itself in deliberative contexts by intimidation, by silencing, by setting the questions and agendas, by not taking up the suggestions of a minority, by claiming expert status, etc. These things must all be guarded against, the best they can. That might require a race-conscious redrawing of constituency boundaries or super majority requirements (where more than a simple majority vote is required).[40]

So keeping an open ear and an open mind is not enough. Taking the views of everyone seriously might well involve unequal effort and fair representation of groups that have been marginalised might require their actual presence in legislatures. Discussion with those who have views similar to mine and those with whom I am used to coming to agreement will involve relatively little effort. But it might take enormous effort and education and goodwill for me to be able to understand, let alone take seriously, the views of someone whose cultural and economic background is very different from my own.

As Judith Baker notes,[41] the effort required is increased when what I am trying to comprehend is the accusation of my own injustice. When a minority claims that those who enjoy the status of the majority have an unfair advantage, it is unsurprising if the majority fails to see any immediate truth in the claim. They might have to work very hard in order to see the problem at all. Surely this phenomenon was at least partly responsible for the fact that most liberal judges and advocates in the apartheid era had difficulty in seeing that they acted with injustice when they applied vicious laws.

There cannot be anything wrong, generally speaking, with giving extra weight to the opinions of some. We think, for instance, that it is conducive to truth-seeking to give special weight to physicists in questions of physics and special weight to first-person reports in questions of what an agent desires. These are reasons – connected to truth – for giving additional weight to the views of particular people.

I have suggested here that controversy regarding those many issues which face contemporary pluralistic societies is not done away with by the pragmatist. No obstacle is placed by the pragmatist in the way of special group rights, from guaranteed representation in a country's most important institutions, to special hunting and fishing rights for displaced indigenous populations, to the right to be educated in one's own language. We might even think that some of these purported rights ought to be enshrined in a constitution so that they are protected from contingent majorities. But neither will the pragmatist have pat answers to questions about whether, say, Sikhs in Canada ought to be exempt from motorcycle helmet laws. Again, the debates will involve the difficult task of weighing values – here the values of, on the one hand, safety regulation and laws being uniformly applicable, and, on the other, making it easy for immigrants to integrate into the mainstream culture and allowing people the scope to live and work while abiding by their cultural or religious convictions.

The pragmatist will say, in advance of the specific debates with their own set of historical, political, and cultural circumstances, that we must promote the flourishing of minority ways of life. But we must not make the mistake, in commending difference, of thinking that any practice is good just because it belongs to a community. Well-established practices are not immune to internal criticism and they are not immune to critical reasons given by outsiders. We need not acquiesce in a practice simply because it is a part of a way of life. We need not think it none of our business to comment or even to interfere. Of course if the disadvantaged group disagrees with us, there is cause for further worry and further complexity. But we are not in principle barred from making our views known.

One must tread with extreme caution here, for all sorts of ideological commitments have been used to justify unwarranted intervention. During the Cold War it was thought by many in Britain and North America to really be in the interests of the people to try to eradicate the Campaign for Nuclear Disarmament 'threat'. But having to be careful does not mean that we cannot act at all. The dangers that exist in making policy and in moral action will not go away, whatever one's philosophy. The question is how to make them less dangerous. The answer, in part, involves keeping in mind how one could go wrong, trying to make the principles upon which one acts as transparent as possible, and trying to find ways of institutionalising fallibilism.

Pluralism, underdetermination, and defeated reasons

Despite pragmatism's framing the notion of truth in terms of agreement and consensus, I have argued that it need not hope for an agreement which will do away with difference. This is a good thing, for there often seems to be no one answer – one answer which is best for all – to a question about what is right or wrong, just or unjust, good or not so good. Sometimes it appears that our moral judgements are underdetermined – that there are two or more equally acceptable, but conflicting, answers to a question about what is right or good. Sometimes, even when we do think that it makes sense to say that one answer is better than the others, we can regret not being able to act on the reasons in favour of the defeated option. And sometimes it appears that all of the potential answers to a question are in some way unsuitable or wrong; that there is no right answer to the question; that our choice is a tragic one, in that no matter what we do, we do something unacceptable.

Non-cognitivists take these phenomena to stand in the way of thinking of moral judgements as being candidates for truth and knowledge. The following are thought to be pillars of an objective discourse: (i) for any well-formed non-indexical statement *p*, *p* must be either true or false; (ii) if a statement has a truth-value – if it is either true or false – the truth-value it has must remain constant from person to person. We have seen that the pragmatist is not as attached to the principle of bivalence (i.e. (i)) as many others are. But if it turned out that bivalence failed across the board for moral beliefs, this would pretty much scuttle the project of thinking of morality as being an objective discourse. The thought is that moral judgements too often, or perhaps always, fall foul of (i) and (ii) and thus they cannot fall under our cognitive scope. The pragmatist who wants to be a cognitivist must provide a view of truth and objectivity on which we can think of moral belief as being truth-apt and still make sense of the phenomena of underdetermination, regret, and tragic choice.

Consider first the fact of underdetermination. It seems that there is no one right answer to questions such as: is the good life the spiritual life or the life of the atheist; is it the life of contemplation or of athletic excellence; is it better to live in a traditional nuclear family or in a commune; ought one to turn one's spare room over to one's struggling brother or to one's more-struggling friend? It is equally acceptable to go either way on these issues. But if we characterise this kind of underdetermination so that 'it is better to live the life of contemplation than the life of athletic excellence' has no determinate truth-value, then bivalence fails for all of these issues. And if we characterise this kind of underdetermination so that the statement is true for me and false for you, then (ii) – the stability of truth-value – seems to fail to hold.

There is an easy way out of this difficulty. The pragmatist/cognitivist can advise that we shift our focus from unwarranted generalisations of the sort 'everyone should try to live the life of contemplation' to statements about what kinds of lives are morally permissible. So it might be true that 'the life of contemplation or of spirituality or of athletic excellence is worthwhile, but not the life of the Nazi or the drug addict'. So the first thing to notice is that the agreement invoked by the pragmatist's account of truth might be disjunctive. We need not think of agreement as being a case of which one way of life is best or which goods are good for all. Rather we might agree that a number of (but not all) incompatible ways of life or a number of (but not all) incompatible things that are valued are reasonable, permissible, or acceptable. Another way of putting this point is that the statements which take truth-values might be of this kind: 'I am permitted to adopt any conception of the good life which does not infringe on others', 'when acceptable values conflict, I may choose the path which best fits with the kind of person I want to be, and others may choose the path that best fits the kind of person they want to be', etc.

We have seen that the disjunctions of values will not include everything. The methodological principle justified by the pragmatist gives us enough to criticise some ways of life and some values as being unacceptable. Those which function through ignoring or denigrating the experiences of others can be criticised. And hard on the heels of this thought is an argument for promoting difference. The plurality of acceptable competing perspectives and beliefs must not merely be allowed, but encouraged, so that we can have a wealth of experiences as inputs to our inquiries. And of course, giving difference a chance to manifest itself will require that the conditions for such views to be articulated and to mature will have to be put in place.

We also have here an explanation of the above kind of underdetermination and disagreement. Because there are different ways in which a human life can go well, we can have a plurality of right answers to our questions.

It is in the making of such choices, in seeing what fits with what I am and with what I want to be, where my freedom lies, where I can discover and invent myself.[42] Sometimes this discovery and invention is dramatic, as in Sartre's example of the young man who must choose either doing what is best for his country and for humanity by joining the French Resistance or being faithful to his desperately needy mother by staying to care for her. But sometimes the discovery is more banal, where we simply make underdetermined choices and have them cumulatively determine what sort of person we become.

The point is that, once considerations about the shape of my life are brought into the decision, the issue might not look so intractable to me. That is, sometimes an individual can compare diverse values. Even if values cannot be aligned on a single metric (say, monetary value, or utility, or pleasure), I can often make a reasoned choice between them. When I choose *A* over *B* because *A* is more in line with who I am and want to be, the choice is not an arbitrary matter. Even if I choose between acceptable or contestable options on a whim, I might be making a reasoned choice, for I can value whimsicality in my life.

Hence, the fact that there may be no one right answer for all need not be tragic. A choice might, of course, be so important and difficult that it tears one apart or tears one's society apart. But when a choice is not so destructive, then we might be grateful for the fact that there are alternative, equally good, answers to some questions.

So we now see one way in which the pragmatist view of truth, while giving us a way of thinking of moral judgements as having truth-values, does not try to wipe away all conflict, difference and diversity. It might be true that some (but not all) ways of life are acceptable or worthwhile. And it might be true that, for me, a certain way of life is best and true that, for you, a very different one is best. Some judgements, to borrow a thought of Blackburn's, are happily relativised (1998: 69).

Let us look at a more serious difficulty – the notion of regret. When I make choices from an underdetermined set, I must of course face the possibility that I cannot have everything I value. If being a serious philosopher does not leave time to be a serious athlete, then if I value both, I am bound to lose something when I choose a style of life. No matter what I choose, regret might be inevitable and the question 'what should I choose?' might appear impossible. None of the candidate answers appear to be wholeheartedly right.

This kind of difficulty is more striking when the question involves how to treat others. Michael Walzer (1973) asks us to imagine a thoroughly decent politician, committed to democracy and to the rule of law, who has just come to power after a terrible civil war. He goes to the capital, which is in the midst of the flagging terrorist campaign, and is told that a number of bombs are set to go off in various apartment buildings around the city in the next twenty-four hours. He must decide whether to go against his principles and torture a captured rebel leader to find out where the bombs are in order save countless lives. Here, we hesitate to say that the right thing to do is to torture, for it seems that it can never be *right* to do such a thing. In such cases, it might appear that there is no right answer to be had, no truth of the matter at stake.

When the issues involve not just the conflicting pulls of an individual's values, but of the swirl of values found amongst people in a society, they look even more impossible – the defeated reasons and the lost values loom even larger. Take, for instance, the issue of whether indigenous groups, who have had their culture run over by a colonising majority, ought to govern themselves. In Canada proposals for self-government remove indigenous peoples from the scope of the Canadian Charter of Human Rights. But the Charter has things going for it and it appeals to many within that group – Native women, for instance. Whatever decision is taken, something will be lost – either autonomy for a badly-wronged group, or human rights protection for groups within that group. Whatever decision might be best in the circumstances, there will be reasons, which will not go away, in favour of other decisions. Notice also that the destruction of an indigenous culture, such as that of the First Nations North Americans by a colonising majority is a kind of injustice that is extremely hard to rectify, for some ways of life cannot be replanted. This is not to say that attempts at redressing the wrongs should not be made, it is just to say that the thought that we might set the situation completely aright is an unhelpful idealisation.

Similarly, the staff of the UN High Commission on Refugees might have to make a decision about whether to return Burmese refugees in Bangladesh to Burma, where they most certainly will be mistreated. The UN has a well-grounded principle against such repatriation. But if it is clear that the Bangladeshi government will return the refugees anyway in the near future, and if it is clear that if the UNHCR cooperates with the return then some exceptions to the repatriation will be allowed, and if it is clear that, on return, the refugees will not be treated as harshly as they have been in the past, then the UNHCR's field workers might assert that repatriation is the only sensible and humane thing to do in the circumstances.[43]

Take also the issue of legal aid for those who cannot pay first-rate law firms to represent them. No one doubts that an accused person has a right to a fair defence before a bewildering law, especially when incarceration looms. And no one doubts that a certificate system, where the accused is issued a voucher which can be redeemed by any practising lawyer, provides better legal service than a public defender system, when it is staffed by stretched and overworked government lawyers. But the staggering cost of legal aid has sent many certificate-issuing governments scrambling to look for a cheaper system. If it really is the case that the entrenched ways in which we have distributed wealth have resulted in the tax burden of a certificate system being too much for a society to bear, then it seems that alternatives must be sought which chip away at the right to a fair trial. And such a decision, even if it is the right decision, is such that we will regret having to make it.

Of course, it will not usually be easy to separate cases in which a conflict of values arises for an individual from those in which the conflict arises for a community. Consider public policy regarding abortion. There are at least two competing and incompatible values – preserving the life of the foetus and preserving the autonomy of the woman. These values might pull against each other in one's own inner life. But even if I am confidently pro-choice, even if I think that it is clear that abortion should be available on demand, I should be able to see that there is some genuine value that the pro-life camp promotes. (And I hope they can see that there is some genuine value that the pro-choice camp promotes.) The fact that there are good reasons for making abortion easily available does not cancel out the reasons for making abortions difficult to obtain. And those reasons might continue to be valid for the confident pro-choice supporter, in that she perhaps will argue that if a foetus is to be aborted, it must be aborted well before the third trimester; in that perhaps she will feel some remorse if she chooses to have an abortion.

The thought that we might set such situations completely aright seems to be an unhelpful idealisation. Moral and political life is characterised by the competing tug of values and conducted against a background history of moral failures. Vexed issues are thick on the ground.

With respect to these unhappy decisions, issues for which all the potential answers to our questions are less than they might be, issues for which we cannot agree upon a disjunction of equally acceptable answers, the pragmatist needs to focus on another sort of thing we might agree upon. We might agree that, *in the circumstances*, a compromise is the best that can be done. Such a compromise might be a trade-off, where all parties get something, but not everything, they wanted. Or it might be that no party thinks the outcome good, but neither do they think it reprehensible. In such cases, we do not think that truth is put on hold because a decision must be taken; we do not think that, if only we could deliberate a little more, we could arrive at something unproblematically right. Rather, we think that this compromise, in the circumstances, just *is* the right decision.

Here we have a way of understanding regret and defeated reasons. The right thing to do might well be to settle for something not altogether good and regret that we could not act on reasons which pulled the other way. So, even though it might be true that, in the circumstances, there is nothing better for the UNHCR to do than to return the refugees, they do so with a heavy heart. The best they can do is strive for the least unhappy of the options or for doing the lesser evil.

We might explain the phenomena of regret and defeated reasons by appealing to the idea of moral failure. The UNHCR encounters layer upon layer of moral failure that weighs on their practical decision. That human society is such that there are political refugees is one such failure, that Burmese dissidents are persecuted in their own country is another, that they encounter discrimination in Bangladesh another, and so on. Given the pervasiveness of moral failure, there will be many situations in which we think that in the circumstances there is a right answer, but one where regret and defeated reasons are heightened. Despite moral failures, despite not being in a position where justice in anything like its full sense can be served, there might be a right thing to do. The UNHCR must act on the strongest set of reasons – that might require that they repatriate, with regret.

So the pragmatist can do justice to the phenomenon of regret – the 'ought' that is not acted upon need not be eliminated from the scene.[44] Thinking that there is a right answer in the circumstances does not erase the reasons for doing what, in the end, was decided not to be best. Those reasons can continue to hold.

It is important to see that with this kind of right answer, we need to actually feel the pull of the defeated reasons. If someone failed to feel the pull of the competing view, we might be tempted to say that he was narrow-minded or lacked imagination or even that he has made an inadequate judgement.[45] Take Walzer's decent politician. If it is indeed best in the circumstances to torture, then one must add the rider 'and to feel terrible about it'. The politician has not had the right moral response if he sees that torture is generally wrong, sees that nonetheless in these circumstances he ought to torture, and when it comes to doing his duty, quite enjoys it and feels no compunction. There is something wrong with what he judges. He has failed to see that, despite the correctness of his act, the reasons for not doing it do not disappear.

So the second way the pragmatist can think of moral judgement as being truth-apt, but nonetheless contestable, is to think of some judgements as being qualified with 'in the circumstances' and 'with regret'. Some conflicts can be resolved, but not neatly resolved – not resolved without residue. As Ruth Barcan-Marcus (1980) argues, the fact that our norms conflict should not straightaway make us attempt to restore consistency. Genuine dilemmas are possible and cannot be resolved by ranking our rules or by appending clauses about exceptions to the rules. The philosopher's response to conflict should not always be to attempt to eradicate it.

Things are even more difficult once we cross a blurred boundary and find ourselves in the territory of tragic choice. Sometimes we will think that a question does not admit of a disjunction of permissible answers, nor of a right answer which is plagued by regret. No matter what we do, we do something so unhappy that we feel tainted by our action; we feel that our hands are stained forever; we feel that the consequences are unbearable. Perhaps the alternatives seem equally evil in some common currency or perhaps doing what might appear to be the right thing destroys something essential, such as dignity or integrity, about one's self.

Consider those tragic choices so horribly exemplified in Nazi concentration camps.[46] The man who has a chance of surviving the camp, and who thinks it very important to survive in order to bear witness, is forced to either load his wife into the gas chamber or die himself. How could one possibly arrive at a right answer here? What can the pragmatist say of such indeterminacy?

The first thing to notice is that we could think of truth-values as being appropriate in tragic choices in that it appears that all of the suggestions as to what is good or just or worth pursuing are false. It might be that what is true is that there is no good or justice or right action in the situation. But when we must find something best to act upon – when the worst case is that in which we do nothing – then this route is perhaps not the most helpful. If a mother in a concentration camp who refuses to choose which of her children are to die sees them all die, then it seems that we are pressed to search for a decision which is best.

The second thing to notice is that many of these seemingly impossible decisions often turn on a conflict with one's dignity, integrity, or identity and that we can be tempted to have an over-robust sense of these. Those who say that they can never travel to a under-developed country because they cannot bear to see such misery are, we feel, self-indulgent or too focused on their own queasy feelings. (And of course, in the country in which they live, similar sites of devastation can be found, so there is also a dose of bad faith.)

We of course do not want to charge everyone who takes it to be paramount that they keep their dignity or integrity intact with self-indulgence. And there might well be cases of overwhelming tragedy where we must say that there just is no decent answer. In such cases, the pragmatist must say that here we find a truth-value gap, or a case where there is no right or wrong thing to do, or a duty-free zone.[47]

We seem to be faced with a continuum here, which ranges from 'right answer with no regret' to 'no acceptable answer at all'. We ought to be prepared for a range of responsiveness to experience and reasons – a range of objectivity, if you like. We expect that some questions would indeed have right or best answers for all and that some questions would have right or best answers for an individual. But others may not.

It is important to see that we are not without explanations of why there is such variance. Some of it might well fall along the lines of certain distinctions, for the class of moral and political judgements is far from homogeneous. Peter Railton, for instance, holds that judgements about value and virtue have a better chance at truth than judgements about duty and rights.[48] And Bernard Williams (1996) and David Wiggins (1976, 1991a) suggest that assertions about what acts and traits fall under thick ethical concepts such as 'kind', 'dishonest', 'treacherous', 'admirable', and 'brutal' can more readily aim at truth than can assertions about what falls under thin ethical concepts such as 'right' and 'wrong'. As Wiggins notes, a practice of correctly applying thick concepts can have its roots in subjective responses to the world, but can nonetheless grow into a genuinely cognitive or objective practice. If some states regularly evoke certain responses, such as 'that's disgusting' or 'that's amusing', we will find ourselves appealing to features of states in order to explain our making these attributions. We will explain and justify our responses by appealing to properties in the world and we can cultivate our responses by becoming more sensitive to the presence of these properties.

Perhaps the fact that resources are scarce makes many judgements less than what they might have been were our resources up to the challenge of our needs; perhaps it is just the plurality of competing values; perhaps, as Hume suggested, human nature exhibits limited generosity.[49] Or perhaps we might detect, as an underlying cause of tragic choice and regret, a conflict between human rights, such as the right to life and liberty and the things that seem to follow (the right to emigrate, to speak freely, to a fair trial, to not be subject to arbitrary arrest or incarceration, etc.). We have seen that pornographic (and one can add, racist) speech seems to throw the right to equality and the right to freedom of expression into conflict. It might be that a number of things are so important to human flourishing that we call them rights, and that these rights could not all be simultaneously satisfied, never mind all satisfied in the economic circumstances.

So, some judgements may command agreement more easily than others. The pragmatist sees that and does not try to idealise moral inquiry by requiring it all to aim at getting the one answer for all. For idealising thoughts – say, were our resources plentiful, then we should distribute them in such and such a way – can be unhelpful. What we are after are judgements in our world, not in a world in which things are very different.

Anyway, we should not want to set up our moral theory or our epistemology so that we do away with the possibility that some issues will prove to be impossible, so that we do away with the situation in which wretched compromise is the best that we can manage. We do not want to eliminate the morally puzzling. To rule out such possibilities would be untrue to the phenomenology or practice of morals – it would be untrue to those occasions upon which we do feel at a loss, where we feel that no matter how hard we persevere, there is no one right answer to be had; or to those situations where we feel regret, even though we did the right thing, that we were unable to act on the opposing considerations. To aim for precision where there may be none would be to do a disservice to the kind of inquiry we are trying to characterise.

It is an interesting question to see how much underdetermination and divergence the model can tolerate without losing its grasp on objectivity. One of the things we can say is that it would be a mistake to think that there is some well-defined cut-off point, if only we could find it.

Another thing we can say is that there will be some determinate answers forthcoming – enough, it is hoped, to support the idea of objectivity. We can predict that, were the views of all to be seriously considered, views charac-

istic of national socialism and patriarchy, for instance, would disappear altogether. We can see that certain perspectives thrive on denying the experience
of others and that pragmatism provides a principled reason for being suspicious of such views. That is, we will indeed expect that some practices will be
damaged by the light of experience. For we have seen that if those who put
forward misogynist, anti-Semitic, and racist views claim that their position is
true, or best, or that which *ought* to be enforced, we have enough to see them
as participating in inquiry. We have enough to see them as bound to the
minimal requirement of taking the experience of others seriously. An
inquirer who does not hold his beliefs open to revision by the recalcitrant
experience of others fails to make genuine assertions and fails to have a
belief which is aimed at the truth.

The view that I have urged is not one which insists that all moral and
political questions must have right answers, whether or not we can ever
know them. That would be a strenuous cognitivism. Neither is it a view that
infers from the fact that morals and politics are rife with unanswerable questions that the notion of a right answer inappropriate. That would be a
strenuous non-cognitivism. I have advocated a cognitivism which is modest,
in that it holds that our moral judgements aspire to truth and have varying
chances of attaining it.

We have seen that the complaint that actual consensus cannot be secured
in a pluralistic society cannot be set against this modest cognitivist view. The
pragmatist agrees that it is likely that we will not all come to think that one
particular thing is the right thing to do in a given situation. But that does
not prevent us from aiming at the truth or from aiming at agreement. For
the agreement with which the pragmatist is concerned is not agreement
about which one way of life is best and is not always agreement about which
is the one best answer to a question.

Pragmatism, that is, should keep well away from two metaphors. It is not
that we need lots of perspectives to choose from in order for the best one to
win in the Armageddon of perspectives. And it is not that we need lots of
perspectives so that they can melt together in the pot and produce the best
amalgam. Rather, one would expect that plurality of belief, at least with
respect to moral issues, would be preserved, were inquiry to continue. And
one would expect that often there will be no answer which is unproblematically right. With these thoughts at the centre of our attention, we can see
how people can be proud of the ways in which they are different and how
they might want to resist assimilation into the dominant culture. We can see
how cultural exchange can go in all directions – we can be receptive to the
thought that we can learn from those who are different from us. And we can
see how we can make of ourselves what we will.

Some brands of deliberative democracy might seem to offer a way of
overcoming disagreement. They might seem to suggest that the results of a
certain kind of deliberation will converge, that everyone will come to see
that an answer to the question at hand is best.[50] That is not the pragmatist's

project. The project is rather to say some things about how best to get agreement where we can, to say what the character of such an agreement is (if the belief would remain the best belief, then it is true), and to say something normative about which methods of inquiry are justified and which are not. But the pragmatist will not, we have seen, try to take shelter from the fact that an issue might be intractable, or that justice might be only partially served, or that the situation for some might remain unjust when the best decision is taken.

We have also seen that the pragmatist does not think that our aim in moral and political deliberation is agreement for agreement's sake or for impartiality's sake. What matters to us is that we reach a belief which takes the experiences and interests of all into account – what matters to us is that we reach the belief that is the best belief, and we call that kind of belief true.[51]

A number of points about our aim in moral deliberation accompany the idea that our moral lives are caught up in the to and fro of competing values and that there might not always be a winner in the competition. First, adjudication between competing answers may not always be what is most important. Rather than aim at a conclusion or at the right answer to a practical question, we might aim at a deeper understanding of others – at greater sensitivity and sophistication in our interpretation of others. Or we might aim at a deeper understanding of ourselves – at making sense of ourselves, of understanding who we are and the kinds of beings we are.[52] Such knowledge is just as important as adding to one's stock of justified belief about what is right or wrong, virtuous or odious.

Here, we have another route to the contextualist thought. We do not need to always think of ourselves as trying to contribute to some public, communal process of inquiry – at what the best answer would be for *us*. For, as we have seen, a decision might be more personal or autobiographical.[53] A decision might be about what is best for me to do in these circumstances, not what everyone should do in these circumstances. In offering reasons for why *p* seems right to me, rather than *q*, I needn't be arguing with an opponent, aiming at getting her to see the light. Rather, I may be explaining to myself, offering reasons to myself, for why I should do one thing rather than another. These reasons will be, if you like, agent-relative reasons – reasons which cannot be stated independently of a particular person's identity and values.

We might, with Krausz (1993: 103) compare this aspect of our moral lives with the evaluation of performances of a score. There may be different reasonable standards of interpretation at play. You might judge *A* to be better than *B* because *A* is more faithful to the score. But I might think that the standard of aesthetic consistency is most important and judge *B* to be better than *A*. There needn't be any overarching standard by which we can judge the competing standards of interpretation and so both conclusions are reasonable. But one may be *the* answer for me, another for you.

Of course, some interpretations will not be reasonable – interpreting a piece by Schubert by trying to map it onto a Spice Girls tune, is simply not a good interpretation. Similarly, the racist's self-understanding – placing himself above others on a scale of worth – is not an acceptable way of understanding oneself. But amongst reasonable interpretations, there is room for the idiosyncratic.

It is important to see, however, that, whatever our intentions, we might find a personal idiosyncratic decision serving as a model for others. This is usually not the case when there are no moral considerations involved in the decision, as when I am deciding whether I prefer blueberry to blackberry jam. Moral considerations can, however, play a part in preferences and when they do, they can have influence. I might prefer Bridgehead Nicaraguan coffee to others because its producers have fair labour practices. This might look like a personal preference, but it can of course affect others – even if I do not campaign or try to browbeat others into buying Bridgehead. It can bring new reasons to light for others.[54]

When Judge Laurie Ackerman resigned from the South African bench because it had to administer apartheid laws, he made a public statement to the effect that it was a personal decision having to do with his own religious beliefs.[55] At the Truth and Reconciliation Commission hearings into the legal order, Ackerman was still anxious to confine the scope of his decision to resign to the personal. Nevertheless, the decision had an undeniable public impact, both at the time as an example for other judges and now, as a reminder that judges could see their way to resigning in protest – that this was an option which was on the table.

So, even when I think of my reasons as being relative to my personal interests and beliefs – even when I aim at getting something right for me, not for the community – they might in fact have a larger scope. I might find that they have a pull on others in similar circumstances. And when they have such pull, it is a misnomer to call them personal, or mere preferences, or reasons entirely relative to my circumstances. Not many reasons and judgements can be so confined.

Another aim that we might have – an aim which stands apart from the aim of finding what belief is best for the community of inquirers – is to keep a discussion going. We might think it good that there is continuing reflection, say, on whether or not there is free will in the face of evidence that genes, brain chemicals, and upbringing determine our actions. We might think that continued reflection is helpful even if we do not think that a decisive answer can ever be forthcoming.

Here the pragmatist, in step with her general position, will argue that we must continue to draw our blurry lines – in this case the lines between when we can be said to be responsible for our actions and when we can be said not to be responsible. It is important to keep on having such discussions and making such judgements in law and in moral deliberation, despite the fact that there may be no way of definitively articulating the principles which stand behind them.

In moral deliberation we try to make policy and decisions in the face of value pluralism, conflict, regret, and tragedy. We can make these judgements by compromising or by settling for something which we know to be not quite right, without first resolving all conflict. Decision-making in the face of uncertainty and disagreement is always difficult, but necessity dictates that it gets done.

Schmitt, coercion, and when we have talked enough

The pragmatist, I have argued, makes good on the promise to speak to and against illiberal views. If the Schmittian claims to have beliefs or claims to aim at the truth, then one can criticise him on the grounds that he has adopted a method of inquiry that is highly unlikely to reach the truth. Or we might say that he fails to get right the practices of assertion, belief, and inquiry, practices in which he sees himself engaging. Indeed Schmitt's own concern with argument and justification led to his eventual falling out with the Nazis.[56] Academics, the Nazis charged, were too intellectual.

It may seem, though, that my arguments fail to get a grip on a certain kind of illiberal position. What do we say about someone who denies that he is a truth-seeker, who denies that he has beliefs which are responsive to reasons, and simply opts to live in a way in which we find repulsive? Here, we must return to Hume's thought that where one is of so perverse a frame of mind, philosophy affords no remedy. We cannot offer reasons to which he will be drawn, which will pull on him.

But we can give *ourselves* reasons for rejecting the view. We will think that, whatever he says, it appears to be a genuine view, something that can be right or wrong. And so, like it or not, he is caught up in the practice of justification and reason-giving.

But we must also consider a position that Schmitt might well have taken, for it poses a slightly different problem for the pragmatist. Schmitt could have engaged in a sociological/psychological argument about human nature. He could have claimed that it is just a fact about human nature that a life goes well if and only if one bands together with self-identified friends against a common enemy. This is a Schmitt who cannot be accused of stopping his ears to the experience of others. For, presumably, the basis of his judgement about human nature would be observation – it would be that the evidence points to human beings doing best in ultra-nationalist communities.

He might have added the argument that the outsider lacks qualification. Her experience is not relevant to a group of which she is not a member, just as my thoughts are not relevant to discussions about high-energy physics or the ins and outs of immunology.

Here the pragmatist will say that, while it is possible that Schmitt is right about human nature, while it is possible that he has accurately captured human flourishing, that view is in fact wrong. The pragmatist's own sociological/psychological argument will be that human beings do best to break down distinctions between friend and enemy, and to think of themselves as belonging to a wider community. But of course, this is a hypothesis – one with plenty going for it, but a hypothesis nonetheless. Here, the pragmatist argues with the Schmittian not on points about methodology and truth-seeking, but on points of where the weight of the evidence lies.

Part of our reasoning here might include the arguments advanced above that pluralism need not be a clash of disparate cultures in different geographical locations. We can find such conflicts within our own culture and even within a given individual. Indeed, in any community – those better-defined because they are based on a common religion and those which are more amorphous – there will be those who chaff against the bit.

Think, for example, of a woman born to and raised by culturally conservative Muslim parents in Canada . She may be torn between loyalty to her parents and attraction to the relative liberty for women in Western society. Or think of a relatively homogeneous society of the Amish or the Hutterites. Such societies are rife with conflicts of loyalties. Cultures or societies are simply not homogenous. Most lives, I suggest, are characterised by conflicting pulls. Even in a stable society approved of by Schmitt, there will be conflict. And there will likely be qualms, provoked by what we think of as liberal democratic values, about the value of shunning those who are not identified as friend.

If individuals and cultures are always divided by disparate values, then Schmitt's idea that there *can* be substantive homogeneity in our communities must be simply wrong. People and societies are too complex and too changeable to be homogeneous.

Indeed, part of the reasoning here will include thoughts about how an outsider can provide fresh perspective, fresh insights from which to learn. Given the tremendous similarity in human response to suffering, to kindness, to affection, there seems no obstacle in principle to having the experience of an outsider be relevant to a group.

I have argued that, at a certain point, we can cease to regard the Schmittian as a genuine inquirer. It follows that, in answering the question 'who is the "we" in the slogan "truth is what we would agree upon"?', we shall want to disqualify some from that group. We can invoke reasons to determine whom to deliberate with; to determine who is a real inquirer. The pragmatist is not committed to a 'we must talk with everyone all the time' attitude. The Schmittian who refuses to take seriously the experience of the other introduces one kind of situation in which we need not talk and we need not deliberate, but there are other kinds as well.

One kind of case, not too far removed from the Schmittian case, is that we might conclude that we ought not to engage in debate with those who deny that the Holocaust occurred. It would of course be wrong-headed to suggest that we should not engage with someone who had been somehow sheltered from and was thus unaware of the horrors of the Second World War, who writes a term paper inquiring into whether or not six million Jews perished at Nazi hands. That would be taking a matter off the inquiry table because we thought that the very inquiry was somehow immoral. This is a thought from which the pragmatist recoils. Had Nazism died the death it deserved after the war, were there no neo-Nazis today who would repeat the sins, inquiry into the details of the Holocaust could be unproblematically conducted. It is only because you do not have to scratch far beneath the surface of today's Holocaust deniers to find their underlying motivation – the promotion of racism – that there is something wrong with their inquiries. On the pragmatism outlined here, the underlying racism gives us reason enough to hold their views and their inquiries under suspicion. They are not serious or genuine inquirers. We can add that engagement with Holocaust deniers might be seen to lend their views legitimacy and, since we do not want to encourage the thought that there is any basis to their denials, it might be decided best to stay out of television debates and the like with the deniers.

There is room in pragmatism for the other decision as well – for the thought that one must debate with the deniers to expose the view for what it is. Notice also that I do stand to learn something from listening to the neo-Nazi. I cannot understand things properly without seeing that such racism is often part of something bigger – it is often about a government failing a certain part of the population. White supremacists, that is, might have some real grievances – often low pay, miserable working conditions, dim prospects. (And of course this was the case with Nazis before the Second World War.) The problem is that they mistakenly and wrongly go on to blame immigrants and others in their midst. They express their grievances by treating others badly. My ability to understand this, while not affecting the judgement I might make about them, can only be a good thing.

So, while the pragmatist might well decide not to engage with someone like a Holocaust denier, she might, on the other hand, decide that engagement is best. My point here is just that pragmatism does not entail that we must always continue to talk, even when we have well-grounded reservations.

In Sidney Lumet's *Twelve Angry Men*, there is a scene where one jury member in a murder trial changes his vote to 'not guilty' simply in order to try to end the discussion. He has tickets to a ballgame. The obvious response to him is the one made by another jury member. If his reason for changing his vote is merely expedient, he is not taking his role of deliberator seriously. Given the nature of a jury at this stage of the proceedings, where disqualification is no longer possible, he must be pressured into giving his sincere thoughts on the matter. But one can imagine contexts, other than a jury, in which, if that attempt at turning him into a sincere inquirer fails, his opinions would simply not be taken into account.

Another kind of situation in which deliberation is not on is when the inquirer simply needs an answer she can immediately act upon, and does not have time to deliberate.[57] Here she would think that she was in the unfortunate position of not being able to adequately inquire. When I must decide whether or not to give my spare change to the *nouveau* poor and probably racist white man begging on the Johannesburg streets, I cannot stop too long to ponder the complexities. I must either give or pass by.

I also need not deliberate if judgement can be simple and quick. If I see a big man kicking a small child, inquiry is not what is called for. Perception of wrongness is enough here. That is, sometimes deliberation is inappropriate because one answer straightaway imposes itself upon us. Here deliberation is bypassed because one seems to know what its upshot would most likely be.

Sometimes deliberation is inappropriate because it can damage a fragile practice.[58] This might be the case with respect to too much inquiry into what one's sexual responses should be. It is not that deliberation is always inappropriate in this domain. Whatever one's urges are, it is wrong to rape one's date and we can certainly deliberate about how best to view various kinds of situations along that continuum (what about considerable pressure that falls short of physical force? what about aggressive seduction?). But thorough, exhaustive, deliberation is not always the best route to what one should do or believe in every aspect of one's life. As Blackburn (1998: 21f) notes, a lover or spouse who deliberates about whether it is her duty to spend time with her partner damages the value of the relationship. She has one thought or one deliberation too many.

So the principle that we must take in evidence and argument is not a principle which must cover all of our actions like a smothering blanket – we do not need to be tenacious pitbull-like inquirers, never letting go of an issue.

Perhaps the idea that deliberation can be set aside will trouble some. Martha Minow, for instance, has a worry about disregarding the views of those who are deemed incompetent. She puts the objection to Rawls' position in *A Theory of Justice*:

> The views of mentally disabled persons, children, and any others deemed to lack capacity for rational thought become relevant only through the imaginations of the 'rational' people who ask what they themselves would want if they were in the position of these incompetent persons.
>
> (Minow 1990: 150)

Minow's precise point against Rawls could not be aimed at the pragmatist, for the pragmatist does not think that the experience of others is taken into account by a thought experiment, where 'rational' people imagine that they are in the position of those others. The pragmatist will want to really listen, as well as she is able, to the voices of those others.

But Minow's question can be asked of any political theorist who focuses on citizens or inquirers agreeing on what is best. For it seems that those who are not thought of as rational will be left out of the conversation. We have seen that the pragmatist, for instance, provides resources by which we can ignore the voices of those who we have reason to think are not genuine inquirers. Presumably, some people with defective cognitive faculties will fall into this category.

Sure enough, to the difficult question of what justice requires for mentally disabled persons and for children, the pragmatist should, I think, reply that the main concern, in many cases, is to make decisions for them, using one's imaginative and empathetic capacities to as far as possible determine what is best for them. As Christine Sypnowich (1996) has argued, it would seem unavoidable that there will be classes of people for whom decisions are bound to be made by the rationally privileged, even if we think that much consultation with, and regard for, the persons involved is required.

Of course, the pragmatist will fully agree with Minow that care must be taken to avoid jumping to the conclusion that some group fails to be genuine inquirers. We can point to countless instances where the powerful have decided that women, blacks, the landless, and others were incompetent in the reasoning business. But, remember, the pragmatist has a built-in commitment to being open to the claims of others. And she has a conception of inquiry which is so thin that the *prima facie* assumption is that everyone is an inquirer. When it is being wondered whether to exclude someone, the entire burden of argument is on the case to exclude. The presumption of inquiry is to include.

That is, those resources which we invoke to disqualify some from the class of genuine truth-seekers are not bludgeons for doing away with any view we dislike. They come into play only with respect to positions which fail to take inquiry or the stuff of inquiry – experience and reasons – seriously. For the most part, what pragmatism insists upon is tolerance – the encouraging of and listening to those who have views different from one's own. And this tolerance is not born of scepticism or of indifference or of mutual incomprehension. It is a tolerance born of optimism about finding beliefs or disjunctions of beliefs which would be acceptable by all.

Notice that the insistence on tolerance here applies not only to communities (each group must tolerate and promote understanding of others), but also to individuals or dissenters within communities. No culture is a monolith, and dissenters from within must be included in the debates, otherwise the principle which the pragmatist has justified will be violated.

We enter a thicket of questions here, in saying just what it means to include others, in saying just what it is to take their experiences seriously. Say a Christian fundamentalist patriarchal man listens to a feminist's account of her experiences of discrimination in the workplace and concludes that by putting her children in day-care she has sinned and that is why she reports the experiences as she does. Or what if he is an extreme Freudian and puts it down to penis envy? Have these men taken her experience seriously?[59] Here, the answer is quite clearly 'no' – their background beliefs prevent them from being able to really comprehend what she reports.

But to try to set out some necessary and sufficient conditions for when someone takes the views of others seriously would be futile. We simply have to go with our best careful analyses of various situations, along with the general thought that first-person characterisations should be given more weight over third-person characterisations. Unless, of course, we have reason to think there is self-deception. The complexities go on and on. It would be a very strange moral epistemology that tried to paint a simple picture of them.

Even when a judgement seems straightforward enough, the complexities do not go away. We have seen that the fact that the pragmatist identifies a principle of inquiry does not entail that he must be an interventionist, quick to coerce those who violate the principle that the experience of others must be taken seriously. There is, as Kymlicka has stressed, a distinction between making a judgement and acting on it.[60] We can be perfectly warranted in condemning an action, but not warranted in trying to put a stop to it. That enforced virginity testing is oppressive and repugnant does not straightaway entail that liberal democratic countries should try to force a revision in such practices in other countries.

For one thing, such coercion is bound to meet with resistance, for it is bound to appear aggressive to an illiberal group or to an unjust regime. Forcing people to believe does not tend to work, although they might be forced to act in certain ways. The long-term success of intervention, however, will depend on getting people to believe that it is right to respect the views of others, wrong to think someone sub-human because of skin colour, etc.

Thus the pragmatist might well recommend debate, advocacy, economic incentive, and other measures over censorship and brute force. As Kernohan argues, economic and persuasive power is more effective in challenging false beliefs about inequality. (1998: 91ff) What we want to do is to get people to *agree* to the principles in question, not just to fall into line with them.

Of course, sometimes situations are so desperate, and people's experiences are being denigrated in such an oppressive way, that our goal might shift from getting people to believe that they ought to respect others to simply ending the oppression. Winning the Nazis over in terms of belief was not a goal of the Allies in their quest to stop Hitler. But notice that whatever success there eventually was in quashing those beliefs (a success which comes into more and more doubt) depended not only on force, but on economic intervention in post-war West Germany.

Thus, our goals in inquiry vary. One way of seeing the Truth and Reconciliation Commission in South Africa is that it was not primarily aimed at getting true answers to questions about what happened during the apartheid decades. And it was not primarily aimed at justice – indeed, what usually gets thought of as justice was bypassed in favour of other goals. The torturer who was truthful and open about his activities was given amnesty, was allowed to escape the demands of justice, if you like. In a society that is not emerging from a history of terrible oppression, it would be wrong for such torturers to be able to exchange truth for freedom. But South Africa is aiming at arriving at a more normal political and legal order and it sees amnesty as essential if that aim is to be fulfilled. The deliberations in the Truth and Reconciliation Commission were primarily aimed at creating a situation where the country can go on, a situation in which society can *recover* from its past.[61]

Perhaps this came out most clearly in Winnie Madikizela Mandela's frustrating testimony, where she refused, against compelling testimony, to admit that she was involved in the killings of some young activists in her football club. When, in the end, Archbishop Tutu pleaded with her to at least say, in an entirely impersonal way, that 'things went badly wrong', the plea was not for anything like the whole truth, but for the merest scrap which would feed the nation's need to receive her back into the fold.[62]

Here, we see yet another example of how our values might conflict – in this instance the value of justice and the value of managing a workable transition from an evil political regime to a democratic one. In this kind of conflict, where the values about the transition are decided to be more important, truth might seem to take a back seat in inquiry. But this is only because a prior decision is taken about the right answer to the following questions: 'What should be done to enable South Africa to come to terms with its past?', 'What is best for the democratic future of South Africa?'

In addition, the values of justice here might also come into conflict with practicalities. Crushing economic problems and a shallow pool of skilled and competent administrators might, for instance, make a truth commission less keen on recommending a wholesale replacement of a tainted civil service.

Much of the discussion in this chapter has circled around the notion of political authority, without alighting on it. Institutions and politicians in any complex modern democracy will have the authority to make countless decisions on behalf of citizens. Not every decision can be made in the arena of public deliberation and not every citizen has the time, expertise, or inclination to deliberate on every issue. The idea of representation – the authority of some to make decisions for those they represent – runs deep in democratic systems of government and, given the size and complexity of modern democracies, it is hard to see how we might do without it. The ordinary citizen hopes to have her voice heard via her elected representative and so how we conceive of representation and how we try to make it work in practice is of the utmost importance.

Many of the elements of a pragmatist conception of authority or the delegation of decision-making should be transparent by now. On the view encouraged here, legitimacy of policy and decisions taken on behalf of others arises when the institutions promote deliberation and when the views of others have been taken seriously. As Warren (1996) argues, on behalf of the deliberative democrat, authority need not be thought of as a relinquishing of one's say or the surrendering of one's judgement. I might, for instance, identify with a group and delegate authority to its leaders. If I can challenge the reasons and justifications given by that decision-making body, if the judgement of the authority is subject to democratic challenge and public accountability, if the authority is committed to offering reasons for its decisions, then I can place my warranted trust in it.[63] Similarly, if I can be properly listened to and if justifications are given for the decisions made, I am bound by the authority of the likes of courts, administrative tribunals, and government decisions.

So authorities are, or could be, part of a dialogue amongst citizens. They can, of course, go wrong. We can find that we have misplaced our trust, that an authority is questionable. But the justifications for this suspicion will rest on the thought that the authority in question has failed to live up to its commitment to take the experiences of others seriously.

Conclusion

It is fitting to return, at the close of this examination of pragmatism and morals, to the principle which Peirce thought should 'be inscribed upon every wall of the city of philosophy: Do not block the path of inquiry' (CP 1.135). This motto strikes me as a worthy guide to philosophy, especially now that principles such as 'setting out the certain foundations for knowledge' seem to have had the wind taken out of their sails. Peirce insisted that a philosophical theory, if it is to be substantial, must have consequences for inquiry. And those consequences ought to promote the practice of inquiry, or at the very least, not place obstacles in its way.

What I hope to have shown is that there are some good reasons for thinking that we can make assertions or have genuine beliefs about what is right and wrong, just and unjust, cruel and kind; that we can inquire about the correctness of those beliefs; that our moral deliberations aim at the truth. And I hope to have shown that if we are to make sense of this, we must conduct ourselves via democratic principles – ones which encourage tolerance, openness, and understanding the experiences of others. By way of contrast, if our philosophical theory says that there is no truth to be had, then it is hard to see how we can satisfy ourselves that the reasons for being tolerant outweigh the reasons for, say, striving to eliminate the other in our midst. The same holds for a correspondence theory of truth, because it almost directly leads to the view that there is no truth about morals and politics. If truth is a matter of a statement's getting the physical world right, then how could we possibly think that statements about what is just and unjust might be true or false? I have not in this book spent a great deal of time on the independent epistemological arguments for pragmatism, but its comparative advantages ought nonetheless to be apparent. True to the phenomenology of morals and true to a democratic vision of inquiry, it gives us something to say to the Schmittian and to ourselves about why intolerance is wrong.

We have seen, however, that the pragmatist position ought to be a modest one. One call for modesty is on the inquirer, who must assume that there is a right answer to the question at hand, but not assume that he has the right answer in hand. The right answer, if there is one, is that which would be arrived at were inquiry to be pursued as far as it could fruitfully go. Thus, the inquirer must be modest also in that he ought to treat the experience of others as having, at least in the first instance, as much weight as his own experience.

The other call for modesty is on the philosopher, who must be content to specify only very general methodological principles, such as the requirement that experience be taken seriously. In the moral domain this principle can be expressed by the familiar thought that what we do in our moral lives is susceptible to the claims made on us by others. About more particular principles, the philosopher must remain agnostic. It is not up to the philosopher alone to say how moral and political deliberation should go.

Notice also that, although I have argued for a radical democracy in inquiry and although this has many practical implications, I have not argued for this or that brand of democracy. It would be immodest of the philosopher to say that she has alighted on the one social/political arrangement that is best. For we must expect that the kinds of democratic political arrangements will differ from place to place, because history, citizens, and neighbours will differ from place to place.

Moral and political theory, that is, should perceive itself as articulating how it is possible for inquirers, immersed as they are in the contingent contexts of their lives and circumstances, to work out for themselves the details about what is right and wrong. As inquirers we proceed as best we can in the situations in which we find ourselves and which we create for ourselves, guided by the thought that experience is the key to truth, knowledge, and objectivity. As Dewey stressed, the pragmatist must see morality and politics as problem-driven, and those problems will vary as social practices, systems of domination and oppression, the religious makeup of a population, and a host of other circumstances vary.

One of the tasks which does remain for the philosopher is to say how it is possible for moral and political judgement to aim at being rational and true. I have offered a picture of how this might be possible – of how we can aim at getting true judgements in a moral and political world which sets limits on that exercise.

So the kind of naturalism[1] I have recommended to the pragmatist is a kind which admonishes us to pay attention to actual inquiry, but which does not preclude aiming at truth and making judgements about what is rational. I hope to have shown that the pragmatist need not and should not seek a transcendental proof for either the pragmatic view of truth or the principles of inquiry which fall out of it. We have seen that the ability to justify principles and the ability to make judgements is not abandoned with the abandonment of certainty. We have good reasons for adopting those methodological principles and we have good reasons for criticising the likes of the crystal-ball reader, the national socialist, and the misogynist. Showing how such criticism is possible is another one of those remaining duties for epistemology and for moral theory, a duty which I have here tried to discharge.

Notes

1 The problem of justification

1 There are other, non-sceptical, routes to the neutrality principle, which will be discussed briefly in Chapter 3.

2 See Dyzenhaus (1996, 1997) for the label 'philosopher of fascism' and for details of Schmitt's view. The translations which follow are from Dyzenhaus (1997).

3 See Scheuerman (1998) for a discussion of this influence, especially on American conservatism.

4 There are other kinds of non-cognitivism, but the expressivist kind is the one which runs in tandem with the sceptical route to the neutrality thesis.

5 See Haack (1993, 1995: 188ff) for good discussions of Rorty's dichotomies.

6 (1989: 189), see also (1991a: 32ff.). For the need to be an actor, not a spectator, see (1998).

7 See Bernstein (1991: 238–9) for this point.

8 See, for instance, Young (1990: 104).

9 The 'or' here is not meant to be the or of equivalence – centering a life around rational debate is not the same as centering it around principles of rational choice.

10 See, for instance, Manin (1987: 348).

11 (1993: 13). I shall take a 'way of life' and a 'conception of the good' as being more or less the same as a comprehensive doctrine, despite the fact that the former may be far less precisely articulated and far less comprehensive than what Rawls has in mind. For unarticulated, unreflective, unsystematic lives can mirror an idea of the good. It is too easy to see the life of, for instance, the occasionally and casually employed recreational drug user, who mostly seems to just hang about, as not having a theory of what is valuable. But on the contrary, such people can speak volumes about what they take to be the valuelessness of the comfortable, boring, conventional ways of life which one tends to think of as being a comprehensive view of the good.

12 Rawls is in favour of neutrality of aim or intention, not of effect or consequence (1993: 193f). See Chapter 3 for discussion and criticism of this distinction.

13 (1993: 137). Rawls, however, rejects the label 'private' and prefers 'non-public' (1993: xix). See (1997: 767) for the statement that candidates for public office and their campaign managers, as well as judges and government officials, must not talk about values which are a part of their comprehensive doctrines.

14 See Raz (1994: 46) for this phrase and for criticism of Rawls' idea.

15 See Raz (1986) and Sher (1997: 84ff) for the argument that the values of unity and stability are asserted by Rawls, and for the general objection that *Political Liberalism* presupposes a comprehensive conception of the good.

16 Rawls (1993: 181n8).

17 Hampton (1993: 302–4) makes a similar point. Donald Ainslie has urged me to think that Rawls might have this to say to the Schmittian: it is an empirical fact that aiming at a homogeneous society leads only to bloodshed. Perhaps that would be Rawls' argument. See Chapter 3 for my own version of it.

18 He is most certainly alluding to Schmitt here. See the preface of the paperback edition of *Political Liberalism* for more talk of Schmitt.

19 I am indebted to Dyzenhaus (1996) for the argument that Rawls' position exemplifies the contradiction Schmitt thought all liberal views suffer from. Because free and equal citizens may well develop views which challenge political liberalism – illiberal views – Rawls is drawn into the battle of truth claims which political liberalism was designed to avoid.

20 This is, of course, a very big 'if' for Rawls.

21 For some anti-thought experimental thoughts, see Ackerman (1980: 327ff).

22 See Gambetta (1998) for this characterisation of bargaining.

23 But see (1997: 413), where he distances himself from this kind of justification.

24 Warren (1995) also discusses Habermas' idea that democratic participation, or participation in a deliberation aimed at mutual understanding, increases one's ability to reason and makes one more aware that mutual respect is required and that common interests are often shared with opponents. See also the papers in Elster (1998) and Christiano (1997) for a discussion of the good effects of deliberation.

25 Nino thinks that the value of democracy lies in the 'moralization of people's preferences'. Democracy and intersubjective discussion are justified because they are the most reliable way of getting knowledge about moral principles – of getting access to moral truth (1996: 107, 113). Nino identifies moral truth with impartiality – with 'impartial attention to the interests of everyone concerned' (113, 117). Then can he justify deliberation, for if we are going to faithfully represent the interests of others, we are better off entering into discussion with them, rather than trying to paternalistically guess at their interests. But no real argument is given for the identification of moral truth with impartiality; it is just taken for granted.

26 Habermas at times uses 'pragmatism' as a name for 'political realism', at times for Rorty's position, and at times to replace the 'performative' in 'performative contradiction'. But his view of validity/truth is so close to the Peircean view that my suggestion is that we can call it a pragmatic account of truth.

27 Most of that structure will go undescribed here. I focus on one strand of Habermas' position – the attempt to justify his brand of deliberative democracy. See Pensky (1995) for an excellent discussion of Habermas and his relationship to German history and politics.

28 See Akeel Bilgrami (1992) for talk of low profile views.

29 See [1973](1980): 255ff. Habermas hinted at the point in (1973).

30 These are Apel's words. See Apel (1990: 24) and Habermas (1990c: 79–80).

31 See (1996), Chapter 3.

32 For the distinction in Habermas, see (1995: 97) and (1990c: 108). For other objections see Benhabib (1992: 40, 68ff). To use Habermas' terminology, the upshot of such objections, including my own, is that we should extend the reach of communicative ethics from the moral to the ethical.

33 Kant's own transcendental argument was to uncover the preconditions of self-consciousness or experience.

34 For an explicit statement that the justification covers the very consensus account of truth, see Apel (1990: 41–7).

35 Apel (1990: 42), see also Habermas, (1990c: 79).

36 It even fails to arise in: 'my arguments are convincing, but I don't expect to convince anyone'. The tension only arises in: 'my arguments are convincing, but I don't think anyone else ought to accept them'.

37 See (1990c: 58). At least, the only influence is the force of better argument.

38 (1990c: 100). If the claim is that he cannot deny these things because he refuses to deny (or assert) anything, then we do not have an argument *in favour* of these things. He also cannot deny that he is a pastrami sandwich, but that does not make him a pastrami sandwich. Despite the wording of the argument, Habermas must mean that it is just a fact that the sceptic is in these circumstances, whether he denies it or asserts it or says nothing.

39 See, for instance, (1990c: 102), (1990d: 199).

40 Tugendhat also cannot understand how Habermas can simply define communicative action so that it rules out so much communication. Habermas, for instance, has a 'curious attitude toward lying', in that, on his definition, it is not a communicative action. See Tugendhat (1992: 437). Michelman (1997: 162–3) also argues that Habermas' claims about communication can be and in fact are contested.

41 At times Habermas seems to suggest merely that communicative action plays an important role in human life. This does not lead to the conclusion that it is impossible for a human being to depart occasionally from communicative action, but perhaps only that it is impossible to dispense for good with it. Pablo DeGreiff set me straight on this point. But notice that the weaker conclusion will not get Habermas what he needs – something strong to say against the likes of the Nazi. For, in William James' terminology, National Socialism might be construed as a brief moral, or in this case, communicative 'holiday'.

42 Though there is, of course, no such recommendation in Habermas' work, to exclude them cognitively from the human community can lead too easily to treating them as less than human.

43 Thus Tugendhat (1992: 436) is right to identify a central tension running through Habermas' work: he wants to offer both a (fallible, empirical) structural analysis of language and a (quasi-transcendental) account of language in the interest of a certain social attitude or value.

44 See Korsgaard (1996) for another of these attempts.

45 Habermas takes the fallibilist to be the enemy sceptic – the one who says that our moral judgements are fallible and hence not valid or invalid (see 1990c: 80ff). This is an odd use of 'fallibilism' and clearly the Peircean variety does not make the above inference.

46 See (1982: 173f) and (1991a: 164ff).

2 Truth, inquiry, and experience

1 See Brent (1993: 31, 61).

2 He says: 'But what else, when one considers it, can our "truth" ever amount to, other than the way in which people would come to think if research were carried sufficiently far? That would seem to be all that our truth ever can be. So good morals are the kind of human behavior that would come to be approved if studies of right behavior were carried sufficiently far' (MS 673, p. 12, see also CP 5.566).

3 Sometimes in (1991), I expressed the pragmatic account of truth in the unhelpful way. This was partly because I was trying to address the standard objections to pragmatism and partly because I did not see just how resolutely one should stick to the better formulation.

4 For an extended argument along these lines, see Misak (1992).

5 See James ([1907](1992): 100) and Misak (1994b) for discussion.

6   Misak (1995), especially pp. 97–127, 152–62, 171–8.
7   For the idea that belief involves the commitment to fact, reality and truth, See Wiggins (1998). See also Haack (1995: 199ff, 1998). There will of course be nuances here – for instance we aim at interesting truth, not at trivial truth.
8   Wiggins (1991b: 148), see Peacocke (1992: 203) for a similar thought.
9   MS 329: 12.
10 Dewey ([1908](1977): 131–2. Dewey sometimes argued that we should carry out the method of science in other areas of inquiry but, as Richardson (1998) argues, Dewey wavered on this point.
11 Or a sentence or a statement. I take the bearers of truth-values to be the contents of beliefs or claims, but will sometimes drop 'the belief that' or 'the claim that'. And, given the holistic nature of justification, inquiry into p will involve inquiry into many other issues.
12 CE 2, 239. This is not unlike McDowell's (1985) account of objectivity, where to be objective is to be independent of any particular experience, but not independent of all experience. Values are values to a sensibility like ours.
13 See Misak (1991) for more on Peirce on definition and signs. Commitment accounts of content have also been recently articulated in Peacocke (1986) and Brandom (1994). For the argument that Peacocke puts too much of a burden on commitments to hold other beliefs and to make inferences, as opposed to the commitment to say what would be the case in the world were the belief true, see Misak (1995: 178–93). I would argue similarly against Brandom.
14 CE2, 483, CE3, 108, CP 5.2, 5.196. This phrase is close to one of James', but his considered formulation of the pragmatic maxim is inferior to Peirce's. See Misak (1994b).
15 We must also not ignore the other aspects, as they help us make sense of meanings over time. Some issues, especially moral ones, will cease to be relevant, or even understandable, as the context in which they are situated changes. If we want to speak of a belief being true or false in 1935 – 'Hitler's dislike of Jews is morally repugnant' or 'Paul Wittgenstein has lost his right arm' – then we need to assume that the meanings of statements are constant. On Peirce's theory of signs, meaning is not entirely fixed by conceptual role or by the sorts of inferences the belief gets caught up in, but also by denotation and connotation. Indeed, the pragmatic aspect of meaning has it that meaning is fixed by the practical, inferential, and *empirical* consequences of the belief. This, of course, is just the beginning of a long answer to how meaning is fixed.
16 Notice that a true belief may be believed, on good grounds, then doubted, on good grounds, then believed again. A true belief is one that *would be* found to be best, were inquiry to be pursued as far as it could fruitfully go.
17 Thus, as Marion David (1994: 66) notes, it does not seem possible to express the DS in ordinary terms; it does not seem possible to elucidate it. Horwich says that the disquotationalist theory of truth can't be written down or fully articulated, for it has an infinite number of axioms (1990: 31). This is the theory's 'single unattractive feature' (1990: 42). We might import a thought of Sellars' (1962: 33) here and think that disquotationalism is more like a telephone directory than a theory.
18 See Ellis (1990) and Craig (1990) for other positions which stress the value of truth and knowledge in the lives of inquirers.
19 See Richardson (1998) for this way of putting the point.
20 Horwich (1990: 2, 37), see also Soames (1984), Field (1986).
21 Sellars (1962: 29). He also makes the point about the coherentist.
22 Of course, the nature of the metaphysical is also a matter of controversy. I take a metaphysical concept to be one which pretends to transcend all possible experi-

ence. See my (1995) for a sustained discussion. Horwich is never clear what he means by 'metaphysical'.

23 See Ellis (1990), Davidson (1996: 274ff), and Jackson, Oppy and Smith (1994: 294–5) for similar sorts of argument. It must be said here that the disquotationalist does think that he can make sense of inquiry. Horwich, for instance, thinks that disquotationalism explains why we aim at truth. True beliefs are beneficial: if one's beliefs include beliefs of the sort 'If I perform action A then state of affairs S will be realized', then I can make the required inferences that will get me what I want, all within the structure of the disquotationalist theory (1990: 22–4, 44–6). The pragmatist will argue here that the aims of inquiry are not purely instrumental. Wanting to satisfy our desires is not the only reason we want the truth.

24 The pragmatist's suggestion is not that one can have a pure disquotational theory of truth at the same time as having a robust theory of truth. Boghossian (1990: 165) must be right that that is not on. Rather the suggestion is that one start with the disquotational thought and then move on to a more substantial, but non-metaphysical theory. And to say that the pragmatist can absorb the disquotational definition of truth is not to suggest that the disquotationalist and the pragmatist can be happy partners. For one thing, many a disquotationalist will think that a theory of truth must be a theory of sentence truth, whereas the pragmatist thinks that truth-values attach to beliefs or assertions. And the disquotationalist will find the pragmatist's willingness to put into question certain principles of logic well beyond the pale.

25 Both Horwich and Wright call their position 'minimalist'. To avoid confusion, I call Horwich's view 'disquotationalism' of the classical or pure kind, and reserve 'minimalism' for Wright's view.

26 Wright takes the disquotationalist to think that truth *must* be merely good assertion. He then argues that truth cannot be so, that the extensions of the two concepts might well diverge (1992: 19, 49, 71). But the disquotationalist will want nothing to do with the claim imputed to her, thinking it a misinterpretation of the DS.

27 His remarks are also directed against Putnam. See Misak (1992) for a similar objection to Putnam's pragmatism.

28 I thank Mary Leng for putting the point this way. And, of course, inquiry into a particular issue will lead to many others.

29 (1992: 38). In (1996a: 920n.9), Wright does not foreclose on the possibility that superassertibility holds everywhere – or at least for every minimally truth-apt discourse. If it turned out that Wright held the global thesis, one would have to see him straightforwardly as a pragmatist. The global thesis, however, seems to be in tension with the direction of argument in (1992).

30 (1992: 29, 204). Not all discourses meet the minimal requirements. Wright thinks that Wittgenstein's point about a private language – for instance, one which is supposed to record sensations – is that it is not disciplined (1992: 141).

31 (1992: 142, 174). This is a striking claim, as it is often held that disquotationalism captures (without talking about spurious facts, states of affairs, and the like) the thought at the heart of the correspondence theory.

32 (1992: 90ff, 175, 222). Another is to show that the discourse is such that we detect matters rather than matters being dependent on how we judge them. Another is to show that appeals to facts have a wide explanatory role; that the subject matter of the discourse figures in the explanations of other things.

33 Blackburn (1989) also makes this suggestion. We have seen, and shall continue to see, that moral knowledge need not take as its model scientific inquiry – it need not see itself as always trying to ascertain whether a hypothesis is true or false. In morals, we may want – as a part of getting the best belief about what is right or wrong, just or unjust – greater self-understanding, greater maturity, etc. Because

these aims are a part of seeking the best belief, bivalence still holds as a regulative assumption. It is still assumed that there is a belief which would be best.

34 Similarly, where the evidence is misleading or is caused in the wrong way, we can invoke the above conditional to make sense of the thought that the true belief is not the one we happen to get stuck with, but the one which would be best, were inquiry to proceed smoothly. This way of coping with statements about the remote past is an improvement on my treatment in (1991), where I focused exclusively on the idea of bivalence being a regulative assumption.

35 Given the connection between bivalence and the law of excluded middle, we must then say that logic here is not classical. However, it would be more than a little odd to try to suggest that, for these discourses, excluded middle is not a logical law, while in others it is. Perhaps the pragmatist here can reject, *tout court*, excluded middle as a logical law (and adopt an institutionist logic), but then reinstate it in most discourses as a theorem. So in most areas of inquiry – in most of our inferences – we could use excluded middle. With respect to conditionals with antecedents from one discourse and consequents from another, we could not use it. Joe Heath suggested this line of argument to me.

36 That refusal is important, for if it is not made, the disquotationalist has plenty of resources with which to render '*x* tastes good' bivalent. Notice also that the pragmatist might think that a discourse about the objective tastiness of non-edible stuff has sufficient discipline to be truth-apt. 'Petrol tastes good' might well have a truth-value.

37 And see the above note regarding the costs for classical logic.

38 Notice that both the pragmatist and the disquotationalist give reasons for revising the thought that we aim at correspondence to mind-independent states of affairs.

39 Horwich (1993: 73), see also Field (1986), (1994b).

40 What Horwich argues is that a moral statement is assertible just if someone thinks it assertible. But when such a statement is slotted into the *DS*, truth comes into the picture.

41 Brandom also argues that when we believe *p*, we commit ourselves to giving reasons. But he seems to not take this commitment to be a constitutive norm of belief or assertion, for he suggests that 'bare assertion' need not come with reasons. One can just think that people with beards are dangerous and be unprepared to give any grounds for this belief (1994: 228–30). He does, however, think that the practice of bare assertion is parasitic on the practice of assertion with commitment to give reasons. My point is a little more exacting. A belief, in order to be a belief, must come with a commitment to give reasons.

42 We can think of this as what is right in verificationism. Nothing in this thought rides on how the term 'verificationism' has often been used. The point could be made just as well by Brandom (1994): beliefs are things that stand as and stand in need of reasons. They are keyed to reasons and reasons count as experience in the extremely broad sense to be explained below. See also Misak (1995) and (1996).

43 See also Wiggins (1991a: 344). This is not to say that a non-cognitivist who says that reasons are not what drives moral judgement is not a genuine believer. It is an argument for why they should see that they are in fact committed to some kind of cognitivism.

44 This nice turn of phrase is Emmet's (1994: 186).

45 For the idea that thought experiments can be a source of compulsion, see CP 3.363, 4.233. Peirce developed a (quantified) deductive logic based on what he called 'existential graphs'.

46 And, of course, there are additional considerations which speak in favour of valuing beliefs that will not be overturned by experience. One might argue that

there is a biological basis for our valuing beliefs which would be forever reliable – that as a species, we have survived because of it.

47 It is of course difficult to say how beliefs might be justified by experience if experience is taken to be something that is 'given'. As Neurath, Popper, and Davidson have argued, only beliefs can stand in justificatory relationships with beliefs. This is not a problem for the account of perception upon which I rely, for it holds that nothing is given to us prior to conceptualisation. For elaboration and for how this view is compatible with the thought that there is a cognition-independent reality, see Misak (1991: 70–9, 126–37).

48 His official view is that he is a disquotationalist about truth, but, as we shall see below, I take him to be committed to some kind of pragmatism. Quine of course is a physicalist and this is the reason he ignores moral judgements. My point is that his physicalism is merely tacked on to his holism.

49 The distinction I wish to undercut is the distinction between (i) judgements which we might inquire into which are responsive to evidence and (ii) judgements which we might inquire into which are not responsive to evidence. That is, it is a distinction drawn within the class of judgements which are the objects of serious investigation. Inquirers should not take (ii) to be a real possibility. This position might well be compatible with a distinction between judgements which are the objects of inquiry and what Putnam (1962) calls single criterion words and corresponding truths such as 'all bachelors are unmarried', which are not the objects of inquiry. See also Wiggins (1994).

50 At least, nothing could serve as evidence that would not also serve as evidence for a more usual hypothesis. And the usual hypothesis has behind it the weight of being the product of our actual inquiries. See Misak (1991: 91–8).

51 See Quine (1990: 12–13, 1975: 80).

52 Quine has not always insisted upon this. His early characterisation of observation is probably broad enough for the pragmatist: 'A sentence is observational insofar as its truth-value, on any occasion, would be agreed to by just about any member of the speech community witnessing the occasion.' (Quine 1974: 39) '2 + 2 = 4' and 'That's beautiful' might be construed as observational on this definition. Later, however, Quine insists that the assent must be prompted by the stimulation of sensory receptors. See (1990: 3).

53 Here is one of the countless differences one might find between kinds of inquiry, which I owe to Alex Oliver. If the inquiry is one in logic, then the move to p from q and $(p \rightarrow q)$ is illicit – it is the fallacy of affirming the consequent. But in scientific inquiry, the move has its place – it is called inference to the best explanation or abductive inference and making it is a sign of creativity. So I think that I can handle Wiggins' worry that my view might discourage us from attending to the differences between moral and empirical inquiry. See Wiggins (1996b: 277).

54 See, for example Levi (1998) and Hookway (1998).

55 See Wiggins (1996a: 278–9). Wright (1992: 101) shows how this is true of the comic – the unintended spoonerisms and muffed anecdotes of the pompous after-dinner speaker are not funny if you know that he is distracted by the fact that his child is seriously ill. Judgements about what is funny might well not be truth-apt – one's sense of humour is less subject to discipline, less subject to judgements of correctness and incorrectness, than one's moral sense.

56 See Jardine (1995: 41f), for the argument that the difference between science and ethics here is not as striking as it first appears. Wright thinks that it is both striking and significant.

57 Hacking (1999).

58 This view might be thought to lead to a kind of moral colonialism – since others cannot see what is there to be seen, 'we' needn't take their judgements seriously.

But on the view of truth offered here, the contrary judgements of others *must* be taken seriously.

59 See Williams (1998: 145ff) for a summary of some of the sociological data here and for the conclusion that minorities must be present in legislatures.

60 See Baker (1998) for this kind of point.

61 Railton (1996a: 74) argues, in a spirit similar to that of the view I set out here, that a moral judgement is true if it would be approved by people in general under conditions of full information, impartiality and the like. 'Full information' and 'impartiality', he says, are vague and indeterminate – under one resolution *p* would be true, under another, *p* would be false. Railton sees no great problem here, for vagueness and indeterminacy are features of all our beliefs. 'There is milk in the fridge' is true if you count the old spill, false if you do not.

62 Of course, good novelists and good novels needn't be moral. But even when a character or a theme in a novel exemplifies an evil, it can get us thinking – it can prompt moral reflection.

63 The point also deals with objections which ask what the pragmatist says about the possibility of a nuclear holocaust or mass hypnosis, freezing, as it were, a set of beliefs. Are those beliefs true just because they in fact will not be improved upon? The pragmatist says that, in such cases, the antecedent of the subjunctive conditional 'were inquiry to be pursued as far as it could fruitfully go, *p* would be agreed upon' would not be fulfilled. That makes no difference to the truth-value of the conditional.

64 See the papers in Bohman and Rehg (1997) for how this thought is often present in contemporary deliberative democracy theorists.

65 Heath takes this point from Melvin Pollner's (1987) study of legal argument. Pollner also suggests that whether or not a person is guilty is assumed to be an objective matter.

3 Moral deliberation

1 My argument is not based on Wittgenstein's considerations against private language, although it has some affinities with that argument. See Misak (1995) for a discussion of Wittgenstein and the broad verificationist criterion which I advocate. See Korsgaard (1996) for a Wittgensteinian attempt at showing how objectivity and reason are public.

2 See Cohen (1989: 27) for an articulation of this problem and Iris Marion Young (1993b, 1995) for the argument that deliberative democracy is so biased.

3 It is not, however, *central* to the pragmatist position that it reject the neutrality principle – the principle that the state should not encourage or discourage conceptions of the good. That rejection is something I recommend to the pragmatist, but declining to adopt my recommendation would not serve to make the position recognisably non-pragmatist.

4 Iris Marion Young has been a champion of this thought. See, for instance (1990: 96ff).

5 See Wiggins (1976: 108) for this way of putting the point.

6 See Dulamge v. Ontario (Police Complaints Commissioner) (1994) 21 O.R. (3d) 356 (Div. Ct.). See S.(R.D.) (1997), 118 C.C.C. (3d) 353 for a case in which a charge of bias was made against a judge who noted that police officers sometimes over-react with non-white suspects.

7 See Ackerman (1980: 11) for the argument from autonomy, see Dworkin (1978, 1983: 2ff) for the argument from equality.

8 See Williams (1998: 182ff) for an excellent summary of how stereotypes are often internalised.

9 Kymlicka, however, has been a defender of neutrality (1989) and he does not set his argument specifically against the neutrality thesis. But in *Multicultural Citizenship*, where the argument appears, he drops talk of neutrality in favour of talk of tolerance, something the pragmatist is happy with.

10 See Sher (1997) for this point and an excellent discussion of non-neutral practices.

11 See his (1989: 883ff), where he takes the distinction from Raz (1986: 17). Rawls joins in the support of justificatory neutrality, or neutrality of aim, as opposed to consequential neutrality, or neutrality of effect (1993: 193f).

12 Sher (1997: 66f) argues against the consequential/justificatory distinction as follows, *a propos* the argument for neutrality from autonomy. If any political arrangement has the consequence of shaping preferences, and thereby of interfering with autonomous choice, a government will not further diminish autonomy if it *intends* to have these effects.

13 It might be thought that the positions which are criticisable on the pragmatist view might be by and large the same positions that would be ruled out by the harm principle of neutrality theorists – the state must be neutral, except with respect to those comprehensive doctrines which can be demonstrated to harm others. But the two groups might well not be coextensive. The restriction of pornography, for instance, is something which the harm principle seems not to have spoken against. But the pragmatist might well initiate the argument that pornography degrades women and thus ought to be prohibited. See Dyzenhaus (1994) for a discussion of this issue.

14 We have seen it argued by Cohen and others that deliberation has the capacity to transform people's preferences for the better. Note that these claims about what moral inquiry can do make little sense if we are not to aim at articulating which conceptions of the good are better than others.

15 Kymlicka (1989: 899f) seems to take state perfectionism to be the alternative to neutrality. I have argued that this is too severe a dichotomy. Indeed, most perfectionists these days will not try to rank ways of life, but will think that a plurality of ways are good. See Hurka (1995) and Sher (1997: 120).

16 (1989: 5–8). We have seen that Habermas articulates a similar view.

17 See Phillips (1993), Baker (1998) and Williams (1998) for the argument that fair representation of disadvantaged groups requires their actual presence in elected assemblies.

18 See Scheurerman (1998) for a discussion of Arendt and Schmitt. Benhabib makes it clear that there are other strains, in tension with this thought, in Arendt's work (Benhabib 1992: 91–4).

19 See Benhabib (1992: 111) and many of the essays in Meehan (1995).

20 See McNaughton (1988) Dancy (1983, 1993) and Bakhurst (1998) for defences of particularism, not always radical.

21 See, for instance, Kritz (1995, vol.1), especially 'Distinguishing Between Transitions: How Circumstances Shape the Available Outcomes'.

22 See Richardson (1995: 111) for the idea that this is what such moral frameworks (mistakenly) aspire to.

23 Hume [1777](1985): 169–70. There is, I think, a Humean root to the kind of position I want to defend (see Misak 1995: 817).

24 See Bakhurst (1998) for a good discussion of this issue with respect to particularism.

25 Dewey [1909](1977): 13.

26 See Bakhurst (1998) for a discussion of how the pragmatist can retain this kind of categorical moral judgement.

27 See Larmore (1987) and (1996) for excellent discussions of these issues.

28 See Lukes (1991: 5f) and Meyerson (1997) for more on this.

29 See Thomas Christiano (1997: 266–67) for this point.

30 See Shapiro (1996: 121) for this way of putting the point. He seems to rush to the other extreme in suggesting that agreement is not a good thing at all – it masks cultish following, strategic behaviour, ignorance, etc.

31 See Christiano (1997: 249) for this point.

32 Wiggins, in various places, has been a champion of this point.

33 See MacIntyre (1981), Taylor (1985), and Sandel (1982) for non-Schmittian communtarian views. Schmitt embraces the communitarian idea that the good is identifiable only within a community and adds that communities other than one's own should be characterised as the enemy.

34 See Michelle Moody-Adams (1997) for an argument, rooted in the anthropological literature, against the idea that different cultures must be seen as having radically different moral systems. Indeed, one may even argue, with Jonathan Lear (1984: 165f), that it has only been relatively recently that we have shifted from the *hope* that we all belong to one community to the *fact* that we all belong to one community. Morality's presenting itself as universal may have in the past been more of an aspiration. But in the present historical period, when societies are pushed together by technological advances and economic and political developments, it has become true.

35 See *The Guardian Weekly* (this piece from the *Washington Post*), February 8, 1998, p. 17.

36 I owe this example to Henry Richardson.

37 This was said by the then Premier of Quebec, Jacques Parizeau. See *The Global and Mail*, October 31, 1995.

38 Since the community I am interested in here is the community of inquirers, or believers, or truth-seekers, animals are left on the sidelines when it comes to deliberation and justification. They are not required to take seriously the experiences of others because they are not making judgements. But of course, we think that there are plenty of first-order reasons to consider their experiences in our moral debates – about whether to eat them, experiment on them, etc.

39 Feminist philosophers have of course brought home this point – to name just a few, see Benhabib (1995) and Noddings (1984). This is not to suggest that women's experience is homogenous, that there is a single woman's voice. See Anzuldua (1990), Moraga and Anzuldua (1983), hooks (1984) and Hill Collins (1990) for the argument against taking women's experience to be uniform.

40 See Williams (1998: 203ff) for an excellent discussion of the range of institutional remedies.

41 Baker (1998). See also Knight and Johnson (1997) and Bohman (1996: 100ff) for discussions of deliberative democracy and equality of influence. Bohman argues, like Baker, that if members of a minority believe that their views are never a recognisable part of the outcome of deliberation, they may no longer be willing to cooperate in political problem-solving. Continued cooperation depends on every deliberator having confidence that he or she will sometimes favourably influence deliberation. And such cooperation is the aim of deliberation on Bohman's account of deliberative democracy.

42 See Charles Taylor (1997), who argues that the unity of a life balances the diversity of values and Wiggins (1991: 126) for the thought that our freedom is located in making underdetermined choices. I do not mean to suggest that we try to ground morality in an individual's identity or in the conception she has of herself. It seems that Korsgaard (1996) attempts to do this.

43 I owe this example and the idea of levels of moral failure, which I use below, to discussion with Joe Carens.

44 See Bernard Williams (1973: 98–100, 175) for the setting of the problem.

45 Blackburn, on this note, (1996: 96) suggests that certain of the ancient sceptics were right when it comes to ethics – often we will see that the weight of opposing

arguments are in balance and we are well advised to suspend judgement and bask in the resulting tranquility. On the pragmatist view offered here, however, this situation does not necessarily result in tranquility or cognitive ease. We might think that there is no right answer, we might learn what we can about ourselves and others, but we might still be unhappy about the fact that we could not reach agreement.

46 See William Styron's *Sophie's Choice* for a vivid portrayal of one such choice.

47 This nice term is Hillel Steiner's (1996), but he does not use it to refer to truth-value gaps.

48 (1996: 60). My view has affinities with Railton's 'idealized subjectivism'.

49 See Gutmann and Thompson (1996: 21f) for the point about Hume, and Calabresi and Bobbitt (1978) for the view that the scarcity of resources is at the bottom of tragic choices.

50 This thought crops up frequently in the volume on deliberative democracy recently edited by James Bohman and William Rehg (1997). Gaus (1997) levels the complaint against deliberative democrats that an actual consensus in a pluralistic society is not possible.

51 As I've tried to show, finding a true belief in the moral domain will often be a matter of balancing the human need to belong – to share a past, language and set of values with others – with abstract principle.

52 See Anderson (1993) and Taylor (1997) for more on this view of what animates our theory of value. Festenstein (1997) sees Dewey as an early exponent of the view.

53 See Bakhurst (1998) for this thought.

54 I owe this example to a conversation with Andrew Kernohan.

55 See Dyzenhaus (1998) for discussion and details.

56 This was an issue with Heidegger as well. See Dyzenhaus (1997).

57 Peirce stressed this point, sometimes too much, so that he often said that in 'vital matters', one must not try to determine the truth, but go on immediate instinct.

58 See Williams (1985: 148, 167–9) and Richardson (1994: 5) on this point and more generally, on when it is appropriate to deliberate.

59 I owe this example to Jerry Gaus.

60 Kymlicka (1995: 164–6). See Tan (1998) for an excellent discussion of this point with respect to Rawls' Law of Peoples.

61 See Bronkhorst (1995) for an excellent discussion of the aims of such commissions.

62 See *The Weekly Mail* December 1997.

63 See Williams (1998) for an excellent discussion of how trust operates in representation.

Conclusion

1 I do not use the term 'naturalism' to mean 'a part of science'. With McDowell (1994, 1995), I take the natural to be a broader category, one which includes our moral sensibilities and other conceptual capacities. By 'naturalism', I mean to signal that we should start in epistemology with our actual practices and beliefs.

Bibliography

Abrams, K. (1988) '"Raising Politics Up": Minority Political Participation and Section 2 of the Voting Rights Act', *New York University Law Review*, 63, 3.

Ackerman, Bruce (1980) *Social Justice in the Liberal State*, New Haven: Yale University Press.

—— (1989) 'Why Dialogue?', *Journal of Philosophy*, lxxxvi.

Ainslie, Donald (forthcoming) 'Questioning Bioethics: AIDS, Sexual Ethics, and the Duty to Warn', *Hastings Centre Report*, Garrison, New York: Hastings Centre.

Anderson, Elizabeth (1991) 'John Stuart Mill and Experiments in Living', *Ethics*, 102, 1.

—— (1993) *Value in Ethics and Economics*, Cambridge, Mass.: Harvard University Press.

Anzuldua, Gloria (1990) *Making Face, Making Soul*, San Francisco: Aunt Lute Foundation Books.

Apel, Karl-Otto [1973](1980) 'The *a priori* of the Communication Community and the Foundations of Ethics: The Problem of a Rational Foundation of Ethics in the Scientific Age', in *Towards a Transformation of Philosophy*, trans. G. Adey and D. Frisby, London: Routledge and Kegan Paul.

—— (1990) 'Is the Ethics of the Ideal Communication Community a Utopia? On the Relationship between Ethics, Utopia, and the Critique of Utopia', in S. Benhabib and F. Dallmayr (eds) *The Communicative Ethics Controversy*, Cambridge, Mass.: The MIT Press.

Arendt, Hannah (1958) *The Human Condition*, Chicago: Chicago University Press.

Baker, Judith (1998) 'Democratic Deliberations, Equality of Influence, and Pragmatism', in C. Misak (ed.) *Pragmatism, Canadian Journal of Philosophy*, supplementary volume.

Bakhurst, David (1998) 'Pragmatism and Moral Knowledge', in C. Misak (ed.) *Pragmatism, Canadian Journal of Philosophy*, supplementary volume.

Barcan-Marcus, Ruth (1980) 'Moral Dilemmas and Consistency', *Journal of Philosophy*, lxxvii, 3.

Benhabib, Selya (1989) 'Liberal Dialogue versus a Critical Theory of Discursive Legitimation in *Liberalism and the Moral Life*', ed. Nancy L. Rosenblum, Cambridge, Mass.: Harvard University Press.

—— (1992) *Situating the Self*, New York: Routledge.

—— (1994) 'Deliberative Rationality and Models of Democratic Legitimacy', *Constellations*, 1.

—— (1995) 'The Debate over Women and Moral Theory Revisited', in Johanna Meehan (ed.) *Feminists Read Habermas*, London: Routledge.

Berlin, Isaiah (1991) *The Crooked Timber of Humanity*, New York: Knopf.

Bernstein, Richard, J. (1991) *The New Constellation: The Ethical-Political Horizon of Modernity/Postmodernity*, Cambridge, Mass.: Polity Press.

Bilgrami, Akeel (1992) *Belief and Meaning*, Oxford: Basil Blackwell.

Blackburn, Simon (1989) 'Manifesting Realism', in P. French *et al.* (ed.), *Midwest Studies in Philosophy*, 10, Minneapolis: University of Minnesota Press.

—— (1993) 'Truth, Realism and the Regulation of Theory', in *Essays in Quasi-Realism*, Oxford: Oxford University Press.

—— (1996) 'Securing the Nots', in W. Sinnott-Armstrong and M. Timmons (eds) *Moral Knowledge? New Readings in Moral Epistemology*, Oxford: Oxford University Press.

—— (1998) *Ruling Passions*, Oxford: Oxford University Press.

Boghossian, Paul (1990) 'The Status of Content', *The Philosophical Review*, 99.

Bohman, James (1996) *Public Deliberation: Pluralism, Complexity, and Democracy*, Cambridge, Mass.: MIT Press.

Bohman, J. and Rehg, W. (eds) (1997) *Deliberative Democracy: Essays on Reason and Politics*, Cambridge, Mass.: MIT Press.

Borradori, G. (1994) *The American Philosopher: Conversations with Quine, Davidson, Putnam, Nozick, Danto, Rorty, Cavell, MacIntyre, and Kuhn*, trans. R. Crocitto, Chicago: University of Chicago Press.

Brandom, Robert (1994) *Making It Explicit*, Cambridge, Mass.: Harvard University Press.

Brent, Joseph (1993) *Charles Sanders Peirce: A Life*, Bloomington and Indianapolis: Indiana University Press.

Brint, M. and Weaver, W. (eds) (1991) *Pragmatism in Law and Society*, Boulder, Col.: Westview Press.

Bronkhorst, Daan (1995) *Truth and Reconciliation: Obstacles and Opportunites for Human Rights*, Amsterdam: Amnesty International.

Brook, Richard (1991) 'Agency and Morality', *Journal of Philosophy*, 88.

Calabresi, Guido and Bobbitt, Philip (1978) *Tragic Choices*, New York: W.W. Norton.

Christiano, Thomas (1997) 'The Significance of Public Deliberation', in J. Bohman and W. Rehg (eds) *Deliberative Democracy*, Cambridge, Mass.: MIT Press.

Cohen, Jean (1993) 'Moral Pluralism and Political Consensus', in D. Copp, J. Hampton, and J. Roemer (eds) *The Idea of Democracy*, Cambridge: Cambridge University Press.

Cohen, Joshua (1986) 'An Epistemic Conception of Democracy', *Ethics*, 97.

—— (1989) 'Deliberation and Democratic Legitimacy', in A. Hamlin and P. Pettit (eds) *The Good Polity*, Oxford: Blackwell.

—— (1993) 'Moral Pluralism and Political Consensus', in D. Copp *et al.* (eds) *The Ideal of Democracy*, Cambridge, Mass.: Cambridge University Press.

—— (1997) 'Procedure and Substance in Deliberative Democracy', in J. Bohman and W. Rehg (eds) *Deliberative Democracy*, Cambridge, Mass.: MIT Press.

—— (1998) 'Democracy and Liberty', in Jon Elster (ed.) *Deliberative Democracy*, Cambridge: Cambridge University Press.

Craig, Edward (1990) *Knowledge and the State of Nature*, Oxford: Oxford University Press.

Dancy, Johnathan (1981) 'On Moral Properties', *Mind*, xc.
—— (1983) 'Ethical Particularism and Morally Relevant Properties', *Mind*, xcii.
—— (1993) *Moral Reasons*, Oxford: Basil Blackwell.
David, Marian (1994) *Correspondence and Disquotation*, Oxford: Oxford University Press.
Davidson, Donald (1974) 'On the Very Idea of a Conceptual Scheme', *Proceedings and Addresses of the American Philosophical Association*, 47.
—— (1983) 'A Coherence Theory of Truth and Knowledge', in D. Henrich (ed.) *Kant oder Hegel?*, Stuttgart: Klett-Cotta.
—— (1996) 'The Folly of Trying to Define Truth', *The Journal of Philosophy*, 93.
Dewey, John (1976) *The Moral Writings of John Dewey*, ed. James Gouinlock, New York: Macmillan.
—— [1908](1977) 'Does Reality Possess Practical Character?', in Jo Ann Boydston (ed.) *John Dewey: The Middle Works, 1899–1924*, vol. 4, Carbondale and Edwardsville: Southern Illinois University Press.
—— [1909](1977) 'The Influence of Darwinism in Philosophy', in Jo Ann Boydston (ed.) *John Dewey: The Middle Works, 1899–1924*, vol. 4, Carbondale and Edwardsville: Southern Illinois University Press.
—— (1984) 'The Public and its Problems', in Jo Ann Boydston (ed.) *John Dewey: The Later Works, 1925–1953*, vol. 2, Carbondale and Edwardsville: Southern Illinois University Press.
Dryzek, John (1990) *Discursive Democracy: Politics, Policy, and Political Science*, Cambridge: Cambridge University Press.
Dworkin, Ronald (1978) 'Liberalism', in S. Hampshire (ed.) *Public and Private Morality*, Cambridge: Cambridge University Press.
—— (1983) 'Neutrality, Equality, and Liberalism', in D. MacLean and C. Mills (eds) *Liberalism Reconsidered*, Totowa, NJ: Rowman and Allanheld.
—— (1985) *A Matter of Principle*, Cambridge, Mass.: Harvard University Press.
—— (1989) 'Liberal Community', *California Law Review*, 77, 3.
Dyzenhaus, David (1994) 'Pornography and Public Reason', *Canadian Journal of Law and Jurisprudence*, 7.
—— (1996) 'Liberalism after the Fall: Schmitt, Rawls and the Problem of Justification', *Philosophy and Social Criticism*, 22.
—— (1997) *Legality and Legitimacy: Carl Schmitt, Hans Kelsen and Hermann Heller in Weimar*, Oxford: Clarendon Press.
—— (1998) *Judging the Judges, Judging Ourselves: Truth, Reconciliation and the Apartheid Legal Order*, Oxford: Hart.
Ellis, Brian (1990) *Truth and Objectivity*, Oxford: Basil Blackwell.
Elster, Jon (1998) *Deliberative Democracy*, Cambridge: Cambridge University Press.
Emmet, Dorothy (1994) *The Role of the Unrealisable*, London: Macmillan.
Estlund, David (1992) 'Making Truth Safe for Democracy', in D. Copp *et al.* (eds) *The Idea of Democracy*, Cambridge: Cambridge University Press.
—— (1997) 'Beyond Fairness and Deliberation: The Epistemic Dimension of Democratic Authority', in J. Bohman and W. Rehg (eds) *Deliberative Democracy*, Cambridge, Mass.: MIT Press.
Festenstein, Matthew (1997) *Pragmatism and Political Theory: From Dewey to Rorty*, Chicago: University of Chicago Press.
Field, Hartry (1986) 'The Deflationary Conception of Truth', in G. MacDonald and C. Wright (eds) *Fact, Science and Morality*, Oxford: Basil Blackwell.

—— (1994a) 'Deflationist Views of Meaning and Content', *Mind*, 103, 411.

—— (1994b) 'Disquotational Truth and Factually Defective Discourse', *The Philosophical Review*, 103, 3.

Fine, Arthur (1986) 'Unnatural Attitudes: Realist and Instrumentalist Attachments to Science', *Mind 95*.

Forbes, G. (1986) 'Truth, Correspondence and Redundancy', in G. MacDonald and C. Wright (eds) *Fact, Science and Morality*, Oxford: Basil Blackwell.

Fraser, N. (1991) 'From Irony to Prophecy to Politics: A Response to Richard Rorty', *Michigan Quarterly Review*, xxx, 2.

Gambetta, Diego (1998) '"Claro!" An Essay on Discursive Machismo', in Jon Elster (ed.) *Deliberative Democracy*, Cambridge: Cambridge University Press.

Gardbaum, S. (1991) 'Why the Liberal State Can Promote Moral Ideas after All', *Harvard Law Review*, 104.

Gaus, Gerald (1997) 'Reason, Justification, and Consensus: Why Democracy Can't Have It All', in J. Bohman and W. Rehg (eds) *Deliberative Democracy*, Cambridge, Mass.: MIT Press.

Guinier, Lani (1994) *The Tyranny of the Majority: Fundamental Fairness in Representative Democracy*, New York: Free Press.

Gutmann, Amy and Thompson, Dennis (1996) *Democracy and Disagreement* Cambridge, Mass.: Harvard University Press.

Haack, Susan (1993) 'Philosophy/philosophy, an Untenable Dualism', *Transactions of the Charles S. Peirce Society*, 29.

—— (1995) *Evidence and Inquiry: Towards Reconstruction in Epistemology*, Oxford: Blackwell.

—— (1998) 'Confessions of an Old-Fashioned Prig', in *Manifesto of a Passionate Moderate: Unfashionable Essays*, Chicago: University of Chicago Press.

Habermas, Jürgen (1971) *Knowledge and Human Interests*, trans. J. Shapiro, Boston: Beacon Press.

—— (1973) 'Wahrheitstheorien' in H. Fahrenbach (ed.) *Wirklichkeit und Reflexion: Festschrift für W. Schulz*, Pfüllingen: Neske..

—— (1982) 'Response to My Critics', in J.B. Thompson and D. Held (eds) *Habermas: Critical Debates*, Boston: MIT Press.

—— (1984) *The Theory of Communicative Action*, trans. T. McCarthy, Boston. Beacon Press.

—— (1989) *The Structural Transformation of the Public Sphere*, trans. T. Burger and F. Lawrence, Cambridge: Cambridge University Press.

—— (1990a) 'Philosophy as Stand-in and Interpreter' in *Moral Consciousness and Communicative Action*, trans. C. Lenhardt and S. Weber Nicholsen, Boston: MIT Press.

—— (1990b) 'Reconstruction and Interpretation in the Social Sciences', in *Moral Consciousness and Communicative Action*, trans. C. Lenhardt and S. Weber Nicholsen, Boston: MIT Press.

—— (1990c) 'Discourse Ethics: Notes on a Program of Philosophical Justification', in *Moral Consciousness and Communicative Action*, trans. C. Lenhardt and S. Weber Nicholsen, Boston: MIT Press.

—— (1990d) 'Morality and Ethical Life: Does Hegel's Critique of Kant Apply to Discourse Ethics?', in *Moral Consciousness and Communicative Action*, trans. C. Lenhardt and S. Weber Nicholsen, Boston: MIT Press.

—— (1991) 'Charles S. Peirce über Kommunikation', in *Text und Kontexte*, Frankfurt: Suhrkamp.

—— (1995) *Between Facts and Norms: Contributions to a Discourse Theory of Law and Democracy*, Cambridge, Mass.: MIT Press.

Hacking, Ian (1982) 'Language, Truth and Reason', in M. Hollis and S. Lukes (eds) *Rationality and Relativism*, Oxford: Basil Blackwell.

—— (1995) *Rewriting the Soul: Multiple Personality and the Sciences of Memory*, Princeton: Princeton University Press.

—— (1999) *The Social Construction of What?*, Cambridge, Mass.: Harvard University Press.

Hampton, Jean (1993) 'The Moral Commitments of Liberalism', in D. Copp, J. Hampton, and J. Roemer (eds) *The Idea of Democracy*, Cambridge: Cambridge University Press.

Hart, H.L.A. (1979) 'Utility and Rights', *Columbia Law Review*, 79.

Heath, Joseph (1998) 'A Pragmatist Theory of Convergence', in C. Misak (ed.) *Pragmatism, Canadian Journal of Philosophy*, supplementary volume.

Held, Virginia (1993) *Feminist Morality*, Chicago: University of Chicago Press.

Hill Collins, Patricia (1990) *Black Feminist Thought*, Cambridge, Mass.: Unwin and Hyman.

hooks, bell (1984) *Feminist Theory: From Margin to Center*, Boston: South End Press.

Hookway, Christopher (1995) 'Fallibilism and Objectivity: Science and Ethics', in J.E.J. Altham and Ross Harrison (eds) *World, Mind, and Ethics: Essays on the Ethical Philosophy of Bernard Williams*, Cambridge: Cambridge University Press.

—— (1998) 'Doubt: Affective States and the Regulation of Inquiry' in C. Misak (ed.) *Pragmatism, Canadian Journal of Philosophy*, supplementary volume.

—— (forthcoming) *Truth, Rationality and Pragmatism: Themes From Peirce*, Oxford: Oxford University Press.

Horwich, Paul (1990) *Truth*, Oxford: Basil Blackwell.

—— (1993) 'Gibbard's Theory of Norms', *Philosophy and Public Affairs*, 22, 1.

—— (1994) 'The Essence of Expressivism', *Analysis,* 54.

Hume, David [1777] (1985) 'The Sceptic', in Eugene F. Miller (ed.) *Essays: Moral, Political and Literary*, Indianapolis: Liberty Classics.

Hurka, Thomas (1995) *Perfectionism*, New York: Oxford University Press.

Ignatieff, Michael (1993) *Blood and Belonging*, Toronto: Viking.

Jackson, Frank, Oppy, Graham, and Smith, Michael (1994) 'Minimalism and Truth-Aptness', *Mind*, 103, 411.

James, William [1907] (1992) 'Pragmatism: A New Name for some Old Ways of Thinking', in D. Olin (ed.) *William James: Pragmatism in Focus*, London: Routledge.

Jardine, Nicholas (1995) 'Science, Ethics and Objectivity', in J.E.J. Altham and Ross Harrison (eds) *World, Mind, and Ethics: Essays on the Ethical Philosophy of Bernard Williams*, Cambridge, Mass.: Cambridge University Press.

Johnson, James (1993) 'Is Talk Really Cheap?', *American Political Science Review*, 87.

Johnson, Mark (1992) 'Objectivity Refigured: Pragmatism without Verificationism', in J. Haldane and C. Wright (eds) *Reality: Representation and Projection*, New York: Oxford University Press.

Jones, Kathleen (1993) *Compassionate Authority: Democracy and the Representation of Women*, New York: Routledge.

Kamm, F.M. (1989) 'Harming Some to Save Others', *Philosophical Studies*, 57.

Kernohan, Andrew (1998) *Liberalism, Equality, and Cultural Oppression*, Cambridge: Cambridge University Press.

Kingwell, Mark (1995) *A Civil Tongue: Justice, Dialogue, and the Politics of Pluralism*, University Park, Pa.: Pennsylvania State University Press.

Knight, Jack and Johnson, James (1997) 'What Sort of Political Equality Does Deliberative Democracy Require?', in J. Bohman and W. Rehg (eds) *Deliberative Democracy*, Cambridge, Mass.: MIT Press.

Korsgaard, Christine (1996) *The Sources of Normativity*, Cambridge: Cambridge University Press.

—— (1997) 'Taking the Law into Our Own Hands: Kant on the Right to Revolution', in A. Reath, B. Herman, and C. Korsgaard (eds) *Reclaiming the History of Ethics: Essays for John Rawls*, Cambridge: Cambridge University Press.

Krausz, Michael (1993) *Rightness and Reasons*, Ithaca, NY: Cornell University Press.

Kritz, Neil (ed.) (1995) *Transitional Justice: How Emerging Democracies Reckon with Former Regimes*, Washington, DC: United States Institute of Peace, 3 vols.

Kuflik, Arthur (1979) 'Morality and Compromise', *Nomos*, xxi.

Kymlicka, Will (1989) 'Liberal Individualism and Liberal Neutrality', *Ethics*, 99, 4.

—— (1990) 'Two Theories of Justice', *Inquiry*, 33.

—— (1995) *Multicultural Citizenship*, Oxford: Oxford University Press.

Larmore, Charles (1987) *Patterns of Moral Complexity*, Cambridge: Cambridge University Press.

—— (1996) *The Morals of Modernity*, Cambridge: Cambridge University Press.

Lear, Jonathan (1984) 'Moral Objectivity', in S.C. Brown (ed.) *Objectivity and Cultural Divergence*, Royal Institute of Philosophy Lecture Series 17, Cambridge: Cambridge University Press.

Levi, Isaac (1998) 'Pragmatism and Change of View', in C. Misak (ed.) *Pragmatism*, *Canadian Journal of Philosophy*, supplementary volume.

Lloyd, Genevieve (1984) *The Man of Reason*, London: Methuen.

Lovibond, S. and Williams, S. (eds) (1996) *Nature, Truth and Value: Essays in Honour of David Wiggins*, Oxford: Basil Blackwell.

Lukes, Steven (1991) *Moral Conflict and Politics*, Oxford: Oxford University Press.

McDowell, John (1979) 'Virtue and Reason', *The Monist*, 62.

—— (1981) 'Non-Cognitivism and Rule-Following', in S. Holtzman and C. Leich (eds) *Wittgenstein: To Follow a Rule*, London: Routledge and Kegan Paul.

—— (1985) 'Values and Secondary Qualities', in T. Honderich (ed.) *Morality and Objectivity: A Tribute to John Mackie*, London: Routledge and Kegan Paul.

—— (1994) *Mind and World*, Cambridge, Mass: Harvard University Press.

—— (1995) 'Two Sorts of Naturalism', in R. Hursthouse, G. Lawrence, and W. Quinn (eds) *Virtues and Reasons: Philippa Foot and Moral Theory*, Oxford: Clarendon Press.

MacIntyre, Alasdair (1981) *After Virtue: A Study in Moral Theory* Notre Dame: University of Notre Dame Press.

Mackie, John (1977) *Ethics: Inventing Right and Wrong*, Harmondsworth: Penguin.

McNaughton, D. (1988) *Moral Vision: An Introduction to Ethics*, New York: Basil Blackwell.

Manin, Bernard (1987) 'On Legitimacy and Political Deliberation', *Political Theory*, 15.

Meehan, Johanna (ed.) (1995), *Feminists Read Habermas*, London: Routledge.

Meyerson, Denise (1997) *Rights Limited*, Cape Town: Juta and Co,

Michelman, Frank (1997) 'How Can the People Ever Make Laws? A Critique of Deliberative Democracy', in J. Bohman and W. Rehg (eds) *Deliberative Democracy*, Cambridge, Mass.: MIT Press.

Migotti, Mark (1998) 'Peirce's Double-aspect Theory of Truth', in C. Misak (ed.) *Pragmatism, Canadian Journal of Philosophy*, supplementary volume.

Mill, John Stuart [1859] (1975) *On Liberty*, New York: Norton.

Minow, Martha (1990) *Making All the Difference: Inclusion, Exclusion, and American Law*, Ithaca, NY: Cornell University Press.

—— (1991) 'From Class Action to Miss Saigon: The Concept of Representation in the Law', *Cleveland State Law Review*, 39.

Misak, Cheryl (1990) 'Pragmatism and Bivalence', *International Studies in the Philosophy of Science*, 4, 2.

—— (1991) *Truth and the End of Inquiry: A Peircean Account of Truth*, Oxford: Clarendon Press.

—— (1992) 'Critical Notice of B. Ellis: *Truth and Objectivity*', *Canadian Journal of Philosophy*, 22, 3.

—— (1994a) 'Pragmatism and the Transcendental Turn in Truth and Ethics', *Transactions of the C.S. Peirce Society*, 30.

—— (1994b) 'Pragmatism in Focus', *Studies in the History and Philosophy of Science*, 25, 1.

—— (1995) *Verificationism: Its History and Prospects*, London: Routledge.

—— (1996) 'Pragmatism, Empiricism, and Morality', in S. Lovibond and S. Williams (eds) *Nature, Truth and Value: Essays in Honour of David Wiggins*, Oxford: Basil Blackwell.

—— (1998) 'Deflating Truth: Pragmatism vs. Minimalism', *The Monist*, 81.

Moller Okin, Susan (1978) *Women in Western Political Thought*, Princeton: Princeton University Press.

Moody-Adams, Michelle (1997) *Fieldwork in Familiar Places*, Cambridge, Mass.: Harvard University Press.

Moon, Donald (1995) 'Practical Discourse and Communicative Ethics', in Stephen K. White (ed.) *The Cambridge Companion to Habermas*, Cambridge: Cambridge University Press.

Moore, G.E. (1907) 'Professor James' "Pragmatism"', *Proceedings of the Aristotelian Society*, 8.

Moraga, Cherrie and Anzuldua, Gloria (1983) *This Bridge Called My Back*, New York: Kitchen Table Press.

Mouffe, Chantal (1994) 'Political Liberalism, Neutrality and the Political', *Ratio Juris*, 7, 3.

Nagel, Thomas (1979) *Mortal Questions*, Cambridge: Cambridge University Press.

Neal, Patrick (1997) *Liberalism and Its Discontents*, London: Macmillan.

Nino, Carlos Santiago (1996) *The Constitution of Deliberative Democracy*, New Haven, CT: Yale University Press.

Noddings, Nel (1984) *Caring*, Los Angeles: University of California Press.

Norris, Christopher (1990) *What's Wrong with Postmodernism: Critical Theory and the Ends of Philosophy*, New York: Harvester Wheatsheaf.

O'Neill, Onora (1989) *The Construction of Reason*, Cambridge: Cambridge University Press.

Pateman, Carol (1988) *The Sexual Contract*, Oxford: Polity Press.

Peacocke, Christopher (1986) *Thoughts: An Essay on Content*, Aristotelian Society Series, 1, Oxford: Basil Blackwell.

—— (1992) *A Study of Concepts*, Cambridge, Mass.: MIT Press.

Peirce, Charles S. (1931) *Collected Papers of Charles Sanders Peirce*, eight vols: vols 1–6, ed. C. Hartshorne and P. Weiss, Cambridge, Mass.: Harvard University Press, 1931–35; vols 7–8, ed. A. Burks, Cambridge, Mass.: Harvard University Press, 1958.

—— (1963) *The Charles S. Peirce Papers,* the Houghton Library, Harvard University, Cambridge, Mass. (30 reels of microfilm), Cambridge, Mass.: Harvard University Library Microreproduction Service.

—— (1976) *The New Elements of Mathematics*, ed. C. Eislie, The Hague: Mouton.

—— (1982–6) *Writings of Charles S. Peirce: A Chronological Edition*, four vols: vol. 1, ed. M.H. Fish *et al.*, Bloomington: Indiana University Press, 1982; vol. 2, ed. E.C. Moore *et al.*, Bloomington: Indiana University Press, 1982; vols 3 and 4, ed. C.J.W. Kloesel, Bloomington: Indiana University Press, 1986.

Pensky, Max (1995) 'Universalism and the Situated Critic', in Stephen K. White (ed.) *The Cambridge Companion to Habermas*, Cambridge: Cambridge University Press.

Pettit, Philip (1997) *Republicanism*, Oxford: Clarendon Press.

Phillips, Anne (1993) *Democracy and Difference*, University Park, Pa.: Pennsylvania State University Press.

—— (1995) *The Politics of Presence: Issues in Democracy and Group Representation*, Oxford: Oxford University Press.

Pollner, Melvin (1987) *Mundane Reason*, Cambridge: Cambridge University Press.

Popper, Karl (1959) *The Logic of Scientific Discovery*, London: Hutchinson.

Pratt, J.B. (1907) 'Truth and its Verification', *The Journal of Philosophy*, 4.

Putnam, Hilary (1962) 'The Analytic and the Synthetic', reprinted in *Mind Language and Reality: Philosophical Papers*, 2, Cambridge: Cambridge University Press.

—— (1979) 'Philosophy of Logic', in *Mathematics, Matter, and Method*, New York: Cambridge University Press.

—— (1987) 'The Diversity of the Sciences: Global versus Local Methodological Approaches', in P. Petit, R. Sylvan, and J. Norman (eds) *Metaphysics and Morality: Essays in Honour of J.J.C. Smart*, Oxford: Basil Blackwell.

—— (1981) *Reason, Truth and History*, Cambridge: Cambridge University Press.

—— (1992) 'A Reconsideration of Deweyan Democracy', in *Renewing Philosophy*, Cambridge, Mass.: Harvard University Press.

—— (1994) 'Pragmatism and Moral Objectivity', in *Words and Life*, Cambridge, Mass.: Harvard University Press.

Przeworski, Adam (1998) 'Deliberation and Ideological Domination', in Jon Elster (ed.) *Deliberative Democracy*, Cambridge: Cambridge University Press.

Quine, W.V.O. (1953) 'Two Dogmas of Empiricism', in *From a Logical Point of View*, Cambridge, Mass: Harvard University Press.

—— (1960) *Word and Object*, Cambridge, Mass.: MIT Press.

—— (1970) *Philosophy of Logic*, Englewood Cliffs, NJ: Prentice Hall, 2nd edn, Harvard University Press, 1986.

—— (1974) *The Roots of Reference*, La Salle, Ill.: Open Court.

—— (1975) 'The Nature of Natural Knowledge', in S. Guttenplan (ed.) *Mind and Language*, Oxford: Clarendon Press.

—— (1981a) 'On the Nature of Moral Values', in *Theories and Things*, Cambridge, Mass.: Belknap Press.

—— (1981b) 'The Pragmatist's Place in Empiricism', in R. Mulvaney and P. Zeltner (eds) *Pragmatism: Its Sources and Prospects*, Columbia: University of South Carolina Press.

—— (1986) 'Reply to Roger Gibson Jr.', in L.E. Hahn and P.A. Schlipp (eds) *The Philosophy of W.V. Quine*, La Salle, Ill.: Open Court.

—— (1987) *Quiddities: An Intermittently Philosophical Dictionary*, Cambridge, Mass.: Harvard University Press.

—— (1990) 'Three Indeterminacies', in R. Barrett and R. Gibson (eds) *Perspectives on Quine*, Oxford: Basil Blackwell.

Railton, Peter (1996a) 'Moral Realism: Prospects and Problems', in W. Sinnott-Armstrong and M. Timmons (eds) *Moral Knowledge? New Readings in Moral Epistemology*, Oxford: Oxford University Press.

—— (1996b) 'Subjective and Objective', in Brad Hooker (ed.) *Truth in Ethics*, Oxford: Basil Blackwell.

Rawls, John (1971) *A Theory of Justice*, Cambridge, Mass.: Belknap Press.

—— (1980) 'Rational and Full Autonomy', *Journal of Philosophy*, 77, 9.

—— [1985](1999) 'Justice as Fairness: Political, not Metaphysical', in *Collected Papers*, ed. S. Freeman, Cambridge, Mass.: Harvard University Press.

—— (1993) *Political Liberalism*, New York: Columbia University Press.

—— (1995) 'Reply to Habermas', *Journal of Philosophy*, 92, 3.

—— (1997) 'The Idea of Public Reason Revisited', *The University of Chicago Law Review*, 64, 3.

Raz, Joseph (1986) *Morality of Freedom*, Oxford: Clarendon Press.

—— (ed.) (1990) *Authority*, New York: New York University Press.

—— (1994) 'Facing Diversity: The Case for Epistemic Abstinence', in *Ethics in the Public Domain*, Oxford: Clarendon Press.

Rehg, William and Bohman, James (1996) 'Discourse and Democracy: The Formal and Informal Bases of Legitimacy', *Journal of Political Philosophy*, 4.

Richardson, Henry (1994) *Practical Reasoning About Final Ends*, Cambridge: Cambridge University Press.

—— (1995) 'Beyond Good and Right: Toward a Constructive Ethical Pragmatism', *Philosophy and Public Affairs*, 24.

—— (1997) 'Democratic Intentions', in J. Bohman and W. Rehg (eds) *Deliberative Democracy*, Cambridge, Mass.: MIT Press.

—— (1998) 'Democratic Deliberation about Ends', in C. Misak (ed.) *Pragmatism*, *Canadian Journal of Philosophy*, supplementary volume.

Rorty, Richard (1980) 'Pragmatism, Relativism, and Irrationalism', *Proceedings and Addresses of the American Philosophical Association*, 53.

—— (1982) *Consequences of Pragmatism (Essays: 1972–1980)*, Minneapolis: University of Minnesota Press.

—— (1988) 'The Priority of Democracy to Philosophy', in M.D. Peterson and R.C. Vaughn (eds) *The Virginia Statute for Religious Freedom: Its Evolution and Consequences in American History*, Cambridge: Cambridge University Press 1988. Reprinted in Rorty 1991a.

—— (1989) *Contingency, Irony and Solidarity*, Cambridge, Cambridge University Press.

—— (1991a) *Objectivity, Relativism and Truth: Philosophical Papers*, 1, Cambridge: Cambridge University Press.

(1991b) 'Feminism and Pragmatism' *Michigan Quarterly Review* 2.

—— (1993) 'Human Rights, Rationality, and Sentimentality', in S. Shute and S. Hurley (eds) *On Human Rights*, New York, NY: Basic Books.

—— (1998) *Achieving Our Country*, Cambridge, Mass.: Harvard University Press.

Ruddick, Sara (1990) *Maternal Thinking*, London: Women's Press.

Sandel, Michael (1982) *Liberalism and the Limits of Justice*, Cambridge: Cambridge University Press.

—— (1996) *Democracy's Discontent: America in Search of a Public Policy*, Cambridge, Mass.: Harvard University Press.

Sartre, Jean-Paul (1975) 'Existentialism is a Humanism', in W. Kaufmann (ed.) *Existentialism from Dostoevsky to Sartre*, New York: Meridian-New American.

Scheuerman, William (1998) *The End of Law: Carl Schmitt's Political and Legal Thought*, New York: Rowman and Littlefield.

Schmitt, Carl ([1932]1976) *The Concept of the Political*, trans. G. Schwab, New Jersey: Rutgers University Press.

Sellars, Wilfred (1962) 'Truth and Correspondence', *Journal of Philosophy*, 59.

—— (1963) 'Empiricism and the Philosophy of Mind', in *Science, Perception and Reality*, London: Routledge and Kegan Paul.

Sennett, Richard (1997) 'Drowning in Syrup', Review of Amitai Etzioni, *The New Golden Rule*, *Times Literary Supplement*, 7 Feb. 1997.

Shapiro, Ian (1996) *Democracy's Place*, Ithaca, NY: Cornell University Press.

Sheffler, Samuel (1987) 'Morality through Thick and Thin', *Philosophical Review*, 96.

Sher, George (1997) *Beyond Neutrality*, Cambridge: Cambridge University Press.

Sismondo, Sergio (1997) 'Deflationary Metaphysics and the Construction of Laboratory Mice', *Metaphilosophy* 28, 3.

Smith, Michael (1996) 'Internalism's Wheel', in Brad Hooker (ed.) *Truth in Ethics*, Oxford: Basil Blackwell.

Soames, Scott (1984) 'What Is A Theory of Truth?', *Journal of Philosophy*, 81.

Spelman, Elizabeth (1988) *Inessential Woman*, Boston: Beacon Press.

Steiner, Hillel (1996) 'Duty-free Zones', *Aristotelian Society Proceedings*, xcvi.

Stocker, Michael (1990) *Plural and Conflicting Values*, Oxford: Oxford University Press.

Stokes, Susan (1998) 'Pathologies of Deliberation', in Jon Elster (ed.) *Deliberative Democracy*, Cambridge: Cambridge University Press.

Styron, William (1976) *Sophie's Choice*, New York: Random House.

Sunstein, C. (1991) 'Preferences and Politics', *Philosophy and Public Affairs*, 20, 1.

Sypnowich, Christine (1993) 'Some Disquiet about "Difference"', *Praxis International*, 13, 2.

—— (1996) 'Impartiality after Difference' *Review of Constitutional Studies*, 3, 2.

Tan, Kok-Chor (1998) 'Liberal Toleration in Rawls' Law of Peoples', *Ethics*, 108.

Taylor, Charles (1985) *Philosophical Papers*, vol. 2, Cambridge: Cambridge University Press.

—— (1989) *Sources of the Self: The Making of the Modern Identity*, Cambridge, Mass.: Harvard University Press.

—— (1997) 'Leading a Life', in Ruth Chang (ed.) *Incommensurability, Incomparability, and Practical Reason*, Cambridge, Mass.: Harvard University Press.

Thomson, Judith (1985) 'The Trolley Problem', *Yale Law Journal*, 94.

Tugendhat, E. (1992) 'Habermas on Communicative Action', in *Philosophische Aufsätze*, Frankfurt: Suhrkamp.

Waldron, J. (1992) 'Minority Cultures and the Cosmopolitan Alternative', *University of Michigan Journal of Law Reform* 25, 3.

Walzer, Michael (1973) 'Political Action: The Problem of Dirty Hands', *Philosophy and Public Affairs*, 2, 2.

—— (1982) 'Pluralism in Political Perspective', in M. Walzer (ed.) *The Politics of Ethnicity*, Cambridge, Mass: Harvard University Press.

Warren, Mark (1992) 'Democratic Theory and Self-transformation', *American Political Science Review*, 86.

—— (1995) 'The Self in Discursive Democracy', in Stephen K. White (ed.) *The Cambridge Companion to Habermas*, Cambridge: Cambridge University Press.

—— (1996) 'Deliberative Democracy and Authority', *American Political Science Review*, 90, 1.

White, M. (1986) 'Quine's Holism', in L.E. Hahn and P.A. Schlipp (eds) *The Philosophy of W.V. Quine*, La Salle, Ill.: Open Court.

Wiggins, David (1976) 'Truth, Invention, and the Meaning of Life', *Proceedings of the British Academy* LXII, reprinted in *Needs, Values, Truth*, Oxford: Basil Blackwell, 2nd edn, 1991.

—— (1987) 'A Sensible Subjectivism?' in *Needs, Values, Truth*, Oxford: Basil Blackwell, 2nd edn, 1991.

—— (1990) 'Moral Cognitivism, Moral Relativism and Motivating Moral Beliefs', *Proceedings of the Aristotelian Society*, 91.

—— (1991a) 'Postscript' to *Needs, Values, Truth*, Oxford: Basil Blackwell, 2nd edn, 1991.

—— (1991b) 'Truth, and Truth as Predicated of Moral Judgements', in *Needs, Values, Truth*, Oxford: Basil Blackwell, 2nd edn, 1991.

—— (1994) 'Putnam's Doctrine of Natural Kind Words and Frege's Doctrines of Sense, Reference, and Extension: Can they Cohere?', in P. Clark and B. Hale (eds) *Reading Putnam*, Oxford: Basil Blackwell.

—— (1995) 'Categorical Requirements: Kant and Hume on the Idea of Duty', in R. Hursthouse, G. Lawrence, and W. Quinn (eds) *Virtues and Reasons: Philippa Foot and Moral Theory*, Oxford: Clarendon Press.

—— (1996a) 'Natural and Artificial Virtues: A Vindication of Hume's Scheme', in R. Crisp (ed.) *How Should One Live?*, Oxford: Clarendon Press.

—— (1996b) 'Responses', in Lovibond and Williams 1996.

—— (1998) 'C.S. Peirce: Belief, Truth, and Going from the Known to the Unknown', in C. Misak (ed.) *Pragmatism*, *Canadian Journal of Philosophy*, supplementary volume.

Williams, Bernard (1973) 'A Critique of Utilitarianism', in J.C.C. Smart and B. Williams (eds) *Utilitarianism For and Against*, Cambridge: Cambridge University Press.

—— (1981) 'The Truth in Relativism', in *Moral Luck*, Cambridge: Cambridge University Press.

—— (1985) *Ethics and the Limits of Philosophy*, Cambridge, Mass.: Harvard University Press.

—— (1996) 'Truth in Ethics', in Brad Hooker (ed.) *Truth in Ethics*, Oxford: Basil Blackwell.

Williams, Melissa (1998) *Voice, Trust, and Memory: Marginalized Groups and the Failings of Liberal Representation*, Princeton, NJ: Princeton University Press.

Wittgenstein, Ludwig (1938) *Lectures and Conversations on Aesthetics, Psychology, and Religious Belief*, Cyril Barrett (ed.), Berkeley: University of California Press.

—— (1968) *Philosophical Investigations*, trans. G.E.M. Anscombe, Oxford: Basil Blackwell, 3rd edn.

Wright, Crispin (1992) *Truth and Objectivity*, Cambridge, Mass.: Harvard University Press.

—— (1996a) 'Response to Commentators', *Philosophy and Phenomenological Research*, LVI, 4.

—— (1996b) 'Truth in Ethics', in Brad Hooker (ed.) *Truth in Ethics*, Oxford: Basil Blackwell.

Young, Iris Marion (1989) 'Polity and Group Difference: A Critique of the Ideal of Universal Citizenship', *Ethics*, 99.

—— (1990) *Justice and the Politics of Difference*, Princeton, NJ: Princeton University Press.

—— (1993a) 'Together in Difference: Transforming the Logic of Group Political Conflict', in J. Squires (ed.) *Principled Positions: Postmodernism and the Rediscovery of Value*, London: Lawrence and Wishart.

—— (1993b) 'Justice and Communicative Democracy', in R. Gottlieb (ed.) *Radical Democracy: Tradition, Counter-tradition, Politics*, Philadelphia, Pa.: Temple University Press.

—— (1995) 'Communication and the Other: Beyond Deliberative Democracy', in S. Benhabib (ed.) *Democracy and Difference: Changing Boundaries of the Political*, Princeton, NJ: Princeton University Press.

—— (1997) 'Difference as a Resource for Democratic Communication', in J. Bohman and W. Rehg (eds) *Deliberative Democracy*, Cambridge, Mass.: MIT Press.

Index